She streaked to the dazzling top in the toughest business in the world. She made her place in the glittering capital of stardom. Yet it never spoiled her. June Allyson really was the girl next door . . . believing in love and family, in truth, in friends, and never losing the sweetness that made her America's favorite . . . even through the scandal of a doomed love that was to tear her heart asunder, even through a tragedy that all but ended her world. Now she tells her story in a book as rich with joy and as drenched in heartbreak as life itself . . .

June Allyson
by
June Allyson

June Allyson

by June Allyson

with Frances Spatz Leighton

BERKLEY BOOKS, NEW YORK

This Berkley book contains the complete
text of the original hardcover edition.

JUNE ALLYSON

A Berkley Book / published by arrangement with
G. P. Putnam's Sons

PRINTING HISTORY
G. P. Putnam's Sons edition published June 1982
Berkley edition / July 1983

ISBN: 0-425-06251-1

ACKNOWLEDGMENTS

I would be totally remiss if I did not acknowledge the dedication and help of my good friend and editor, Ellis Amburn, in New York, and Lucile Hertz and Sylvia Stewart, in Washington.

I would like to dedicate my book to
Pam, Rick and David

A special dedication goes to Jerry Cohn,
my very close friend— and manager—who
taught me the true meaning of the word friendship.

Contents

PART I: A MOST IMPROBABLE STAR   9

PART II: RICHARD   63

PART III: DOWNHILL ALL THE WAY   155

PART IV: THE TUNNEL   217

JUNE ALLYSON

1

A MOST
IMPROBABLE
STAR

1

"HEY! GET IN!" A chauffeur-driven limousine stopped and the back door swung open. I looked up, shocked. I was not about to get into a strange car, especially a big black limousine, but suddenly I realized it was Judy Garland yelling at me from the back seat. "Come on, damn it. The light's changing." I hopped in and Judy laughed. "What did you think I was going to do, kidnap you?"

"Of course," I said, laughing too.

"I've seen you around the set, watching me and Mickey rehearse. What are you going to do in *Girl Crazy?*"

Didn't she know? I gulped. "I hate to say it but I'm supposed to sing a song."

She laughed. "Well, damn it, don't be apologetic. I'll bet you've got a great voice. And if you can't sing it, fake it. You'll do fine."

"Thanks for the vote of confidence."

"By the way, what were you doing on that corner?"

I told her that was where I got my third bus every morning to get to the studio.

"Oh yes," she groaned. "Our famous godforsaken Culver City. Only MGM would think of building there."

She was fun and easy and the absence of star attitude put me totally at ease. Judy Garland had been my idol and here she was as plain as an old shoe, dressed in slacks and with little makeup, and talking to me as if we were old friends. And soon we were. I told her that a Judy Garland song had gotten me into show business.

She said, "Me? I got you into this crappy business? Then someday you'll hate me. Whatever you do, don't let Papa Mayer send you out to entertain at birthday parties. They'll treat you like hired help." Judy explained that Louis B. Mayer, head of MGM, had sent her to various stars' homes to entertain at their parties. She had to eat in the kitchen, she said, and she felt like a part-time servant.

" 'This is the way you will get experience,' Papa Mayer told me. The only one I really liked doing," Judy added, "was Clark Gable's party. I was stuffed into a big fake birthday cake and I popped out at Clark Gable and sang 'Dear Mr. Gable.' I was fourteen at the time. And you know what? A couple months ago I ran into Clark and he hugged me and said, 'I just had a birthday but I didn't dare have a cake—I was afraid you'd pop out at me again, Judy.' "

As we approached the studio, I told Judy that I had to sing my song to Mickey Rooney and she told me Mickey was a dream to work with but not to be shocked at anything he might do. He was a pesky practical joker and had even set off a stink bomb in front of her dressing room during one of their early movies.

I felt incredibly lucky, in my first movie role, to be singing a song to Mickey Rooney, who had topped the popularity polls for years in succession over Spencer Tracy and even over Clark Gable.

Thank God I did my first movie scene with him. He was surprisingly sensitive to my needs and helped me through a nerve-racking day.

After rehearsals we started shooting. I was terrified by the complexity of movie acting—trying to remember all the things you have to do—simultaneously or in sequence—flirt with Mickey, sing, hold the note, move to that mark, smile, look there, hold that note. I had a sexy song and I was supposed to shove Mickey around a lot during the number. He was a rich smart-alek kid who comes to a nightclub. I was supposed to be a Betty Hutton type, a little tough, and as the singer with the club band I was supposed to start singing and then come down from the bandstand, single Mickey Rooney out, and torment him. And I did—I sure did. In my slinky satin gown, I came on strong, singing "Treat Me Rough." I didn't let Mickey alone for a minute, and bit by bit he responded to me and ended up onstage dancing and playing up to me; we finished the song as a duet.

I could not believe they were satisfied with the first take, but they were. It was a lucky thing because I don't know whether I could have lasted a second round. I made it to the rest room and threw up.

Forever after, when people asked me what the hardest thing was for me in acting, I would say, "Singing a song." I could not read music so I had to memorize everything. Everyone was watching. Everything had to be perfect. I would dance and I would sing and I would throw up. I would sing and I would throw up again. I learned not to eat much until the end of the day. Other stars, like Judy Garland, ate to soothe their nerves and ended up endlessly fighting fat. I starved to soothe mine and ended up with low blood sugar.

I didn't know that during *Girl Crazy* I would make a lasting friendship. The new friend was Judy Garland and through the years we would cry on each other's shoulders and laugh together as our fortunes zoomed up and down.

Mickey was like a big brother. Never again would I act with anyone who was greater at helping me along and making me look good by playing to me. I'm sure that had he wanted to, he could have made me all but invisible by drawing attention to himself. It would have been easy for such a master craftsman, but Mickey was a generous human being. He was a clown on the set. He would stand with his back to the camera mugging and trying to break up Judy Garland and ruin the take. I thought I'd started young, but Mickey had been in show business since he was six, playing a midget in a movie short.

When we were in *Girl Crazy*, Mickey was married to Ava Gardner less than a year and already his marriage was on the rocks and he would soon be divorced. Judy told me how MGM had trumped up a romance between Mickey and her. It bothered her that Mickey would escort her to a premiere or to an Oscar night as his official date, decreed by the studio, only to dump her at the theater for some leggy beauty who was there waiting for him.

Later, when Mickey Rooney had gained his reputation of changing partners and marrying over and over again, Judy reminisced, saying, "Everyone thought me and Mickey were so cute together and were going to get married someday. He could've at least asked! He asked everybody else."

She laughed a bit ruefully.

Judy seemed to be no luckier than Mickey in the romance department. In 1943, when we appeared in *Girl Crazy*, she was separated from her first husband, David Rose, and getting ready for a divorce.

During one of the breaks that day I filmed my song with Mickey, Judy came over to me; I was standing on the sidelines and watching. She wanted to know how her song had helped me get into show business and I told her about skipping school in the seventh grade on a bet to audition on Broadway. "I didn't even know you needed sheet music to give the piano player," I said. "Actually you were the first sheet music I bought for later auditions."

"Kid, you sound like my beginnings. The only thing you

didn't have was a stage mother to drag you around. So be grateful."

I told Judy I was anxious to send money to help my mother in New York and she sighed and said she could hardly remember how young she had been when she started supporting her mother by singing wherever they could get a booking. "Was your mother onstage?" she asked.

"Heavens, no," I told her.

"Well, mine was," she said. "Or wanted to be and I'm supposed to be the star she wanted to be."

As we became closer friends, we would get together between scenes in her dressing room and sometimes she would bemoan the fact that she was not glamorous like other stars. "Who would you like to look like?" I asked.

"Lana Turner," she said without a moment's hesitation. "*That* is beauty."

"Well, you've always been my idol," I said to comfort her.

"Knock it off, Junie," she said. "All I am is a girl who can sing. Haven't you heard that Papa Mayer calls me 'the little hunchback'?"

From then on, Judy Garland took the new kid, me, under-wing. I copied her style, wearing slacks everywhere. At the studio she protected me from teasing on the set and generally showed me the ropes.

On days when Judy wasn't shooting, she would send her limousine to take me to the studio and back. I loved bobbing along in the wake of her stardom. MGM had signed her when she was only twelve years old. And this, my first movie, *Girl Crazy*, was Judy's twentieth.

We would stay in her dressing room and talk for hours, discovering all we had in common. We'd suffered through many of the same problems growing up. We both had fathers with drinking problems. She adored her dad. My father was seldom around and I resented that. Judy said she had never discussed this with anyone else but she, too, had been deprived of her father's company. Her mother dragged her around the country to put in stage appearances as "Baby Frances," while her father stayed home running a small movie house. I had always been angry that my father did not come to see me. Only once did he come to our house in New York. He waited outside with a bicycle for me when I was six or seven. I carefully stored the bike in the basement that night only to find that it had been stolen when I went to get it in the morning.

When my daddy wanted to see me, through my childhood, he called my grandmother. After she died, he had to go through my mother. She would send me out to meet Daddy at such and such a corner. I'd take the subway and arrive early at the right corner and wait and he might never arrive. Sometimes I'd see him reel out of a cheap bar and head for me and we'd walk around and he'd treat me to lunch or an ice cream sundae. Sometimes I'd have to wait outside a bar while he made a quick trip in and out.

Judy Garland listened to me gravely as I told her about my childhood; then her eyes filled with tears and she said, "I had just gotten my break and been signed by MGM when my father died, before ever seeing me in a single movie. I didn't cry. Not at the funeral and not for nine days afterwards. And then I locked myself in my room and cried and screamed and vomited for a whole day and night."

I could not believe how similar our reactions had been. I told her my father was still alive but my grandmother had been the center of my life. Mother and I had lived with her and she had taken care of me while my mother worked. Her arms around me had been the most precious thing in my life and my protection against the world. When she died, I did not cry for three days but just sat locked in my room—and then I cried for seven days and would not be consoled.

Judy was proud that it was her father who had been with her

7

when she went for her audition before the great head of the MGM studio, Louis B. Mayer. Three months later her father was dead of meningitis.

Coincidentally, my father started me on the way to a dancing career. When I was allowed to see him, I told him how I'd make grandmother laugh with my gymnastic hijinks. I'd put my leg around my neck or do the splits while crossing my eyes. Daddy said, "You're going to be a dancer."

My heart leaped when I realized he really meant it. "Come," he went on, "there's a tap-dance school right near here and I'm going to enroll you right now." The first lesson was fine. The second lesson, I did not seem quite so welcome and the third lesson, I was barred from the door. I could not come back, I was told, until my lessons were paid for.

I never mentioned it to my father. I was afraid he would not come to see me again if I embarrassed him. Even a six-year-old child knows that.

But now I had a goal. I would save my own money and enroll in the dance school. I earned money by ghostwriting homework for my classmates. Some were too lazy to copy from my handwriting to their own. I charged extra to forge their handwriting. I was left-handed and had to learn to write with my right hand. After that, any kind of writing was easy.

Every penny was put aside for dancing lessons—every nickel from ghostwriting and running errands and my weekly allowance. At last, I saw an ad and enrolled and paid $20—almost my entire savings—for the whole dance course. This time I did not get even one lesson. When I arrived to start dancing, there was a sign on the door: CLOSED FOR BANKRUPTCY. I finally learned to dance by watching Fred Astaire's *The Gay Divorcee* seventeen times. I played hooky and spent whole days in the movie house, taking along the lunch I had packed for school, making sure to arrive home at the right time. *Flying Down to Rio* had me flying around the room when I got home, practicing what I had seen Fred Astaire and Ginger Rogers do.

When I was about eight I was almost killed in a freak accident while I was riding my bike. There had been a storm and the wind and heavy rains had loosened a dead branch on a huge tree near our house. Neighbors had been complaining about this rotten tree but the city had conveniently ignored their protests. Then the thing fell on me, totaling the bike, killing my dog, and breaking half the bones in my body. I had to learn to walk all over again. A swimming instructor—Marie Spinosa—gave a summer of her life to rebuild my muscles and get me on my feet again.

When Mother attempted to collect damages, city officials denied the existence of the tree, which had mysteriously disappeared in the night. She had to go to court waving newspaper clippings with pictures of my freak accident to prove it all and was lucky to get $100 from the city.

In my hospital bed I looked adoringly at the doctor who had taken a great interest in me and experienced my first crush—it made me want to live. I determined, as I watched him working over me, that I would grow up to be a doctor. It looked like my dancing days were over.

My mother had known abject poverty ever since my father left home when I was only six years old. We were even poorer after my grandmother died. After the accident and expensive therapy, we were desperate. Sometimes my mother would not eat dinner when I was eating and I'd ask why. She would say she wasn't hungry, but later I realized there was only enough food for one. Once I came home from school to find all the furniture out on the street. I cannot remember how many times we moved, sometimes to different addresses in the Bronx and once to a little town in upstate New York. Mother took whatever job she could—telephone switchboard, cashier in a restaurant and even a printing job making personalized checkbooks. The restaurant jobs were best because sometimes she could bring home food.

My greatest fear was that my mother would send me away. Once I was sent to a farm, supposedly for my health. I was taught to milk a cow, but I climbed a haystack and sat crying until they called my mother, who came to get me. I could not bear to be away from her and developed a lifetime fear of being alone and of the dark.

Even worse was the time my mother took me to stay "just a while" with a very stern aunt. I thought my aunt had become more friendly because she showed me a photo album with a picture of my father. I was so thrilled I later took the picture and put it under my pillow. The next morning I forgot to put it back and, confronted by my aunt's wrath when she found it under my pillow, I lied and said I hadn't put it there. She announced she did not want a liar in her house and dragged me outside where she made me wait in an icy rain on the porch until she phoned my mother and insisted that she leave her job and come get me immediately. The door opened once and I thought my aunt had relented. But I was wrong. She was throwing my suitcase out.

In time I recovered completely from my injuries, graduating from a wheelchair to crutches and finally a brace. I found that I could dance again, even in the brace, and soon I was bragging to my girlfriends in school that I could dance "as good as Ginger Rogers." One of them said, "Prove it."

I could afford to be cocky. I was safe. I said, "I can't prove it because there is no chance of dancing with her. I'm here and she's in Hollywood. Just bring her here and I'll prove it."

My repertoire of dance routines now included scenes from other Astaire-Rogers movies—*Shall We Dance?*, *Roberta*, *Top Hat* and *Follow the Fleet*. A girlfriend triumphantly showed up at school one day with a notice ripped out of a newspaper about tryouts for a Broadway musical comedy chorus line.

"Is that how they get them?" I asked, reading the clipping, which was headed "Auditions."

"I guess so," she said. "I dare you. I'll bet you a quarter you can't dance good enough to get into *that*."

"Sure I can," I said, before I even stopped to consider whether I had the right clothes or training. "What's the address?" I was in junior high—what did I know about tryouts? The other girls were tittering.

I had seen in movies that chorus girls practice in shorts and so I arrived for tryouts, newspaper in hand and a pair of shorts under my skirt. *I* was ready. Most of the girls—there were about a hundred—looked taller, considerably older, well endowed, and vastly more sophisticated. Naturally they did—to a seventh grader.

"Where's your music?" asked the piano player when my turn came. I had noticed girls were handing him music before they started to sing and saying "Key of C" or something, but the significance hadn't really registered. "What music?" I asked. I was starting to look scared and he could see it. He softened a bit. "Okay, what do you want to sing?"

"What song do you want to hear?" I asked, trying to indicate a huge repertoire. The whole place broke out in laughter. I finally called out the name of a popular song of the day. Fortunately, he did not ask me my key—since it was obvious I wouldn't know—and he put it down low enough for me to sing comfortably.

By some miracle, I was told to come back the next day—and the next day and the next. The final day came and the piano player groaned "Oh God" as I stepped up. He started to play the same music he had gotten used to and hated. I had a terrible sinking feeling that I wasn't going to make it, but from way back in the theater I heard a voice in the darkness—"No, no, hold it."

I stopped singing in midword. The voice continued, "Please, you've got to hire her, because if you don't, he'll come back and sing again and I can't stand it." There was a big horselaugh at the end of his little speech.

I won the quarter—the hardest money I ever earned. I'd paid out much more than that running back and forth to Times Square on the subway for auditions. I had landed my first Broadway show, *Sing Out the News*. Mother was less than thrilled. "What about your schooling?" she said. "I'm going to insist that you keep on with your schooling." It proved impossible, of course. *Sing Out the News* was a hit and now I had daily performances on Broadway. I was also running around to auditions, trying for bigger roles. Mother finally accepted the fact that school was over forever for her daughter, the Broadway showgirl.

The choreographer in the *Sing Out the News* company had a picturesque but very disconcerting habit—he instructed the chorus line by pointing his toe at us—and one day he pointed his toe at me, with an emphatic kick, and said, "Ella, we've got to change that name. What name do you like?" Others were listening in. I was Ella Geisman—short for Eleanor.

I said, nervously, "I think I like Allyson. It's a family name." I felt that my identity, my very being, was at stake. "Fine," he said. "Allyson Something would be a great name." I couldn't think of a thing. He turned to another dancer and pointed his toe at him. "What month do you like?" he asked the startled chorus boy. "June," came the quick answer. The choreographer swung his toe at me and announced, "Allyson. June. June Allyson, that's it." I was so glad the fellow hadn't liked August or October or I'd have been known as Augie or Oggie. I liked my new name very much.

Staying in show business proved hard for the newly christened June Allyson. I was fired in the next few years from many chorus lines for being too small, too young, too innocent looking—and then there was my ridiculous dancing, self-taught. Once I danced off the wrong side of the stage. I wondered where everybody else was, but it was too late to go chasing back across the stage looking for them now—*fired*. New show, new scene. Right left, right left. I was kicking left right—*fired*.

It was possibly time to try something else. I went out on a modeling call not because I thought I could be a model but because I thought they might use me in a crowd scene where they needed to fill up space. To my delight I was hired—not just for a mob scene but as a solo. I had no portfolio or even one picture to show, yet they picked me out of a crowd of twenty-five or thirty girls. I was one of three or four chosen and we were instructed to report for work the next day. Our measurements were taken before we left—we were told that we'd be posing in bathing suits. When I arrived the next day, I was a little disappointed that the bathing suit wasn't a little sexier. It looked more like a tennis outfit or shorts.

But who was I to inquire or tell them how to run their business? When the ad finally appeared in a magazine, everyone in the neighborhood saw it before I did. It was one of those horrible before-and-after ads—and I was the sad-looking *before* part. "If you don't use this product, here is how you will look"—that's what it said under my picture. "But if you use this product, here is how you will look"—and there were the girls with bosoms out to there. So much for modeling.

After the modeling fiasco, I went sheepishly back to the chorus line. It wasn't any easier. I was still strictly amateur. Sometimes I'd be on probation—warned I had to shape up by the next rehearsal. Once a fellow chorine, Miriam Franklin, who would later marry Gene Nelson, took pity on me and coached me in professional dancing. It didn't always help. Sometimes out of pity directors would give me my own bit part just to keep me from disrupting the chorus line.

After *Sing Out the News* I had bungled and bamboozled my

way through Very Warm for May and Higher and Higher. Now came Panama Hattie and my dancing was as atrocious as ever. Ethel Merman saved me. How I loved that girl—she wouldn't let them fire me. She chose me to do a little schtick with her. Betty Hutton was the second lead in Panama Hattie and Richard Rodgers picked me to be Betty's understudy. "But don't expect anything to happen to Betty," Mr. Rodgers warned me. "She's a big strapping girl in bouncing good health. So don't worry, June. You'll never need to go on for her but it will be good experience for you." Richard Rodgers may not have been anxious for me to go on in Betty Hutton's place, but he certainly wasn't speaking for me. I studied every move Betty made and memorized every line. I can't say that I wished Betty ill—I just wished me awfully well.

I acquired a place of my own and a boyfriend. Well, it wasn't exactly a place of my very own—I had two roommates. But it definitely was a boyfriend of my own. He was Tommy Mitchell and he was a singer in Broadway productions. As a matter of fact, he had been onstage with me in Sing Out the News and he had sung with a quartet.

Tommy came from an old conservative family in the South. He told me they frowned on his dating a chorus girl, and yet he insisted we were officially engaged. "They just don't approve of show business," he said. "Or of drinking because they heard how it has ruined so many famous people such as John Barrymore."

I said, "Tommy, tell me one thing. If your parents hate show business so much, how can they accept your working in the chorus?"

"I guess they make an exception for me." I'm sure it would have made life easier for Tommy if I'd given up my ambition to make it on Broadway. He loved me too much to ask me to do that.

Tommy was handsome. Tall and lean, he could have passed

for Jimmy Stewart's brother. The first gift I bought a man, I bought for him. It wasn't expensive but it was the best I could do and he loved it—a camera.

We had three beds in our room at The American Woman's Club, on Fifty-seventh Street—an all-female residence. Jane Ball, who was also in *Panama Hattie*, was one of my roommates. After the show, Jane and I would run over to moonlight at the Copacabana, padding out their chorus line. Jane ended up marrying the boss of the Copa, Monte Proser, and bearing him five strapping sons. The third roommate was a secretary-artist and she was the only one among us who had a decent winter coat. When you had a good job interview or great date, you wore the coat. I learned to baste it up and push up the sleeves or it would have looked as if the coat were wearing me.

Tommy Mitchell was amused when I showed him our room. It looked like a cyclone had a rummage sale. Gentlemen visitors were permitted between 6:00 and 8:00 but the door always had to be kept open. There was a strict food rule. You could bring in simple items like muffins and milk but you were not permitted to cook, according to the New York fire code.

I acquired a hot plate and lived on eggs. When the security officer knocked, and he always did at the first sniff of cooking food, I would quickly put the hot plate out on the fire escape. My room was not the only one to be raided for food, and the security man kept busy. I remember when he finally caught me dead to rights, with the window open and the snow blowing in and me trying to wave away the odor of frying eggs. I was terrified as he stood there glowering at me and then he rasped, "You can bring it in now."

"What?" I had asked innocently.

"Those eggs that are getting snowbound on the fire escape. I'm not going to turn you in. You just go ahead and use that hot plate from now on. But for God's sake, don't burn the place down." Bless him.

Richard Rodgers was wrong. Even a star in bouncing good health can develop spots—which Betty Hutton did. They were diagnosed as measles and I was on.

Ethel Merman was so great to me. The first night I went on for Betty Hutton, Ethel let me share her star's dressing room. Otherwise I would have been running up and down three flights of spiral stairs to the chorus dressing rooms. And she made me feel like a star by sending me a bouquet of spring flowers—delivered to the dressing room.

They were the first flowers I had ever received.

At the performance the audience roared. It was clear—they *liked* me. Richard Rodgers liked me too and offered me the role in the national road company of *Panama Hattie*. I was overcome and immediately accepted.

George Abbott, the great Broadway impresario, was casting a new musical, *Best Foot Forward*, and word must have got around to him that he ought to take a look at this kooky little kid who was going on for Betty Hutton. He sent for me.

"Miss Allyson, I thought we'd seen the last of you for a minute there. At one point in *Panama Hattie*, the chorus boys are throwing you so high you disappear altogether under the proscenium. You're so light you just fly right out of sight. It's like a magic act—now you see her, now you don't." I surely wasn't about to tell him that after those great flights I would go to the rest room and throw up.

I made a funny face. "Well, if it's magic you want . . ."

He looked at me with affection. "We need a funny little girl like you to ham up some scenes with Nancy Walker. She's a budding comedy star."

Best Foot Forward was the story of a school prom. A self-centered actress—played by Rosemary Lane—needs publicity to pep up her career and accepts when she's invited to a college prom.

I said no. I had my principles. I had already promised Richard Rodgers to go on the road with *Panama Hattie*.

Abbott look startled.

"Have you signed yet?"

"No, but I couldn't break a promise to Mr. Rodgers." Abbott just sat there shaking his head as I left his office.

Without telling me, Abbott went to see Mr. Rodgers and he said, "Give her a break. It's a good part." I was surprised when Mr. Rodgers called me in and asked me what I wanted to do. I said, "Oh, I'm going on the tour. I promised you and I can't go back on a promise." He said, "You can sign for the tour with us but do you think that is wise when you have the chance of a Broadway show with George Abbott?"

"I can't think about that because I promised you."

He looked amused and baffled. "Well, you can start to think about it now because we have just fired you."

"Oh, thank you, Mr. Rodgers," I said. Suddenly he was laughing but I was earnestly jumping up and down and pumping his hand.

In *Best Foot Forward* I loved going into my great show-stopper, "The Three B's," with my sidekicks—Nancy Walker and Erlene Schools. The three B's stood for Beethoven, Brahms and Bach. In the song, written by Hugh Martin and Ralph Blaine, we complained that what we really wanted the B's to stand for was Barrelhouse, Boogie Woogie and Blues. I sang the barrelhouse, Nancy the boogie and Erlene the blues. I also had a solo song, "What Do You Think I Am?" and for the finale, I sang with the cast that now much overused and abused classic, "Buckle Down Winsockie."

One night an excited buzz went around backstage—"Dick Powell is out front." We were all standing onstage and Rosemary Lane was saying, "Really? Where, *where?*" as she peeped through the curtain to locate him. I was just a featured player so

I waited until the stars of the show had their turn before I took a peep at the screen idol. There he was, seventh row center.

Wouldn't he be surprised, I thought as I looked through the curtain at him, to know how many times I had skipped school to go see him in a movie? No, I suppose not. Didn't every girl drool over America's singing idol—star of both *Gold Diggers* and *20 Million Sweethearts* with Ginger Rogers, and scores more—like *42nd Street* and *Naughty But Nice*. Next to Fred Astaire, he was my favorite.

A thrill passed through me. Dark wavy hair, handsome boyish grin. They were all there, just like in his movies.

It's protocol for visiting celebrities to make an appearance backstage after the show. Dick Powell's had the air of excitement usually reserved for heads of state. No one went to the dressing rooms—we all stayed in costume onstage. When he arrived everyone clustered around him and I envied Rosemary Lane as he kissed her. I was not among the crowd. Shy, I watched from the spiral staircase, where I was sitting, joyous to be observing it all. Suddenly I noticed that Rosemary and Dick had turned and were looking up at me.

Rosemary would report to me later that Dick had said, "There's that little midget who came onstage and then she opened her mouth and out boomed this big husky voice. It just knocked me out. She's got a voice like Jimmy Durante's—only June Allyson's is froggier. Can I meet her?"

At that point Rosemary called up to me—"Come on down and meet Dick Powell, honey." I guess I came down pigeon-toed—Joan Blondell said so later and it's true I still walk that way. Rosemary said, "Junie, this is someone who asked to meet you—Dick Powell." I looked up, way up, and put out my hand and he held it, grinning down at me, "So here's the little girl with the funny voice." I just continued looking up at him as he held my hand. My mouth was open, but nothing was coming out. I was not uncomfortable, though, and broke into a smile.

Vaguely I became aware that his wife, Joan Blondell, was also there, but no one introduced us and quickly the moment passed and someone else was grabbing Dick and talking to him.

Joan's account of this meeting—in *Center Door Fancy*, a fictionalized autobiography—is loaded against me. She wrote that I simpered and came down the steps pigeon-toed and cooed that I slept with his *letter* under my pillow every night. I had no letter. I never wrote a fan letter. I had no picture or letter from him or any star. It was ridiculous, but then, so was her charge that I had stolen her husband away—starting that night. Dick Powell recorded his own account of our first meeting in his diary, and it differs substantially from Joan's.

New York. October 11:
Why I bother to put this down I don't know except that she certainly is the cutest thing anybody ever saw. Last night, I went to catch *Best Foot Forward* and there was this little blond character named June Allyson who sang so loud that the veins stood out on her neck like garden hose. I sat and guffawed through the whole routine. Really a funny act although I doubt if the producer meant it that way.

Anyway, this afternoon I had to attend a formal luncheon and I got stuck with the most stubborn hunk of chicken I've ever had the displeasure of eating. It took all my attention and I was struggling with it until I guess my face turned red. Then, suddenly, I felt someone's eyes on me and I looked up. And there was this same cute little character from the show last night and she was convulsed with laughter. At me! I don't know whether or not I particularly like that kid—but she sure is cute.

The backstage visit of Dick Powell certainly raised my status in the company. Suddenly Rosemary Lane drew closer to me, sharing many confidences about her dear friend Dick Powell—how nice he was, how unlike the usual arrogant movie star. She was fascinated that he had singled me out from everyone and insisted on meeting me. So was I.

One night, between acts of *Best Foot Forward*, I heard the cast talking excitedly about Hollywood—"Have you heard the news?"

"No," I said. "What news?"

"We're all going to Hollywood. *Best Foot Forward* is going to be made into a movie by Metro-Goldwyn-Mayer and everybody's going to be in it."

"Everybody?"

"Everybody."

Wrong. One of my trio, with whom I stopped the show every night as we sang "The Three B's," was not going—Erlene Schools, who was to be replaced by a starlet named Gloria DeHaven. Nancy Walker was going, so at least part of the trio would be intact. Erlene Schools was crushed and later I heard that she took her own life. I was shocked when I heard the news. How much did the disappointment over not going to Hollywood have to do with it? I wondered.

Rosemary Lane was also left behind. Instead MGM was using the sexy, tall, Lucille Ball. Dear Rosemary Lane of the famous Lane Sisters—she treated me with kindness and never with the condescension other stars reserve for chorus and featured players. I would miss her.

I would miss everyone. And New York. And Broadway. And Willoughby's, where I'd emoted for hours trying to pick the right camera for my dear Tommy. I was going to Hollywood and he was going to war. Who knew where he would be going, but this was 1943 and as he put it, "Nothing lasts forever." Maybe by the time the dreadful war was over and Tommy was back, I would be so famous even his snooty family would accept me.

Full of emotion, I made my last visit to Mother, and she filled me with advice, repeating the adages that had been handed down to her: "There is always hope . . . You're known by the company you keep . . . Nothing succeeds like success . . . and, when the going gets tough, the tough get going."

I tried not to cry, telling her I would make it up to her for the long years of deprivation after the accident—and before the accident.

"Don't make promises you cannot keep," she said sternly, trying to fight back her own tears. She held me close. "Don't you know, I want only your happiness and nothing for me, dear."

"And I'll help you take care of Arthur, too," I said, stopping her. "You'll see." Mother had remarried and Arthur was my half brother. I loved him dearly.

And suddenly, I, who had never been out of the state of New York unless you counted New Jersey—was on my way to Hollywood, running through Pennsylvania Station in New York City. I had everything I owned, all stuffed into the scruffy little borrowed suitcase Tommy was carrying for me.

And in the little makeup case in my hand were the things most dear to me, my bits of costume jewelry and, most important of all, the photographs of all those dear to me. "I'll never change when I become a star," I told Tommy, striding beside me as I ran to keep up. "Oh no, never. And I'll invite everyone to come see me in Hollywood."

People were looking at me as if they knew there was something special about me. I wanted to shout, "Hey, look, everybody! I'm going to Hollywood." And I'm at the train door and it's my big goodbye scene and I look down. And I'm still wearing my fuzzy wuzzy bedroom slippers. So that's why people were looking. What a comedown.

"Goodbye, goodbye . . ."

Shoes, shoes. Just barely aboard the train and already facing my first crisis. My best and only good shoes had been left sitting beside my bed, ready to be put on. I certainly hadn't counted on an expenditure of seven dollars, maybe even ten, for a pair of shoes before I received my first Hollywood paycheck. I had $21 in my purse, my total wealth.

As I sat in the train, excited yet fearful about the future, I realized that I knew two people in Hollywood and wondered if I would ever see them again. The first, I had just barely met—Dick Powell. The second, I had dated and he had gotten to Hollywood a year ahead of me—in 1942—Van Johnson.

Of course they hadn't been what you would call romantic dates. Van had been a dancer in the chorus of *Pal Joey* and we would meet after the show and go to the Automat—Dutch treat, each feeding our own nickels into the slots.

But Van *had* bought me a box of chocolates and gallantly let me eat all the dark ones, my favorites, while he ate the light. We laughed constantly. I told him, "People are always thinking there's something wrong with my voice, that I have a sore throat or something." Van predicted my voice would help me make it big and called it my "million dollar laryngitis."

I'd have settled for a half million.

2

I HAD ALWAYS had a fantasy of what it would be like when I arrived in Hollywood—welcoming committees for the national heroine, newsreel cameras, flashbulbs popping. Wrong! Reality found me arriving alone in a crowded wartime train station in my houseshoes—to good news and bad.

The good news was that a studio representative was at the station to meet me and he recognized me. If he hadn't it might have taken my last cent to get to my hotel—I had only $10 left. The bad news was that I was already on six weeks' layoff without pay because my movie, *Best Foot Forward*, was not ready yet for the cameras.

I wondered why I had ever left Broadway. I wondered what saying of my mother's would cover this situation. And then I remembered—"It's always darkest before the dawn." Dawn came in the form of *Girl Crazy* and I was placed on the payroll.

I moved into my first apartment—a place on Wilshire that cost $40 a month. It wasn't much but at least I had a kitchen, a step up from the hot plate out the window at the old American Woman's Club. Now I cooked not only eggs but pancakes—my new culinary triumph.

Money. My own money at last. A decent meal at last and a new pair of shoes. I finally got that great check for my first week. I danced around the room with it. I was paid $125 a week, with ten percent or a fat $12.50 going to my agent. All of $112.50 for me. I felt rich—until I saw how quickly money melted away in Hollywood, where some hotshot stars gave tips as big as my weekly salary. With Judy Garland's friendship and Mickey Rooney's kind help I began to feel I belonged in Hollywood.

Papa Mayer didn't send me to entertain stars in their homes, but the studio did something equally terrifying for a newcomer like me. As part of the war effort MGM decided to send Gloria DeHaven, Nancy Walker and me to entertain and cheer up the troops who were in wartime hospitals. Gloria, Nancy and I would spread out and each take a different ward. Usually there would be great applause and the boys would hardly let me go and I would sing and talk on and on. One day after I'd sung and gone into a little dance routine I was stunned by complete silence. Not a clap. I paused, confused and frightened and not sure whether to continue—did they hate me?

Finally, one fellow yelled out, "Sing it, June!" I sang another song and danced some more—but again there was silence. Suddenly I realized what the problem was and I almost choked—this was an amputation ward. These boys had lost arms, and those with one hand were considered the lucky ones. I pulled myself together and called for requests. After that I stayed on and sang whatever song they wanted. Only after I got out of the ward did I fall to pieces.

I was relieved but apprehensive when *Best Foot Forward* was finally ready to go before the cameras with the little comedy trio for "The Three B's"—Nancy Walker and I and the girl who had gotten her start in a Charlie Chaplin movie as a child, Gloria DeHaven.

Gloria and I would eventually become good friends, but the person who was most important to me in that critical year was a tall, slightly tough talking but glamorous redhead who would be in three movies with me before the year was up—or rather, I would have bit parts in three of her movies.

In 1943, when I met Lucille Ball, she had not yet turned herself into the wacky wife of I Love Lucy fame but was dressed and coiffed and turned out as a dazzling showgirl type in her role as the haughty motion picture star. Lucille Ball and I were together again in Thousands Cheer, in which my bit was nothing to cheer about, and Meet the People, for which I was never even given a script or told who else would be in it—I was just handed a song for yet another cameo role and told to learn it and be ready to sing it. I think it was called "I'd Like to Recognize This Tune," and I remember telling Lucille Ball "I'd like to recognize where I'm going. I think it's nowhere. That's where."

"What are you saying?" she asked.

"I'm saying I'm giving up." Next to Judy, Lucy had become my best friend, and she would not let me leave Hollywood in 1943, when I was beginning to fear I might never be anything more than a bit player, singing a song and throwing up with nervousness afterward.

"You can't go," Lucy told me. "You've worked too hard to get here and you're going to make it. Look at me." Then she launched into stories of her past, how she had been a stagestruck kid like me who had come to New York at fifteen to study drama. "The school wouldn't take me because I was too much of a shrinking violet to be an actress," she said, adding, "Yeah, yeah, it's hard to believe and look at me now. And once I got to Hollywood nobody could make me go home."

The way she had gotten to Hollywood was that she became a model and was discovered by a Hollywood agent who spotted her in a cigarette ad. She had been told she could be a chorus girl in Roman Scandals if she would leave for Hollywood immediately; she was on the next train. The 1933 Eddie Cantor musical was her start.

I looked at Lucy and thought of the difference between us—how lonely and frustrated I was and how she had a full life, husband, friends and everything and was a *star.* I wanted to express this, but all I could blubber was, "Yes, but you're *tall.*"

We were sitting on the sidelines that day, watching Kathryn Grayson sing. Lucy turned and fixed me with a hard stare.

"What did you say?"

"I said as soon as I finish my next commitment, I'm going to fold my tent and steal away. After *Meet the People.* I don't mean to be ungrateful, but I was hot in New York—"

"Big fish in a little pond."

"Oh, Lucy, don't you see? I was just starting to get somewhere on Broadway. Hollywood is just not for me. I'll never get real parts. I can't even earn enough for my medical education. I want to go to medical school before it's too late."

"Medical education? Are you crazy? You just settle down and dig your toes in. Don't you dare run away. Where would you go, anyway?"

"Back to New York," I said, "where they care about me."

"Well, you can't jump back and forth. You're here now and you're going to stay. I won't let you go back. You're going to laugh at this someday."

I was watching my friend Lucille do a scene from *Meet the People* one day when I became aware of someone I had seen before. Dick Powell. There was a box on wheels about fifteen feet away with a telephone mounted on it and he was standing there talking on the phone and smiling at me.

I had to get a closer look. I walked over and stood nearby, staring at those incredible blue eyes. He put his hand over the receiver and said, "What's the matter? Is something wrong?"

"Oh no. I'm just waiting to use the phone."

I was crushed. He hadn't even recognized me. He didn't

remember he had wanted to meet me backstage in New York. All right, he didn't know my name so I pretended I didn't know his.

"I'll be off in just a minute," he said. He hung up and I still stood there looking at him in a daze—he looked back as if to say, "What's wrong with her?" and walked away. I started frantically dialing numbers, hoping no one would answer. Should I remind Dick Powell that he had asked Rosemary Lane to introduce us? I was too shy to. For a moment I thought he'd remembered me because he was walking back my way. But he only wanted to use the phone again and stood there absently waiting for me to finish.

"Nobody's home," I said, hanging up the phone.

I soon found out why he was at MGM. He was going to be the star in the upcoming *Meet the People*. And though I got palpitations every time he looked at me, I felt I was getting nowhere with him—and besides, he was taken.

Still, it was thrilling when Dick suddenly invited several starlets and young actors from the *People* cast to his home for a barbecue. He was just being kind. He knew we had no money. I learned it was typical of Dick Powell to befriend beginners. Jane Powell, he told me, had taken both his advice and his name—for luck. Her real name was Suzanne Bruce and she had asked him if he'd mind if she took his name. "Jane Powell is a fantastic talent," he said. "I was happy to advise her."

I looked around me as I stood in the Powells' home, curious to see how a real movie star lived. I met Joan Blondell for the first time—and her mother. Her mother could never remember my name but referred to me throughout the evening as "the cute one." This woman sat and monopolized me for what seemed like hours, telling me endless stories about Joan.

This wasn't exactly what I had come for, but I was all ears, nevertheless, to learn anything and everything I could about the woman who was married to Dick. Joan had been a vaudeville brat, traveling as a child with her touring parents through Europe, Australia and the Orient. Her father, Eddie Blondell, was one of the original Katzenjammer Kids. Joan had been Miss Dallas when she was only seventeen.

Other sessions followed. It became a pattern. At these meetings we discussed how to handle scripts and studio officials and how to judge roles. Dick Powell sat in the middle of this little band of ambitious youth, answering questions which added up to a course in how to get ahead in Hollywood. As he put it, "You're only as welcome as your last picture." He looked around the group and commented, "It will be interesting to see who's still among us ten years from now and who's back home working in the shoe store. And who's in trouble for not saving enough money to pay Uncle Sam."

He told us all to feel free to call him if we needed counsel on a specific problem. Eventually I told Dick how hurt I'd felt when he hadn't recognized me at the portable phone and he just laughed. There was still no romance.

MGM now took a moment to assess my career to date and decided they could do without me. I had made it safely through my six months of probation but I had not yet come to the attention of Papa Mayer and now I was on the list to be dropped at the end of my first year. I was not to receive the seven-year contract I had dreamed about when I'd first arrived in Hollywood. I was to be dumped.

But I didn't know it. I had been planning to leave Hollywood, but that was all behind me now that I had Dick Powell as a mentor. I had changed my mind and was ready to stay and fight for a movie career. Only later would I learn what had been going on behind scenes, in fine paneled offices. I had flunked all my classes—the don't-close-your-eyes-when-you-smile class, the how-to-sound-like-a-girl-not-a-boy class, the lisp-remedial class.

It was producer Joe Pasternak who went to Papa Mayer and said, "You have a kid on the drop list, a kid I think it's wrong to drop." He added, "I don't even know why. She isn't pretty. She certainly isn't sexy. She sings fairly well but we've got Judy Garland and Jane Powell and Kathryn Grayson. She doesn't dance all that well, either. But she's got something. Would you do me a favor and take a look at this test where we talk to her and make her walk?"

"Okay, if you want me to look, I'll look," said Louis Mayer, "but remember, I'm very busy."

"This will only take a few minutes," Pasternak assured him, getting ready to dim the lights. "I don't want you to pay attention to how she's dressed or how she walks. I just want you to be aware of how she listens. And watch her eyes." L. B. Mayer later told me he didn't know what the heck he was supposed to be watching, but when the lights came back on, he said, "You know, you're right. I don't know what she's got either but it's something and if you want to use her in a picture, go ahead."

"Fine. I think I want to use her in *Two Girls and a Sailor* as balance to Gloria DeHaven. I can see them together."

For the moment my head was out of the noose.

I guess I made a mistake when I called Dick Powell at home. Joan answered and she seemed to be in a bad mood. I said Dick had given me his number to call if I needed help. She did not seem interested in what my trouble could be and irritably called Dick to the phone. Then she came back on and said, with biting sarcasm, "You want my husband? Well, you can have him." Dick was on the phone and I tried to hide my embarrassment as I said, "I've got a script from MGM and they want me to do this picture called *Two Girls and a Sailor*."

He said, "That's good."

"Would you please read it and help me with it?"

"Sure. I'll be out at MGM Wednesday doing retakes—bring it to the studio."

I gave him my script—my only copy. That was how much I trusted him. He was like a god to me, someone who knew everything. He was older and wiser. Much older—more than twenty years. I was in awe of him. He called me on Thursday and said, "I'd like to talk to you about this part."

I said, "Okay," thinking he meant to talk at the studio. He suggested the Brown Derby for lunch. As we sat down he startled and frightened me. "I don't want your feelings to be hurt," he said, "but you can't play the part they want you to play. You have to play the plain sister." The studio had cast me as the beautiful sister and Gloria DeHaven as the plain one. The plain girl had spicier lines but the parts were equal. They were grooming Gloria DeHaven for stardom.

"I can't believe what I'm hearing," I said, poking at my Cobb Salad. My mood plunged as Richard talked on.

"There are two lines in the script that absolutely negate your doing the role of the beautiful sister and they are when the grandfather asks Gloria, 'Is your sister as pretty as you?' and she says, 'Oh, prettier, much prettier.' Nobody is going to believe that. Gloria is a real beauty. So what I want you to do is go in and tell Mr. Mayer that you want to test for the role of the plain sister."

I was terrified. Me go in and tell Papa Mayer what to do? Richard was going merrily along, ignoring the dismayed look on my face. "And when he agrees, which you will make him do, I want you to go home and cut off your hair. Just straight across bangs and short, straight sides and don't use any makeup in the test."

I went staggering out of the restaurant. I knew I was going to somehow get up the courage to do what Dick Powell had advised. Such was my blind trust in his judgment that I did not for a moment consider disagreeing with or ignoring what he said.

Now all I needed was guts. I had no trouble getting in to see Papa Mayer, who loved playing the father figure with his starlets. When he heard what I wanted, he made a face but said,

"All right. You can test for the plain sister. We have people who know how to cast and they are paid to cast. But if you want to test, you can test." He shrugged his shoulders and threw out his hands in resignation. I thanked him effusively and almost ran out of the office.

It was hard to cut my hair but I did it and again Dick Powell had been right. Papa Mayer saw the test and called me in. "You are absolutely right," he beamed. "We are switching the roles."

At last I had a real role. At last my career was getting started. And at last the studio told me how close I had been to being dropped completely—about a hairsbreadth away.

I shuddered as I reflected on what Papa Mayer must have thought of my audacity. I bumped into Lucille Ball in the MGM commissary. Now that I was off the drop list and a full-fledged star, I could thank Lucille for convincing me not to go back to New York when times were bleak. "I'm glad I stayed in Hollywood," I said. "It grows on one."

"Yes," she said, "and you have grown on it, Junie, and that's even better."

3

JOAN BLONDELL was convinced that I was after her husband. I wasn't, even though Dick Powell gave me palpitations and shortness of breath just to look at him. I tried not to think of him—except as my mentor. Anyway, I was having other problems.

My romantic life was certainly confused. Anytime I found a man to my liking, Papa Mayer found it to *his* disliking. For example, I was getting interested in David Rose, who had been taking me out. David was still married to Judy Garland but they were separated.

I had checked with Judy because I would not hurt her for the world. She didn't mind my dating David and said he was very nice but she wanted nothing more to do with him. David and I and Gene Kelly and Betsy Blair often double-dated or we'd go picnicking on the studio grounds.

As a young starlet, I was given the Papa Mayer pep talk that all the little starlets received. We were to be models of good behavior. We represented the studio and were not to have publicity in the gossip columns that embarrassed the studio. If we behaved, we might become great stars at MGM. The choice was ours. Understood? Dismissed. We were ushered out.

The one thing Judy and I could never agree about was L. B.

Mayer. She feared and hated him because he never gave her a chance to rest and relax during or between pictures. I feared and loved him because he had given me my chance and he was the strong father-figure I had always yearned for.

I would go marching into L. B. Mayer's office and tell him my problem and he would lecture me sternly and tell me what to do. I rather liked our relationship and enjoyed charming him. It was when *he* summoned *me* that I knew I was in hot water. Invariably it would be that he didn't want me to see this boy or that. They were not right for a young lady who was going to be a star someday—*if* she did what Papa Mayer said.

I said, "Yes, sir." I did not argue. I wanted to be a star and I wanted to be a star at MGM, the hottest studio of the '40's. One thing I respect about Louis B. Mayer is that I never saw him once call an MGM star on the carpet at those unavoidable times when a cruel rumor without foundation was circulated. Every major actress gets whispered about, usually at about the time she first hits it big. With me it was the nymphomaniac thing. While I was still a virgin, a rumor went around that the "sweet young thing" image was a pose and that I really craved sex. "She's not Goody Two Shoes, she's Goody Round Heels," said the malicious ones. Someone had to explain to me what "round heels" meant—a girl easily toppled backward into bed. This kind of thing hurts but it goes with the territory of being a celebrity. If Papa Mayer heard this rumor, he dismissed it. There can be no question that he did in fact hear it because he had a great spy system and knew *everything*. He knew what you had for breakfast.

The subject was not roses when Louis B. Mayer called me on the carpet one day, but rather David Rose, whom I was dating fairly regularly by now.

"Is it true that you are going out with David Rose?"

"Yes, sir, he's very nice and I'm learning a lot about music from him."

"Buy a book. If you care about your reputation, you cannot

be seen with a married man—a twice-married man—no matter what he's teaching you about music. Don't you know he's Judy Garland's husband?"

"Oh, but they're getting a divorce. And Judy says it's okay."

"So when he gets it, it will be his second divorce. So it is not okay and this must stop immediately."

"Yes, sir."

David Rose may not have made a success of his marriages to Martha Raye and Judy Garland but he was a lovely, gentle person and a gifted composer. I was pleased to be singled out by the man who had composed "So in Love" and "Our Waltz." Years later Judy would tell me what had made her fall out of love with him—she had gotten pregnant early in the marriage and David had not stopped her from getting an abortion. "A baby would have interfered with the shooting schedule of some film I was doing," Judy told me. "I finally got the abortion to keep from making the studio angry, but the marriage was never the same. Something was gone. It broke my heart."

When I was in Papa Mayer's office arguing about David Rose that day, I finally said, "Who do you want me to date if I can't date David?"

"I know just the boy," Papa Mayer said immediately. "Your co-star in Two Sailors and a Girl, Van Johnson. To the fans you're already a romantic couple at MGM. Now all you need to do is make it official."

"But Mr. Mayer, Van and I have been old friends ever since New York."

"Good. Then it's settled. I'll tell Van to call you. Go out with Van. Get this David Rose out of your system. Every bobbysoxer in America's swooning over Van Johnson. Look what a lucky girl you are, June." Van Johnson and I went out on a series of official dates—to premieres and industry functions—arranged by the studio. Eventually we were to see the phenomenon of joint Van Johnson-June Allyson fan clubs.

Van was a national craze and teenage heartthrob and I had my first taste of mass hysteria as his frequent date—his fans waited in the hundreds wherever we went. Some nights were so bad we didn't dare leave the studio—there was that kind of unruly crowd outside the gates at Culver City. When they started really getting rough—trying to tear off clothes and yank hair—Van simply went into hiding. It would cause people to call Van Johnson arrogant, but they could not be more mistaken about this man who always went to great lengths to be kind to the hordes of swooning, screeching fans who were invading his privacy and trying to turn his life into a farce.

I was always amused at the irony of our big romance which MGM manufactured. While all the intimate details were fabricated by the publicity department, Van and I continued our platonic friendship. At a fancy restaurant Van winked at me as he picked up the tab and said, kind of muttering in his funny way, "Let's see now, what's your share?" I gave him my sweetest smile and said, "If the arithmetic is too much, maybe the waiter can help you." Then we both roared, remembering our Automat days in Manhattan.

"Just a private joke," Van said to eavesdroppers leaning over to enjoy our tabletalk.

The fan magazines especially liked the combination of Van Johnson and me and were panting for a marriage—and so were the fans, even writing to suggest a name for our first child. It was Van, Jr., if a son; and Vanjee, if a daughter, to rhyme with Angie, and yet keep the letter "J" for my name. After *Two Girls and a Sailor* Van Johnson and I did so many war movies together that the studio joke was that no one would ever know how many missions Van had flown over my dressing room. But the only man who really made my heart flutter was, of course, Dick Powell.

With Papa Mayer's blessing, I was also dating Peter Lawford. If I had married either Van or Peter, Papa Mayer would have made it a studio event.

For a short time I dated Jack Kennedy. I didn't know his father was an ambassador and I certainly didn't know I was being pursued by a future President of the United States. He was just a very thin, tall fellow with a boyish grin and nice eyes. My impression was that he was under contract to Metro or wanted to be. We had seen each other around the studio and one day he asked me to dinner and took me to a nice place. It wasn't even Dutch treat. We laughed a lot. He reminded me of Peter Lawford—both had the same charm and fun-loving ways.

Peter Lawford had a funny little quirk about his shoes. He loved his velvet slippers—little velvet loafers with gold emblems on the instep. He padded around in them on the set and even wore them to parties. I was often over at Peter Lawford's house. I never was as close to him as I was to Van, but I grew very fond of him in a mildly romantic way. We had a lot of fun. I loved his devil-may-care attitude and his British accent fascinated me. So did his mother and father, who were *teddibly* British. Peter's father was addressed as Sir Sidney and his mother, Lady Lawford. I was told that Sir Sidney had been a high-ranking military man in England before coming to the States, and that Peter was in line to succeed his father in the title but that he gave up his claim in order to be an American citizen.

I couldn't have cared less about titles. What amused me, years later, was what Peter said about his mother's reaction to his marriage to Patricia Kennedy, whose father was an ambassador and whose brother would one day be President of the United States. His mother had not been too pleased with the marriage, initially, and had said what a pity it was he hadn't married someone "more suitable"—someone of the British peerage.

After *Two Girls and a Sailor* was finished, the studio was sure it had a blockbuster and sent me to New York with Nancy Walker on a personal appearance tour. I kept hoping Dick Powell, who had engineered this success, would call to tell me what he thought of my performance. He had told me he and Joan were going to a sneak preview in L.A.

The phone rang in my New York hotel room at midnight and I was groggy with sleep until I heard a voice say, "This is Dick Powell." Now fully awake, I said, "Oh, hi. Did you see the picture?"

"Yes, I did. All I can say is it's your picture." I had never heard the expression before and thought he was saying it's just another picture—as in "It's your picture and you're stuck with it."

"Oh," I said disappointed.

"Oh, June, do I have to teach you everything? That means you steal the show—the movie is yours. And you know what else it means?"

"No."

"It means I think you're going to be a star."

I was so choked up I couldn't speak.

"What are you doing?" he asked.

"It's the middle of the night. I'm in bed."

"Well get up and get dressed."

"Get dressed? What for?"

"I'm going to meet you downstairs in your lobby in twenty minutes."

"Aren't you in Hollywood?"

"Would I be saying this if I were, dummy? We'll go somewhere and celebrate with a cup of coffee." I flew around the room throwing on my clothes and rushed to the lobby.

The first thing he did was walk me over to the newsstand and casually pick up a newspaper. The headline said, JOAN BLONDELL AND DICK POWELL SEPARATE. That was the way he told me that he and Joan were through. I suddenly remembered the phone call when Joan had answered. But I said nothing. I was walking on air. He took me to Sardi's and a lot of people looked at us rather strangely, having seen the headlines, too. I noticed

Dick didn't seem nervous when Walter Winchell stopped by our table to chat.

So began our courtship. When I got back to Los Angeles, he started taking me to parties. He wasn't hiding anything but it was a delicate situation. People at the studio stopped smiling at me, registering their disapproval without saying anything. Papa Mayer called me in and said it didn't look good for a young starlet with a great future ahead of her to be going with an older man who was married.

"But he's getting a divorce," I said in a small voice.

"It's the same thing. He's still married. I want you to think about it. Like my own daughter, I tell you to think of how it looks."

"Yes, sir," I said and crept out as quickly as I could. But I knew there was nothing to talk about. I was madly in love with Richard—by now I was calling him Richard though I was the only one who ever did. Now we were even more careful of where we were seen in public—I knew I shouldn't appear to be flaunting my love in the disapproving face of Papa Mayer. One place that became our refuge was Lucy Ball's home. She welcomed me into her inner circle of friends.

I began to meet people of such vast talent and success that I started to have my first overwhelming feelings of insecurity. How could I ever fit in? These were more mature stars and celebrities who had arrived long ago. I didn't even know what they were laughing about half the time. Richard would coach me, "Just go ahead and laugh if everyone else is laughing, honey, and then I'll explain it to you later."

So when a joke ended, I laughed louder than anyone and I would turn my head sideways and look wise as in, "You know me, pal." And sometimes in my eagerness, I laughed when I shouldn't have and Richard would have to explain that, too— why it *wasn't* funny. A less sophisticated man would have been terribly embarrassed. Usually Richard was merely amused. Except about caviar.

Caviar. I had never had caviar before, and suddenly Richard was taking me to Hollywood parties where they always served it. I didn't know what it was but I thought it was divine. It would be in a bowl with the trimmings of crumbled hard-boiled egg, sour cream and chopped chives surrounding it and a tray of little wafers and squares of rye bread.

I learned to build my own—doing what everyone else did. Caviar on the bottom, a sprinkling of everything on top and I loved it. I would eat it and eat it. I had no idea it came from a fish.

We were at a particularly posh party at Jack Benny's when I said, "Richard, what is this thing that I love so much?" I was pointing to the caviar. He looked sheepishly around as if afraid someone had heard me. "That's caviar," he said in a low tone.

"Caviar!" I exclaimed. "So *that's* caviar! What's it made of?"

"Hush," he said. "I'll explain it later."

And he did, giving a whole speech on the famous little fish eggs and how the best came from the beluga, a white sturgeon of the Caspian Sea and the Black Sea.

"Fish eggs or not, I still love it," I said, writing down the word "beluga." Richard's birthday was coming up—November 14—and I knew just what to surprise him with. I bought a huge tin of the best beluga and placed it all on a tray in front of the sofa where Richard had his evening cocktail while I sipped a Coke or ginger ale. I meant to merely taste it but by the time Richard got to my place to start the birthday celebration, there were only a few globs left. I had cleaned out the whole bowl and I was stuffed.

When I saw the look on his face, I rushed to get him his

birthday present. He opened it and took out two pearl-handled antique guns. "Flattop," he said, shaking his head, "don't you know you're taking your life in your hands to give me guns at a time like this?"

Richard presented me with my first gift—a book, *Messer Marco Polo* by Donn Byrne. He had owned it for many years—it was copyrighted 1921—and treasured it and he wanted me to read it and be inspired by it too. Richard made a little speech about how the great Venetian adventurer had amazed the world by sailing to China in the thirteenth century. "Make only big plans," he told me. I kept it beside my bed and when I got to page 44, I saw that he had written my name in the margin and was deeply touched as I read: "She is not a cold and beautiful princess. . . . she is warm as the sun in early June, and she may be beautiful and a princess, but we all think of her as Golden Bells, the little girl in the Chinese garden."

Richard had moved out of his home, leaving Joan and getting an apartment of his own, but soon he gave it up and moved in with his father at Toluca Lake because he hated to come home at night to an empty apartment. He took me over to meet his dad and I could see that the old gentleman was ailing now and needed him. The next day, he said to Richard, "Son, who was that cute little boy you brought here last night?"

Richard said, "Pa, that's who I'm dating. That's who I love." His dad exploded, "That little boy?" They got along fine except for the times when his dad got into Richard's hundred-year-old scotch. Richard was saving it for an important occasion but the old gent clucked and said, "Son, nothing's too good for your father."

I realized I had a take-charge guy. Soon after I started dating Richard, I found my whole lifestyle changing. He insisted I move to a larger apartment—one with a bedroom—and hire a housekeeper to look after me. He had his own reasons, as well, for having her there. He wanted to be able to have dinner with me at home whenever we felt like it. And he was determined to protect my reputation.

I did not think of defying him, even though the housekeeper's salary came out of my humble—by Hollywood standards—salary. I used my slim savings to have the porch enclosed so that it could become a bedroom for the housekeeper. Since Richard seemed to know what he was doing, I even let him hire her. He chose Bess Van Dyke, a dignified, cultured woman who had gray hair and was quite motherly. But she had a no-nonsense air about her, too, and I felt safe and secure with her.

The first time Bess Van Dyke cooked dinner for me, Richard came as my first guest, bearing flowers. The table was correctly set and I suddenly realized that I didn't know the proper way to eat. I observed Richard and followed suit. I was the kid who had lived on hamburgers and fried eggs out the window. What did I know about beautifully appointed tables? But the next day I started learning. I went to the library and took out an armload of books on etiquette. I read women's magazines and cut out all the pictures which showed tables set with lovely silverware and linens.

The talk was lively and far-ranging at our intimate dinners. I was going to college with Professor Powell lecturing on many subjects. When he asked me what my philosophy of life was, I told him, happily: "If you see someone without a smile, give him yours."

Richard almost fell off the chair laughing. "Oh God, don't ever let her change!"

I don't know if Richard knew how much I was learning from him but I suspect he did. Sometimes he would leaf through a magazine with me and show me what he thought was good taste and what was not. Soon I was ready to sit down at elegant formal dinners with ease.

It was good to have a starring role in a hit movie at last. I was determined never to be on that drop list again. By now people were starting to imitate me. The croaky voice was in. Peter Pan collars were in. And my little lisp was in. Little did anyone know how many hours I spent checking through the script and changing words with the dreaded "s" sounds to something easier for me to say. And people wrote in asking how to learn to sing like me.

Now that I was a star, I was wondering what had taken me so long, but others were saying "meteoric rise" and "overnight success." It didn't matter. The main thing was I finally felt I belonged. Every day was an adventure. I loved the premieres, the parties, the role of the movie star, even if I couldn't believe it had happened to me. Richard warned, "Believe me, it wears off. Honey, I've been through it—and not just once."

"Please take me to the big party at the Ronald Colmans'," I insisted. "I've got to go. I promised. And you'll have fun. You'll see."

"Okay, but just remember, what's a party to you is work to me. So if I give you the high sign, let's get out of there and disappear early."

Then, when we arrived at the party, Richard was the most social creature there and I just walked around clinging to him, afraid to say a word. Richard later told some friends, "When Ronald Colman walked into the room, Idiothead here looked at him as if he were the King of England and Colman looked at her as if he agreed completely."

We stayed the whole evening. "Why don't you just drift around and talk to people," Richard urged. "Strike out on your own."

"I can't," I said, terrified. "I don't know what to talk to them about."

Richard sighed. "You'll learn." I did learn but by the time I could hold my own socially, the thrill was gone and I preferred to stay home, just enjoying Richard and a few friends.

In those early days in Hollywood, I was at war with

myself—sometimes I clowned around and acted as if I were having a great time. Other times I sat in a corner. The truth is—I was an introvert in training to be an extrovert.

Now I was being driven as hard at MGM as Judy Garland, with movies back to back. As soon as I completed one film, I was hurrying to wardrobe for the next. In rapid succession came *Music for Millions*, *Her Highness and the Bellboy*, *The Sailor Takes a Wife*, and *Two Sisters from Boston*.

I loved hearing all the inside stories around the studio. Several of the stories concerned Gloria DeHaven and me. One was that we were feuding because of the switch in our *Two Girls and a Sailor* roles with Van Johnson. That wasn't true. We were and are good friends. Another was a story of the flying teeth and that one was true. It happened in a scene with Jimmy Durante in *Two Girls and a Sailor*. We were in an empty warehouse and Jimmy was hiding there and supposed to frighten me and Gloria. He certainly did. He let out such a bloodcurdling sound that Gloria screamed for real and the caps she was wearing over her teeth to make them look perfect flew out and went sailing right to me before landing on the floor. The horrified look on my face as I watched the teeth sail by stayed in and remained as part of the movie.

Margaret O'Brien and I were known around MGM as "The Town Criers." Any role that called for a lot of tears was automatically earmarked for either Maggie or me. Since this put us in a class by ourselves, we formed our own mutual admiration society. During the filming of *Music for Millions* in 1944, little Maggie O'Brien's picture was the only one I kept on my dresser.

When Maggie had a big crying scene—not just a pucker-up—her aunt Marissa or her mother would walk off the set with her and talk to her for ten or fifteen minutes. Maggie would come back and cry forever. I never knew what they said to her and I never asked. When I had to cry, I didn't walk away but I had to be quiet within myself. I stood there telling myself, "I'm not going to cry," and the tears always started flowing.

In *Music for Millions* I was in an all-girl band—I played the bass fiddle—and Maggie was my little sister. My husband was overseas in the war and I didn't know whether he was dead or alive. I cried my bitter tears and Maggie kept telling me I needn't worry, he'd come back because "he promised to bring me a Japanese saw-ward." I heard so much about that "saw-ward" from Maggie that I started pronouncing it her way—on camera. The crew thought this was funny but the director yelled "Cut!" Sometimes I started talking like Maggie even on dates.

In 1945, *Her Highness and the Bellboy* thrust me up against the greatest competition of that era, Hedy Lamarr, said to be the most beautiful woman in the world. I would just stare, entranced, at her profile. No doubt about it, she was stunning and she knew how to look at a man with an intimate little smile that turned him on.

Every time I tried to copy that kind of look, it was viewed as comedy—Junie, the clown. Junie trying to look cute. I resigned myself—it would never be Junie the sexpot. At least MGM had no trouble over me with the Legion of Decency. It was a joke around Metro officials that I was the only one on the lot whose cleavage the Hays Office never had to come down to check.

Robert Walker also co-starred with me in *Her Highness and the Bellboy*. Working with him was a strange and exhilarating experience. He was intense and moody. For no reason he would disappear from the set and we couldn't find him for hours. Once we found him sitting on the roof just surveying the world and we took his picture before he knew it. He always seemed to be hiding some hurt.

Shooting a scene with Bob was a once-in-a-lifetime experience. No other actor I've worked with could make a scene more true—Bob could make you feel the scene with him as something urgent and surging with life. During the filming of *Her Highness and the Bellboy*, he said to me, "I'm absolutely miserable when I don't measure up to my own standards doing a scene."

I'll never forget one disappearance. There used to be a café outside the MGM gate, on a little side street. When Bob didn't come back, we went out to investigate. He had smashed his hand through a mirror over there. Instead of calling the studio for medical help, he had taken himself to a doctor. A lot of stitches were required and Robert didn't come back to work for several days.

Many around the studio felt sorry for Robert Walker and knew he was involved in a terrible love triangle. As Bob put it, "My personal life has been completely wrecked by David Selznick's obsession for my wife. What can you do to fight such a powerful man?" Jennifer Jones was to divorce him shortly after this conversation. At another time he said, "Selznick was so jealous of me that he had a clause put in my wife's contract forbidding her to be photographed with me." Robert Walker was young and handsome; Selznick was older and plainer. But he was already assured of eternal fame for having produced *Gone With the Wind*.

Robert explained to Judy Garland and me during a visit that David Selznick had entered their lives when he and Jennifer were trying to get started on the New York stage and were happy young marrieds with two little sons. Happy except that they were barely eking out a living—he in radio and she as a part-time hat model. Desperate to get into acting, Jennifer, who was still just plain Phyllis Isley, went to see David Selznick, who she heard was in town auditioning stage actresses for *Claudia*. She was so nervous about how she was reading her lines that she burst into tears. The average actress would have been dismissed from the audition, but something about Phyllis touched the producer's heart and he asked her to stay. No, she didn't get the part. But she got a contract to go to Hollywood, and a new name, Jennifer Jones. Robert Walker followed Jennifer to Hollywood.

"My life has been hell ever since," he told Judy and me, "because of Selznick's demands on my wife's time. It's hopeless. We made one last attempt to salvage our life together—we got Selznick to let us co-star in *Since You Went Away*." That had been the year before, in 1944, and both the movie and the marriage were finished at the same time—all but the divorce.

Prophetically, Bob Walker was killed off in *Since You Went Away* after a haystack scene with Jennifer. His actual suicide followed by a few years. Robert had married once more but that marriage had been doomed to a short life, too.

I saw Jennifer at parties, looking beautiful of course and so well groomed—one of the best-dressed women of Hollywood—but she spoke now and then of being lonely, and I believed her. There was sadness in her eyes. Now Selznick is gone. Walker is gone. Only Jennifer has survived—still reserved and sweet in manner and now married to the great art collector and tycoon Norton Simon. But something good remains of the union of Jennifer and Robert—Robert Walker, Jr. He is an exact copy of his father and a fine actor.

Whenever I look back at my career and all my co-stars, I think of Robert Walker and I almost cry. I wish I could have helped him, but at the time I thought *I* was the one who needed help, not he. I was pitted against such beauties in my movies with him that I was preoccupied with my own problems.

I was to do two other movies with Robert Walker. They were *The Sailor Takes a Wife* and *Till the Clouds Roll By*. Happily the latter found me reunited with Judy Garland.

Till the Clouds Roll By had so many big names that it couldn't even be produced today—it would take the national budget. They were Judy Garland, Van Johnson, Frank Sinatra, Robert Walker, Kathryn Grayson, Van Heflin, Dinah Shore, Lena Horne, Angela Lansbury, and me. It was the life story of

Jerome Kern, the great musical composer, and no, I didn't play his wife but I did get to sing the title song and dance under an umbrella.

Judy Garland wasn't his wife either. She was Marilyn Miller, the queen of musical comedy, and Judy got to sing "Look for the Silver Lining." Robert Walker played the composer—convincingly—and Dorothy Patrick was Mrs. Kern. Frank Sinatra appeared in a cameo performance, singing "Ol' Man River."

Kathryn Grayson had the patience of Job. She remained unruffled no matter what was happening on the set. If the director blew up or she had to repeat a difficult song due to the fault of her partner's acting, she smiled her sympathetic little smile and carried on. I was made of weaker stuff. I could not stand temperament around me.

I admired Kathryn as a woman and I admired her singing talent. Most singers, when they reach for high notes, have to contort their faces to make beautiful sounds. Kathryn Grayson could hit the highest note possible and look even more beautiful doing it. I think she was one of the most beautiful girls ever to come to Hollywood. Papa Mayer had heard her sing at a music festival when she was still in high school, still Zelma Hedrick.

It was one of life's ironies that Kathryn Grayson did not perceive herself as beautiful or successful. She was disappointed because she hadn't attained her real goal in life, which was to be an opera singer. Kathryn Grayson was nicknamed Stinky and Conky but I never used these names—I knew what it felt like to have every nickname under the sun. I shared the Stinky moniker with Kathryn but that was the only one of the names Richard had given me—Flattop, Idiot Child, Idiothead, Junie face.

Richard had helped me with my career and now he wanted my thinking on something important to him. "I have a script I want you to read," he said. "I really want your opinion of what you think of it. Will you do it?"

"Sure, if it's important to you."

"The title is *Murder, My Sweet*. Isn't that great?"

"Yeah, it sounds pretty sinister." I read the script and loved it. "It couldn't be more exciting," I told Richard the next night. "Who's supposed to play in it?"

"Me," he said. "Can you see me as the tough private eye?"

"Heavens, never. That would be terrible. That isn't you at all. Don't do it. You'll be ruined. Everybody will laugh."

Richard didn't argue with me. Instead he just took back the script. Soon afterward I read in the trades that he had been signed to star as detective Philip Marlowe. It was a good thing that he hadn't taken my advice because *Murder, My Sweet* was a smash hit and marked the start of a new career for Dick Powell in tough-guy roles.

4

RICHARD WAS a hard man to lead to the altar. He would be sitting in my living room when I'd get calls from other fellows asking me for dates. Naturally, I turned them down. Richard pretended he didn't notice, which hurt my feelings.

I tried the opposite tack. I goaded him by dating other men and pretending I was serious but he just played along with my game. He said, "I'll come to the same restaurant as you and your date and look the guy over and see if I think he's right for you." At the restaurant Richard would sit alone at a distant table and always give me the same sign once he saw my date—he'd shake his head no and go thumbs down.

I don't know what I'd have done had he gone thumbs up! Gossip columnists never seemed to catch on that we were in the same restaurant together at different tables. And, of course, I was making Papa Mayer happy by being seen around town with men other than the taboo Dick Powell.

I grew desperate. Now on every phone call that came through, even if it was Judy Garland, I pretended I was talking to a fellow and made quaint rejoinders like "Oh sure, I haven't forgotten you." Still Richard didn't pop the question.

I reviewed my strategy. Maybe the problem was that he was

used to more sophisticated girls. I borrowed a scrapbook from his dad and learned about Richard's early career; his romantic triumphs were also featured. Glamour and sophistication were obviously what he was used to. Richard had been linked romantically with his co-star in *20 Million Sweethearts*, Ginger Rogers. Then there was his co-star in *Dames*, Ruby Keeler. When Ruby was separated from Al Jolson, she stirred up a minor scandal by moving to a house near Richard's bachelor pad. And then there was Rosemary Lane. They had been a continuing romantic saga in the press.

Richard had snatched another beauty from the arms of Buddy Rogers, the actor who later married Mary Pickford. That was actress Mary Brian, whom he had started to date when he was master of ceremonies at the Stanley Theater in Pittsburgh and she had been booked as a visiting Hollywood star. Columnists had a field day with them.

Richard had certainly given Lew Ayres a run for his money when he was dating Ginger Rogers. One columnist wrote, "Dick, they say, wants all of Ginger's time. And gets it. Doesn't even want Ginger to see Lew, so that looks serious on Dick's part. As for how serious it is on Ginger's part—well, at this writing she's been obeying her new boyfriend implicitly."

And hadn't he married glamour gal Joan Blondell? Obviously he preferred sophistication. I went to Bullock's and bought a slinky black gown, long false eyelashes and other paraphernalia and I put my hair up. Richard was taking me to Ciro's and I was ready. But when he saw me, he was speechless. He slumped on a couch in the living room.

"What's the matter?" I said. "Aren't you ready?"

"I'm ready," he said, "but you're not."

"Don't you want me to be devastating?"

He pulled me down on his lap. "You look like everything I'm trying to get away from, so when you take off that dress and that warpaint and become June Allyson again, we'll go."

When I appeared again, all scrubbed, with just a touch of lipstick, and my usual Peter Pan collar, Richard grabbed me and started smooching. "Whew, you scared me that time," he said. "If I want sophistication I know where to find it. I'm here because being around you is like being in a fresh breeze. So don't go dramatic on me, right?"

"Yes, sir," I said. "Goody Two Shoes reporting for duty."

"Let's go," he said. "No, wait a minute." He kissed me again. "Monkeyface, I love you."

I came to realize that my biggest competition for Richard's affection was not another woman at all but his boat, the *Santana*. When he said "she" I knew whom he meant—the *Santana*. And *she* always needed something. "She needs to be scraped . . . She needs to have me take a look at that sail—I think I saw a weak spot . . . I noticed a spot on *her* stern and it may mean *she* needs a paint job." Obviously the way to this man's heart wasn't through his stomach but his boat—so I set about wooing his boat.

I spent full days on it and under it, helping scrape. I ooed and aahed over it and told it—in his hearing—how beautiful it was. I spent an entire week running the thick railing wire through a plastic tubing so a person—particularly Richard—would not hurt his hands on the rough surface. All this was without even the reward of a day on the high seas. But finally Richard said, "Come on, I'm going to take *her* out and you can come along. We'll go to Catalina."

"I've been waiting for this," I said. "I'll help."

"Sure," he said. "Just don't get in the way. *She* moves pretty fast and I'm going to be very busy for a while." Everything was fine in the quiet bay and a little less fine in the open ocean. But things got really rough on the way back. I told Richard I was getting seasick. The only way he could keep me out of his way was to tie me to the mast with a rope around my middle. Eventually, I couldn't stand it. Weaving back and forth in the choppy sea did me in. "Richard," I screamed above the wind, "I'm going to throw up!"

"I can't take care of you," he screamed back. "I have a boat to get back."

I yelled once more, "I'm going to throw up."

"Not on her deck!" he yelled. "Just hold it a second, hang in there." He handed me a big aluminum bucket. Lashed to the mast, I upchucked until I thought the lining of my stomach was coming out.

Jimmy Cagney had been with Richard on the day that he bought the *Santana*, a sixty-four-foot yawl. Richard had loved the *Santana* for some time, admiring the way she held her sails, her architecture, her beauty. We were lounging with Jimmy, watching the *Santana* come into the slip. "She's a beauty, June—the only boat in the bay with no dry rot," he observed. I was hungry for some sweet words about me and not about dry rot, but he was talking about the woman he loved so I shut up.

Jimmy Cagney then told how the *Santana* had previously been owned by Ray Milland. "We watched this creature of beauty make her proud way to shore, getting ready to dock. The captain failed to put her in reverse fast enough and the *Santana* ran right up over the dock with a mighty crunch of wood." James had looked over at Richard and said, "Well, chum—she's yours. And if you play your cards right, you'll get a good deal." They had ambled over like a couple of beachcombers, Richard and Jimmy in scruffy sweaters and knitted caps.

As Richard put it, "She was mine before the afternoon was over."

Richard and I and Bogie and Betty Bacall were courting at the same time—and on boats—and that brought the four of us together. Richard and Bogie became close friends and Betty and I became friends but not exactly intimates. We were just too different. I admired Lauren Bacall for the way she had stormed Hollywood. We had one enormous thing in common besides boats, in that both Lauren and I were overshadowed by our men and let them run the show and our lives. One day on the *Santana*, Bogie looked over at Betty and me sitting on the deck and said to Richard, with his slightly sinister smile, "Look at them. We had to pick the two babes with the croakingest voices in Hollywood." We both gave them dirty looks and Richard said, "Junie's my son, you know. She gets mistaken for a boy on the telephone all the time."

"Yeah, Andy Hardy," said Bogie, who was always insulting Betty, too. She'd just insult him back and it would be hilarious. They sounded like they hated each other but all you had to do was look at Bogie to see he worshiped Betty. When he looked at her he seemed to be feeling "This is my world." And her love for Bogie was a beautiful thing to see. Later, when Humphrey Bogart became so ill with cancer, Betty was great and never pampered him. We went over to visit when Bogie could no longer walk downstairs and an elevator had been installed.

Bogie rode down for his cocktail hour and Betty talked just as tough to him as ever—"Damn it, get your own drink." She never made him feel like an invalid—she never stopped being the Betty he loved.

She seemed so calm and collected, but she didn't fool me. I had seen the real Betty when we filmed *Woman's World* together and were doing a scene in which we each had to pick up a champagne glass and turn and survey the room.

I looked at Betty's glass and her hand was shaking—I couldn't believe it. She saw my look and whispered, off camera, "I'm so nervous." That was when I realized Lauren Bacall did not have the inner security she displayed to the world. Inside, she was very vulnerable. When Betty wrote her memoir I found it so painful I had to keep putting the book down—it was too much like my own story.

In *Guys and Dolls* there is a song that tells how, if you are miserably in love and can't get a guy, a person can develop a cold—well, a person can also develop a bad case of shingles from nerves, and I did—right around my middle. I couldn't kick and scream and moan and groan as I wanted to. I just had to keep smiling as the cameras rolled. All my patience with Richard and our predicament was getting me nowhere. I realized that he had to wait a full year for his divorce to be final, but as Judy Garland had put it so eloquently about Mickey Rooney, "He could of at least asked."

My life was a mess and no wonder I had shingles. On top of this, I was working too hard and when I almost fainted on the set, the studio doctor discovered that I had low blood sugar, saying, "You'll have to get some rest and start eating right." Now Louis B. Mayer could really play the role of Papa to the hilt, supervising my diet. He made me eat in the executive dining room.

Predictably a rumor started up that I was having an affair with the MGM mogul, who, it was said, enjoyed dating starlets. I had to take a lot of ribbing and innuendos and cracks like, "You'd better be careful, June. We hear Mayer likes young girls."

"Well, I'm safe," I said. "He thinks I'm a boy." Still it hurt. The Hollywood gossips were persisting in their notion that I was a hot number. There were so many rumors by now that I was the playgirl of the western world that I simply gave up denying anything. I confided in Lana Turner at MGM and she consoled me by saying, "After reading about the twentieth new romance I'm supposed to be having this month, all I can say is I only wish I had the time."

Papa Mayer summoned me to his office in the middle of my misery and shingles and pointed an accusatory finger at me. "You are still dating Dick Powell." I nodded yes. "I want it to stop," he said, I nodded no.

"I love Richard. I really do."

"Love, love. You are just a child. What do you know about love? Go home and think about it. I don't want you to ruin your future. Now, what are you going to do?"

"I'm going to think about it." My eyes smarted as I walked the long mile to his door. What did *he* know about love?

Richard and I went into hiding. I spent more time on the boat and at Lucille Ball's house. Actually, my housekeeper, dear as she was, was such a straitlaced Victorian that I felt more comfortable over at Lucy's. So did Richard. Even though Lucy was married to orchestra leader Desi Arnaz, she, too, seemed to be going it alone. "We're not ships that pass in the night so much as cars that pass in the morning," Lucy commented. "I'll be on my way to the studio in the early morning hours and Desi will be on his way home and we'll spot each other on the highway and park and talk a while. This is supposed to be married life?"

I never laid eyes on Desi even when I was a frequent guest in his home. Later when I watched them in *I Love Lucy*, I thought, What irony—the fans think this is the ideal marriage. Their friends knew Lucy and Desi had considered divorce as early as 1944 but had hung on until 1960, trying to bridge their great differences. Lucy and Desi still had no children in the early days of our friendship though they had been married since about 1940. Their first child, Lucie, was not born until they'd been married ten or eleven years.

On one particularly desperate day I decided this was it! I was tired of running and hiding. Richard was taking me to an out-of-the-way nightclub for dining and dancing—where Papa Mayer's spies were not apt to find us. I wanted to blurt out, "Look, fellah, you're divorced and you're not talking about marriage and I demand to know why." But of course that would have been the worst thing I could do.

Be subtle, I cautioned myself. All evening as we sat in the fine nightclub eating, I was very quiet. I wasn't trying to amuse him with my usual patter. I wasn't making him laugh. I was reaching for words but nothing came. We danced a little to the music of a small band.

He drove me home and we sat in the car awhile as we always

did when we were arriving home late—Bess, my human watch-dog, was inside, waiting up for me. His kisses seemed unusually sweet that night. I knew that if we kept on this way I was either going to be very hurt or what was currently called "a fallen woman."

Richard opened the car door and started to get out. He always came around to help me out, but this time I stopped him before his foot hit the ground. "Wait a minute," I heard myself saying.

"What's wrong, June?"

"Nothing's wrong."

"Something's wrong. I've been trying to figure it out all the way home."

"I just want to ask you something."

He slammed the door. "I knew something was wrong. What is it?"

I swallowed and stumbled a bit. "Well, I would like to know what your intentions are."

"About what?" But that was as far as I could go. Richard nodded then and said, "You want to know about marriage."

"Yes, I do." Thank God, that was over. Richard said, "Oh, honey, I love you very, very, very much but I have no intention of ever getting married again."

"Well, in that case I don't think we should see each other again."

"That's silly. Why should we *not* see each other again?"

"Because I love you and if you don't want to marry me, I don't want to see you anymore."

He tried to bluster and talk me out of it but I held firm and said no and I wouldn't even let him walk me to the door. I got out of the car by myself and bid him a cavalier goodnight with a wave of my hand. My back was turned so he couldn't see the front view of that lighthearted wave.

"Do you have any better offers?" he called out the window.

56

"Two," I said defiantly and stumbled up the porch steps with tears streaming down my face. I had one—Tommy—but two seemed the least a girl should have at a time like this. I could hardly see to get the key in the lock. All I could think was, *Will he call tonight?*

I knew it would take him a full hour to drive out to Toluca Lake where he lived with his father. Richard always called me each night after we'd been together to tell me he was home safely and say goodnight. The phone rang at the usual time and I said with a tearful voice, "Hellllllooo."

He said, "It's me. I got home safely."

And still sobbing, I said, "Ffffine. That's ffffine."

"Are you crying?"

His voice sounded a little disgusted and I said, "Certainly not."

He said, "Oh, for God's sake," and hung up. That's it, I told myself, tears flowing. Maybe I'd just pack up and go back to New York and marry Tommy Mitchell.

Later there was a pounding on the door. When I opened it, Richard came in like a tired man who has had it. He plopped himself on the couch and said, "All right. If you want to get married, we'll get married." He sounded like he had done twelve hours' hard work. It was the most unromantic proposal ever uttered. Wearily, he added, "You know I love you."

I threw my arms around him. "I love you too, Tommy." For a full second I didn't realize what I had done. Richard pulled away from me and gave me a dirty look. "Who the hell is Tommy?" I started to explain but suddenly Richard was roaring with laughter and so was I. "When would you like to get married?" he said, sobering up. It was late July. I said, "Is August too soon?" That broke him up completely.

We planned to be married August 19, 1945, and Bonnie and Johnny Green generously insisted we use their home in Holmby Hills for the big event. John was MGM's musical director and Bonnie had become like family to me. They would have to serve as family for both of us. Richard's father was now in a nursing home and my mother had just remarried and said she couldn't make the trip West.

Now that I was formally engaged to Richard, there was one phone call I had to make and I dreaded it. It was my "Dear John" call to Tommy, who had just returned to New York from military service. I didn't have to do much explaining. As soon as I started, he cut in. "I've been reading about you in the newspapers," he said, sounding a little disappointed. "And Joan Blondell and all that."

"We're getting married," I said. "This isn't what you might think. I love him and we're getting married."

"Oh," he said and there was a long pause. "It won't work, you know."

My heart sank. "What do you mean, Tommy? Why won't it work?"

"There are too many differences—age mostly. But get it out of your system and when it's over I'll still be here. Call me." I hung up and cried.

Oddly, I seemed to be having second thoughts about marrying Richard. "I feel so strange," I told him. "You know, everybody is saying you left Joan for me and I'm the home-breaker. The villain."

"I know it and I'm sorry," Richard said, "but I can't go around shouting that it isn't true and that she left me first for Mike Todd. I hope they'll be very happy together but I doubt it."

He was right about that. When Joan Blondell and Mike Todd finally married in 1947, it turned out to be a stormy relationship riddled with financial problems and lasting only three years.

The day I met Mike Todd years later—the only time I saw him—I really put my foot in it. There was a whole group stand-

58

ing around at a party and Mike was with Elizabeth Taylor and when I was introduced to him, I wanted to say something friendly—after all, I'd heard so much about him from Richard.

"Oh, Mike," I purred. "You and I have so much in common. We're practically family, you know." He was looking at me so blankly that I felt compelled to forge on. "You used to be married to my husband's wife, Joan Blondell."

His eyes turned to steel and he gave me the dirtiest look I'd ever seen and turned away without a word. I felt terrible. I wanted to say, "What have I done? I didn't mean anything."

Mike Todd must have forgotten that for a moment in the '40's he and Joan Blondell had made each other happy. I, too, was happy for Joan and relieved not to have to feel sorry for her anymore. She had scored a hit in a great supporting role in *A Tree Grows In Brooklyn*, in which she played the role of the slightly blowsy aunt whose conduct is no better than it has to be.

Evidently Joan was not equally happy for me. In *Center Door Fancy*, Joan gave me the name of Amy, possibly after the selfish sister in *Little Women* who steals Jo's boyfriend and marries him. How bitter she must have been to have written about me: "Doesn't he know about his Amy? Everybody else does. Her reputation is in the public domain. She's a tramp dressed like a little kid. She was a call girl in New York—exhibitions 'her specialty.'" I could not believe it. How untrue, how cruel.

I was not aware that Richard was going to announce our upcoming nuptials in the gossip columns, but that's the way things are done in Hollywood. He leaked the news to Louella Parsons, which made her archenemy and competitor, Hedda Hopper, furious with me. Hedda would never believe I had not been at the bottom of it and the episode got me off on the wrong foot with her.

Louis B. Mayer read the item in Parsons and immediately

sent for me. In no uncertain terms he told me that I could not marry Dick Powell. "I told you I didn't want you to see him," Papa said with great disapproval. "And now you are going to marry him. I have to read such news in the paper. Is it true?"

"Yes, sir."

"Dick Powell is too old. He's a has-been. And he's a divorced man. What are you doing to yourself, child? Your career will be over. This will ruin you."

"I don't care."

"You'll end up having to take care of him if you live that long."

"I don't care." He couldn't believe his ears, and small wonder—it was the first time I'd ever defied him. I stood up and said, all in one breath, "I am going to marry him whatever you do because I love him and he loves me and you can fire me." I stalked out.

And the heavens didn't fall and if they had I wouldn't have noticed because I was getting married and I was busy figuring out which of my suits to be married in. But suddenly I realized I had another problem and I went to see Papa Mayer again.

He beamed as I came in, sure that I was about to apologize for my outburst. Or that I was not going to get married after all. But instead, I said, "Papa, I have a father somewhere but I don't know where he is. Can you give me away?"

He looked dumbstruck. He sat there with his mouth open. Then he said, "I'd be happy to," with a very strange look, and he gave me a little hug. Having several daughters of his own, I guess he knew when to give up.

The night before the wedding I was in a state of nerves. For some reason, I still wasn't sure Richard would show up for his own wedding. "He has a perfect excuse," I told my maid of honor, Jane Wilkie, who was there helping me get through the jitters. "He has a horrible cold."

He had been doing his own stunt work in icy waters. Before the long night was over, I would have my own problems. I had tried to fix eggs for Jane, a magazine writer, and had dropped the platter in my nervousness, then cut a gash in my finger while picking up the pieces.

Jane and I ran around town—me with my finger held up high in a towel—trying to find a doctor who was still open, a drugstore or even a friendly face. Finally, a druggist administered first aid and sent us to a hospital emergency room. It took seven stitches to close me up.

Four hours before the wedding I showed up with a big bandaged finger at Bonnie and John's house, dressed in my wedding finery and ready to go. I was taking no chances. I stood most of the time looking out the upstairs bedroom window, waiting for Richard's arrival. I did not want to sit down and get creases in the gray suit I was wearing—the only thing I had that was dignified enough for a wedding.

How typical! I was four hours early and Richard was an hour late. I was relieved when I saw him and suddenly I was in the living room and there were banks of flowers and I was marching to the front of the room where Richard and the judge waited. Richard's best man was A. Morgan Maree, who handled Richard's money—and who, by now, also handled mine, though what it was being invested in only Richard knew.

Of course no Hollywood wedding is complete without one's agent and so my agent, Johnny Hyde, was there. He wasn't just my agent, he represented a lot of stars including Linda Darnell. But he would become famous as Marilyn Monroe's boyfriend, who wrecked his own frail health over her career. I loved having tiny Johnny there, not just because he was a friend but because he made me feel tall in comparison.

I was proud to be on the arm of Papa Mayer, head of the whole studio, from whom all blessings flowed. I looked around at all these people dear to me and I almost choked up. Jane Wilkie, my maid of honor, Richard in his business suit, Bess, a very proper lady in black hat and dress with old-fashioned white collar, and Bonnie and John, who had even lent their home.

The judge was saying something but I was confused—"Do you take this man . . . ?"

"Who?"

There were chuckles around me. "Oh yes, yes," I said, coming to.

After a reception at the LaRue restaurant, we were at last going home—to our home. Richard had almost had to pull me out of LaRue's because it had begun to occur to me that I would soon be alone with a man who had been very married and really knew what he was doing—and I didn't.

We got to the apartment—the big apartment that would be home for a while—and I spent as much time as I could in the bathroom getting ready. I had bought a knockout wedding nightgown—white satin with a filmy white robe and satin slippers. I came out absolutely terrified and said, "Would you like a glass of milk?"

"Fine," he said. So, laughingly, I got that and as he was polishing it off, I said, "How about some soda crackers?"

After the third glass of milk, Richard looked at me and said, "Honey, let's go to bed. I'm too tired, anyway."

I hadn't fooled him, but what a relief.

The next day he took me to the *Santana*, and there we finally had our wedding night in broad daylight. How I regretted pushing all those crackers on him. What had I been afraid of—this was truly the gold at the end of the rainbow. I didn't want to get off the boat, ever. But in three days, we got an urgent call from the nursing home.

We arrived to find doctor and nurses frantically working over his father, and the doctor hitting him over and over in the chest. Richard took me outside and said, "I don't want you to see this." Two hours later Richard came out and said, "He's gone."

And so was our honeymoon. I prayed: "Don't let this happen to me with Richard." Something was telling me that there was nothing I could do about it and this was the shadow of things to come.

RICHARD

5

EVERYONE MARRIES a stranger. But I, more than others. I knew all about Joan Blondell. I had been a guest in her home many times. But all of a sudden, I read in some ancient article about my husband that there had been a wife before Joan. A Mildred somebody.

I confronted Richard. Was it true?

"Oh yes," he said. "That's the truth. It was a boyhood romance. She used to come visit some neighbors and I thought marriage was proof of my manhood. But it was never much of a marriage and we parted friends. She hated show business."

"Why do all the fan magazines call Joan Blondell your first wife? Why was it kept secret?"

"The studios wanted it that way. I was their bachelor star. The gay blade. Available. But I made no bones about it. The studios knew. And when I dated girls I was serious about, before I married Joan, I did not hide it from them. But I didn't particularly want you to find out."

"Why?"

"I don't know. I guess I didn't want to disillusion you. I'm crazy in love with you, you know."

"Oh, Richard," I said, "I'm crazy in love with you too but

you better make up your mind right now I'm your third and last wife."

"Roger and over," he said, grinning. "I'm glad you know. I hate deception. And if anyone leaves this marriage, it will be you, not me. This is it." He swept me up in his arms and carried me to bed. "I never knew love could be so sweet and beautiful," he said afterward. "There's a lot of lovemaking going on in the world but real love is rare."

I tried never to pry into Richard's business, but having learned that I was his third wife and not his second, I could not resist asking him why he had gotten a divorce from Mildred. "I tell you this only so you will never do it. We'd be traveling from one job to another and we'd stop for hamburgers. She'd protest that she wasn't hungry and didn't want anything to go. But as we drove, no sooner had I taken the first bite than she would say, 'Can I please have a bite?' and then proceed to finish the whole thing. I spent most of my time hungry and the only solution was divorce."

He simply refused to be serious about anything depressing.

How wonderful it was to be married and not to have to worry about money anymore. Richard said, "Just tell any store to send the bill to the house. I'll take care of it." Ah, sweet music.

I took off for Adrian's like a shot. Adrian dressed a lot of stars and created the broad-shouldered look that Joan Crawford made famous. I'd always dreamed of owning an Adrian suit. I found the elegant salon intimidating at first—how does one talk to these people? I didn't even know exactly what I wanted, I just wanted an Adrian suit. In the back of my mind, I was even a little afraid they might ask me to leave. Before I came to Hollywood, I had wandered into Tiffany's, wearing pigtails and flat shoes, and they had asked me to please leave. But the sales people at Adrian's made me feel right at home, even congratulating me on the popular *Two Girls and a Sailor*.

They brought me all kinds of luscious materials and I ordered a suit made of a most gorgeous white cashmere, never, of course, inquiring about the price. I didn't think you would bring up money in such an atmosphere.

There were several fittings, and finally I left the salon in triumph, with my new suit. "Send the bill to my house," I said.

I went home and told Richard, "I have a surprise for you," and I modeled the new suit.

"Very nice," he said. "What did it cost?"

I had no answer.

"You mean you don't know?"

"You don't go into Adrian's, for goodness sakes, and talk about money."

"That's news to me. Other people do. You will take that suit back and ask the price and if it's beyond what I think is reasonable—which is $250—you will leave it there."

I didn't argue. "Oh, all right," I grumbled.

It was a humiliating experience, but I took the suit back and even I was aghast to hear it was $1,500. I said, "I'm so sorry but Richard doesn't like the suit. He just doesn't like it."

They were wonderful and said, "That's perfectly all right. We understand." They even wanted to show me some other things. I said, "I'll bring Richard in." They never saw me again.

But other stores did.

One day Richard came home with a photo of a mansion with lavish grounds and said, "Would you like to live there?"

"Wow, that would be wonderful! Is that the house we're going to move to from this apartment?"

"It might be if you keep spending money the way you do. That's the Motion Picture Relief Home."

Richard was full of contradictions in money matters. As if to make it up to me for the Adrian suit, now that I had learned my lesson, Richard bought me a fur coat. Mercifully, all I had been told was that the coat had been made for another customer who was dissatisfied. The words "second hand" were never mentioned.

Fit? It fitted like a tent but I rolled up the sleeves and said, "I love cuffs. It fits me perfectly." I was so afraid that if I complained the coat would walk out the door. It didn't dawn on me that I could ask to have it cut down. And a "slightly used" stole had been tossed into the deal.

He would say, "Do you really need that blouse?" and then I wouldn't buy it. But he'd suddenly buy an extra little motorboat he didn't need or a very expensive car or plane. Sometimes I felt that I'd married a total stranger.

Of course Richard married a stranger, too. I was afraid of everything—cats, people who didn't like me, being alone, the dark, catching some illness. I was a genuine certifiable hypochondriac.

On top of that, I needed constant reassurance of Richard's love. Richard confided to his male friends that in order to get any paperwork done, he had to get up at 5 A.M. and sneak into his bedroom-study to complete it before I woke up.

When I overheard him voicing this complaint I told him, "Can I help it if I can't get enough of you and want to be with you every minute that you're home?"

He said, "I want to be with you too, Monkeyface, but I'm used to a lot of space around me. This isn't just for me—I'm doing it for you too. So help me—I'm aiming to get to the top of the mountain."

"Why?" I asked.

He looked at me a long time before answering. "I guess so I can finally relax and quit climbing."

"Good," I said. "Let me know when you get there. I sure thought *this* was the top of the mountain."

Poor Dick Powell had married a nest of fears. I was always

going to him to dispel some specter I'd raised. One day I confessed to him that I was afraid of Hedda Hopper because she said mean things about me. Richard said, "When people say cruel things, just smile and be sweet in return and let them shame themselves."

He was a joy to live with. Richard usually acted as if he didn't have a care in the world. Take the matter of noise and noisemaking. Richard was a noisy man. He was always either whistling or singing. He whistled when he came into the house; he said he always knew when I was mad at him—he'd listen and if I didn't whistle back he knew I was angry about something. He whistled as he worked on the boat, even cleaning the bilge. He whistled as he walked—and he talked a lot. And he cried. He wasn't ashamed of crying. I was surprised to see that a grown man could wipe away tears and not feel less manly because of it. He cried with happiness and he cried over the deaths of people he did not know that well. He wept, for example, when a female film editor he hardly knew died, and he said, "It's such a terrible waste for a talented woman to be struck down in the prime of her life."

Richard couldn't stand moodiness and he couldn't stand temper. He was always intense and wound up like a spring, but he could just lie back and relax, too, especially if he felt anger coming on. When he was a kid, Richard had gotten into a big fight with one of his brothers and he had gotten his bee-bee gun and taken aim at his brother. "I was so angry everything was white. I could have killed him and I almost did. The bee-bee hit near his eye. And that is the last time I ever lost my temper." When he felt his temper rising, he would say, "God is love," and he would just slow down.

Working on the boat was always a good way for Richard to work out his frustrations. He would scrub for hours or work all day on the bilge and at the end of the day he'd be smiling and whistling again.

RICHARD

Richard did everything better than I did. He swam better—
he played tennis better—golf better. He could fly a plane. He
could ski better, too, but who broke a shoulder? Not me. We
had just arrived at the Sun Valley ski lodge and I was still in our
suite unpacking when I got a phone call. Richard couldn't wait
to get to the ski slope and I hadn't tried to stop him—I told him
I'd meet him for lunch at the Round House.

"I'm hurrying," I told him as soon as I heard his voice.
"Don't worry. I'll be there. I'm almost on my way."

"Hold it a minute, honey," Richard said, sounding just a tad
strange. "Don't meet me where you're supposed to meet me."

"Why?"

"Because obviously I'm not there."

"Okay, where are you?"

"I'm in the hospital."

"What are you doing there, Richard? Are you sick?"

"No," he said. "I'm not sick but I think I broke my goddamn
shoulder."

That was Richard—the kind of man who, even with the pain
of a broken shoulder that is about to be set, would say with his
usual bravado, "Just a minute, Doc, I've got to call my wife.
She'll be worried."

Richard tried to be fair and kind but he was not a phony.
Once, when a very disliked mogul died and there were few to
mourn him, some important studio executives came to Richard
and said, "Will you please do the eulogy for the poor soul? We
can't find anybody." Richard said, "Look, I didn't like the son of
a bitch while he was alive and I don't like the son of a bitch now
he's dead. I'm not going to be a hypocrite."

I was not the most efficient of wives, though now and then I
tried. God knows I tried. Once Richard had to go to New York
to make a speech and I packed everything for him—even his
evening studs and cuff links, even his dinner jacket. Everything
but his pants.

He never let me help him again. But he did give a simple direction now and then and whether I did as requested depended on the choice of words he used. Once he said, "You've *got to* get these pants to the cleaners. I need them back tomorrow. Are you listening to this order?"

"I heard you," I said. But when he got home the trousers were right where he had left them. I had done my "got to" in returning that Adrian suit and had a psychological block against those words from then on, which made me simply forget.

Jimmy Cagney had been close friends with Richard and Joan Blondell when they were married. I felt a little left out at first because, in effect, I'd inherited Jimmy from Joan. James Cagney and Joan Blondell had been unknowns together in the Broadway musical *Penny Arcade*, and they had been brought to Hollywood in 1930 to repeat their roles in the film version that would be entitled *Sinner's Holiday*. Dick Powell had joined Jimmy and Joan to make the hit 1933 movie extravaganza *Footlight Parade*.

Soon Jimmy's sweet nature won me over and I became his friend. I loved to hear Jimmy and Richard talk about the jobs they'd had before becoming actors. Richard bragged about being a kid singer and manager of a grocery store and even a rabbit breeder. But he couldn't say, as Jimmy could, that he had been a female impersonator onstage and had worked in a poolroom as a racker. "No, Jimmy," Richard said, "I didn't have those advantages."

One of the biggest adjustments in marriage had to do with Dick's children by his marriage to Joan.

I was startled when Richard said one day, "Junie, will you please go to my old house and pick up Ellen? Joan wants her to come live with us."

"What?" I said, shocked.

"Joan said she wants . . ."

"I heard you," I cut him off. "But shouldn't you be the one to get your child?"

"No, Junie face," he said. "You're better at this kind of thing. Just say hello and say you've come for Ellen. Ellen will love you. You're about the same size and she'll be like a little sister."

"How can Joan want her child to go? I could never let a child of mine go. I don't understand."

"Just do it for me, please. Joan is having problems now in many ways and Mike Todd is giving her a hard time. It's bad for the kids. And it's really Ellen's decision. She wants to come live with us."

"Oh, I'm not prying. It's just that I would love a child so much I wouldn't want it to go. But I'm glad Ellen is coming to stay with us. Oh, I think that's wonderful."

So June, the bride, was on her way to instant motherhood.

At Joan Blondell's someone let me in and then Joan came down the staircase majestically. I looked up, transfixed, and with each step I felt she was getting taller and more regal and I was shrinking like Alice in Wonderland.

Joan looked at me with her enormous blue eyes and said, "Ellen and I have talked this over and it's what she wants to do—live with you. And I guess it's better." My feeling was that Ellen did not want to be around her mother's rugged relationship with Mike Todd.

"Just be good to her," said Joan, softening a little. "Just be kind to her and love her."

"Yes, ma'am." I didn't know what else to say, I felt so intimidated. And then Joan called upstairs to Ellen, and Ellen was hurrying downstairs with her suitcase and making straight for the door as I followed her.

Somehow, because of the children, there was always a slight shadow of Joan Blondell across our marriage. Richard called it

71

"having a civilized divorce." I called it "East Lynn, Revisited."

Ellen came to live with us for a while and then came to stay with us periodically from then on. I was always happy to see her—though completely baffled by her underlying unhappiness. I wanted so to push a little of my own happiness into her. But I may have pushed too hard. We were friends but never the sister team Richard had hoped for. Sometimes both children—Ellen and her older brother Norman—stayed with us.

Our marriage was certainly different. Instead of saying, "I'm going to make a good cook out of you," Richard said, "and now I'm going to make a sailor of you." We were out on the water quite a lot. Humphrey Bogart and Lauren Bacall watched us coming into port on the *Santana*, and Bogie was almost drooling. "When are you going to sell me that boat?" he yelled.

"Never!" Richard called back. Richard was proud that the *Santana* was known in racing circles. "She's the queen of the sailing vessels," he said.

"Is the *Santana* named for some person?" I asked.

"No," he said, "it's named for a wind. The Santa Ana."

We'd often take Bogie and Betty with us on the *Santana*, and Bogie examined every square foot of the boat with a passion that surpassed even Richard's. Betty looked at the men engaged in deep boat-conversation and commented, "What can you say? They're both crazy."

I was beginning to catch the fever myself. I was learning to operate the boat under sail and under power. Richard was just beginning to trust me at the helm. One day he started the lesson as usual with the admonition, "Remember, Flattop, a boat has no brakes."

"I know that," I groaned. "You've told me that a million times."

"This time I'm adding something else. When you are under

power, any ship or boat coming on your starboard side has the right of way."

"Okay, I'm memorizing that. You've told me that before, too."

"It bears repeating," he said. We switched eventually from sails to power and Richard let me handle the boat while he took the sails down. He said, "Just keep her on course." I was having a wonderful time. I was the captain. I yelled, above the motor, "Hey, Richard, there go Bogie and Betty passing us in their boat. Can I turn around and follow them?"

"Sure," he said, "easy does it." He watched me as I turned the boat around. I turned to Richard again and yelled, "They're going too fast. I'm losing them." He shook his head. "Don't try to catch up with them." But I felt fully competent so I reached down and gave it a little more throttle. I loved the breeze in my face and the glorious view as Richard worked with the sails and I felt I could even go all the way to China with what I knew about boats.

I suddenly looked to the right and there, coming at me, was a tiny blue sailboat. The right of way—was that boat starboard? Was I? I yelled, "Richard, what should I do?" He looked at the boat and back at me and shrugged. "Hit it," he said. As if there were a choice. Already the kids who had been in the boat had jumped overboard—they knew a Sunday driver when they saw one.

We fished them out of the water and Richard paid them well for the boat they themselves had made and had a good laugh with them. They were thrilled when they realized Dick Powell's dingy wife, June Allyson, had done this to them and they could hardly wait to tell their friends. I was mortified. I apologized to the kids. I apologized to Richard. I apologized to the boat—the *Santana*. The only thing that seemed to really bother Richard was the streak of blue paint where the *Santana* had neatly cut the boat in two.

"I'm so relieved," I said. "You can just have that part painted over." He looked at me as if I had suggested he scrap his beloved. "That would be a patch job. You could always see it." And even though she had recently undergone a paint job, she got a completely new one.

When it came to boats, men could be cattier than women. Richard and his boating friends, Bogie and John Wayne, knew everything about boats and made nasty cracks about this boat and that. They sat like drugstore cowboys watching the yachts and it sounded as if they were gossiping about a woman. "She has a fat behind . . . Get a load of that keel . . . She's got more sway than a B girl." I was with them when John Wayne leaned over and smugly commented about a lovely yacht going by, "She's full of dry rot." It was the ultimate insult one could give a boat. Richard and he sat there shaking their heads.

Humphrey Bogart was determined to own the *Santana*. Persistence paid off—one day Bogie caught Richard in the right mood and suddenly Bogie was the proud owner of the *Santana*. Richard came close to crying that night as he told our friends. "Hell, I just got tired of seeing Bogie looking like a twelve-year-old kid mooning over my boat. He wore me down."

The next time we saw Bogie and Betty, Bogie was all smiles and totally obsessed with the *Santana*. Betty turned to me and said in a low, sour voice, as only Betty could, "Thanks—a lot."

When Bogie died in 1957, Betty came through with the perfect symbol of understanding of her man. It moved me when I saw it there on the altar—a replica of the *Santana* encased in glass and sitting proud. It was like saying the spirit of Bogie lived on. If it hadn't been sacrilegious at a time like that, I'd have been tempted to put on my Humphrey Bogart voice and say to Betty, "Here's looking at you, kid."

Next to boats, Richard loved planes. First he had an Ercoupe craft that seated two. Then he traded that in for an Avion that

74

seated four. Finally, he graduated to a Bonanza that seated six. I was a very uneasy rider in all of them and, by nagging, I finally made Richard quit piloting his own plane.

I hated planes. I hated flying. It was bad enough that Richard bought planes and piloted himself, but he even prevailed on me to climb into the cockpit with him and take off into the wild blue yonder. "Remember how seasick you used to get on the boat," Richard said, "and how you love it now—it will be the same with planes. You'll be demanding your own plane someday." I doubted it as I trembled beside him, staring at the strange gauges on the instrument panel to avoid looking down at the ground.

"Richard," I asked, "is the fuel gauge in a plane the same as in a car?"

"Of course, Flattop," he said, disgusted by my ignorance.

"Well then, I think we're out of gas."

He looked and yelped, "Oh God, I've got to land!" It was no time to feel smug. I held my breath as he looked down and said, "Christ, we're over the Air Force base and private planes are forbidden to land! Well, I'll try." He spoke into the radio, "Out of fuel and request permission to land." Permission was denied and he was directed to a small base nearby. "It's a tiny field but I can make it," he reassured me. "No, you don't!" I screamed. "Call them back and say you're coming in." The little plane could probably have landed in a good-sized living room, but distrusting planes as I did, I wanted the biggest, longest landing strip in the world. Groaning that he would probably lose his license, Richard again called Muroc Field, which would later be Edwards Air Force Base, and said, "Mayday, am coming in for landing. Out of fuel." He did not add, "And with a hysterical woman beside me."

As Richard put the plane down, it was obvious that a lot of angry officers were marching over to intercept us. "Okay," said Richard grimly, "it's your show. I understand they don't shoot women."

He pushed the dome back and I climbed out and yelled, "Hi. I'm June Allyson."

There were big smiles below. "You don't have to tell us. We'd know you anywhere," they called and soon were helping me down, clustering around me and inviting me to lunch. "Great," I said, marching right along, answering questions about the flight such as altitude and wind resistance. I was just repeating things I had heard Richard say, hoping they would think I was the pilot. I looked back and there was Richard trailing behind like a lost lamb. "Oh, I want you to meet my husband," I said, waiting for him to catch up.

"Yes," said Richard. "I'm her co-pilot." And they all laughed.

"But what June failed to realize," he would say later, "was that the pilot always sits to the left. And as we took off, all refueled, there was such a high wind that we had to take off crossfield instead of downfield. So June is still giving an imitation of a pilot and she has her hands on the dual controls and is doing everything I'm doing and looking out now and then to laugh and wave to the crowd that had gathered.

"So I fixed her. Just as we were beginning to get up steam, I pulled back on the controls and Junie disappeared underneath the panel. We took off almost straight up. I guess they knew who was flying the plane then."

"Yeah, and I'll never forgive you," I added.

The rumor factory and some gossip columnists gave our marriage about six months. On our six-months' anniversary, Richard gave a surprise party for me. There was a huge cake and lettered on it by an expert pastry chef was the legend: WHO SAID IT WOULDN'T LAST?

6

WHEN WE WERE first married, I had some vague notion that somehow we would eventually live in Richard's house—which showed how naïve I was, because it never happened. Joan Blondell remained in the house and we stayed in the apartment while Richard looked for a house for us. Before Christmas, he found one in Brentwood Park, on Cliffwood Drive, right around the corner from Joan Crawford. I was impressed when Richard told me who our new neighbor would be. And even more impressed when he took me out to Brentwood to see our new home.

"Well, how do you like this house?" asked Richard, matter of factly.

"It's beautiful," I said. "It's perfect." I kept repeating these phrases about everything I saw, inside and out.

But Richard was singing a different tune— "We'll knock out that wall. And that wall. This whole front can go out a hundred feet." I thought it was some madness that would soon pass but I realized he wasn't kidding when moving day came and I found myself in a completely gutted house, with sleeping quarters in a dressing room. A mattress on the floor and a tarpaper wall against the elements—that was it. I realized that any burglar with a penknife could break in—but then, what would he get?

Later would come the very precious things—antiques, lovely furniture, and braided rugs—we always had braided rugs from then on, except in our very last house. Paul Grannard, Richard's favorite decorator, came over with many swatches of material and I sat there in amazement as he and Dick discussed pros and cons of patterns and weaves. I was happy with whatever Richard chose. Nobody asked my opinion, and I didn't volunteer. Didn't all men do the choosing?

By the time Richard was finished, the house was totally different from the one I had first seen—elegant yet homey—and I settled down to foreverness.

Now at last, I thought Richard would let me add a few touches of my own. Wrong. I tried expensive antique tables and chairs and they went back. I tried paintings and they went back even faster. There was only thing that Richard had a passion for and would never send back—lamps.

Before we were married, he had admired an antique made into a lamp and I took my cue from that. My wedding present to him was a solid brass antique scale of justice which I had the antique shop convert into a four-foot-tall lamp. Now I went through a period in which I made everything I found into a lamp. An early movie projector which I found in a shop became another unusual lamp—people marveled and still do. Old telephones, churns, anything old made splendid lamps.

I even had a few of Richard's old hunting rifles made into lamps. He was delighted. He would tease me, saying, "I'm going hunting. I wonder which lamp I should take."

It wasn't quite the same when it came to trying to buy shirts and ties and other articles of clothing for my man. At first I was so happy to see him beam at the gifts I had chosen and murmur something like "That's great" or "That will do just fine" as he threw away the wrap. But still, I never saw him wear one of the fanciful ties or unusual shirts and one day I found out why. He was giving them as gifts and rewards to prop men and butchers and bakers and even the lawn man.

For this I had slaved over a hot counter, making up my mind?

My old fiancé, Tommy, came to visit us at Brentwood, and he wasn't alone. He hadn't waited long to marry someone else— a long-stemmed beauty who was a model. Tommy had left show business and had blossomed into a fashion photographer. He loved to tell how his first camera had come from "June Allyson, future star."

Richard had been most gracious toward my ex-boyfriend. Could I be less gracious when he invited his ex-wife to dinner? I rose to the occasion and even insisted that I take care of the steaks on the outside grill so Dick could be properly attentive to his guest. Pushing hospitality to the ultimate, I told everyone to go ahead and have the first course.

Nobody objected. I kept a lonely vigil over the steaks in the deepening dusk. It started to mist and finally to rain. I looked inside through the window. The candles were glowing. Richard was sitting at one end of the table and Joan, elegantly gowned, was at the other end, a child on either side, and they were intensely engaged in conversation. I went in with my steaks, hair damp and matted, and I felt like the maid. It was a perfect picture and there was no room for me and all I could think of to say was, "Where do I sit?" I bit my lip to keep from bawling and said, "Oh, I see, over there."

The next time Joan came to dinner, I had a butler and I was in an evening gown and standing at the head of the table, indicating where Joan Blondell was to sit.

My neighbor Joan Crawford was very aware of my presence. I kept getting notes from her inviting me to lunch. I was shy and kept turning her down. Maybe shy isn't the word. Terrified of her would be more like it. She had been in so many movies and was such a great star. How would I act? What would I have to talk about? Richard finally said, "You must go. It's ridiculous for you to turn down the opportunity to meet Joan Crawford and get to know her. You can learn from her."

"But what will I say?"

"You don't have to say anything. Listen. If your own mouth is open, you're not learning. You're only learning when you're listening."

"I just hope there are a lot of other people and I don't have to talk much." I hoped in vain. I was the only guest. When I rang the doorbell of the large house, Joan herself opened the door, greeting me warmly, taking both my hands and even giving me a little kiss on the cheek.

I thanked her for the lovely roses she had sent me when we'd moved in and praised her home. And then I paused, wondering where to go from there. I needn't have worried about what I was going to say with Joan Crawford. Proudly she launched into her busy schedule, the demands on her, the number of times she had to change clothes before the day was over—three times was par—and how she had learned the secrets of looking taller and could teach them to me.

She looked at me suddenly as if I needed help, demanding to know how tall I was. I was surprised that she wasn't much taller than I and I told her my height—5 foot 1½. She laughed, "I'm only 5 foot 4½," she said, "but I hold my head as a queen would." And wear high heels that are like stilts, I thought. She led me into the living room but we didn't sit down. It didn't look like a room that got much use. There were no rugs around and the floor was so shiny, like something in a movie, not real life. The furniture was impeccable, with cushions so perfectly fluffed that you didn't dare disturb them. She led me to a less imposing sitting room, where we finally sat down and continued our conversation about the demands on her time and how she answered every fan letter herself. Didn't I?

"No," I said, "but the studio shows me some." I started to tell her about a few amusing letters but she was no longer interested in my fan mail and was ordering a servant to get Christina, adding, "I want you to meet my lovely daughter."

Christina Crawford, a gentle, blond little girl, curtsied formally and said, "How do you do?"—then promptly sat down and never moved or said another word. An uneasy feeling crept over me. I knew I should be trying to draw the child out but Joan never left a gap in her dialogue and then lunch was announced and we went into the dining room. I found it impossible to concentrate on the food when a child was sitting there and saying nothing and her mother was treating her as if she didn't exist.

I had seen a movie of Fred Astaire and Joan Crawford's and now I tried to tell her how he had inspired me. She made a wry face and cut me off. "Hmph, I helped him get started in movies," she said. "I was his first dancing partner. *Dancing Lady*. Nobody remembers that. Only Ginger, Ginger, Ginger. I gave him the glamour he needed."

"But Adele was first," I broke in defensively. "His sister."

"Oh, my dear—that was stage. That was stage. But I made him look so good in *Dancing Lady* that RKO grabbed him away. And that's how he happened to team up with Ginger Rogers. I wonder what would have happened if he'd stayed at MGM and we'd have been a team?"

I could see this was no time to talk of my career or anything but hers. She launched into *Mildred Pierce*, her latest achievement, and how even the grips had told her what a wonderful job she had done. And on and on. No interest in me.

For goodness sake—I had just finished a picture with the estimable Robert Walker and I could tell her all kinds of things about that. We could compare notes. Wasn't she going to ask me anything about what I'd been working on lately?

I could feel myself sinking lower and lower in my chair until

I felt about seven years old, like Christina, across the table from me. At first I'd been afraid to talk. Now I wasn't permitted to talk.

The self-adoration of Joan Crawford continued. I tried to be a good listener. I decided that was what Joan had wanted after all—not so much a friend as an audience. I comforted myself with the thought that this would be a limited run and soon, oh please soon, we would get up from the table and I could suddenly remember what I had to do at home.

Now Joan was holding forth on the subject of silver. She pointed to the shelves of silver that lined the wall and said they were a priceless collection from the family of her former husband, Franchot Tone.

By now my face had frozen into a permanent smile as I tried to follow Joan's patter, including how she had hated the name Joan Crawford when the studio had run a contest and that name had been the winner—only coming to as I realized Joan was saying, "Don't you agree?"

She had gone from the name back to her favorite topic of A Star's Life and was waiting for my response to the comment that "A star's life is so lonely."

"I guess I'm not that much of a star yet," I mumbled. I wanted to add, "You don't have to be lonely. You can do things with Christina." But again, I didn't. Obviously her skin was too thick by now for any advice, no matter how well-intentioned, to penetrate.

Now we were walking out to the large foyer again and Joan paused and said, "Have you noticed how quiet Christina is?"

I was even more uncomfortable, not knowing what Joan was leading up to, and I hemmed and hawed, finally allowing, "Yes, she did seem quiet."

Joan looked at Christina, who was looking elsewhere, and said, "Christina is getting the silent treatment." Again I didn't say anything although I longed to blurt out, "For God's sake, what for?"

Joan must have been waiting for some reaction from me, too, but when none came, she said. "Christina knows what she did, don't you, Christina?" It was clearly a rhetorical question. Christina nodded mutely.

"Christina," Joan said regally and with feigned patience, "go upstairs and find the box that is all wrapped up." She sighed before continuing, "And then bring it here."

Christina walked slowly away and I was terrified that this was going to be another present for me. The only present I wanted was to be able to make a quick exit.

Christina was soon back with a huge box beautifully wrapped and tied with satin bows. My first reaction was relief that the package wasn't for me and my second was shock and disbelief as Joan told Christina what she must do with the package.

"Sit on that bench," said Joan, waiting until Christina complied. "You know that is the birthday present you are supposed to take to the party this afternoon. And for punishment for what you did, you will sit on that bench holding that box until the party is over." Joan had wanted a witness to this humiliation.

I could hardly wait to get outside. I felt like throwing up. How could a person do this to anyone, let alone a child? Somehow I said goodbye to Joan, thanked her for lunch, and said an awkward goodbye to Christina, who had an equally strained face and couldn't answer. I hurried down the front path and along the sidewalk home, almost stumbling as tears blurred my vision.

What was going on? What was it all about? I said, "Oh, God, don't let me ever treat a child that way!"

I never returned the luncheon invitation to Joan. I was never her friend. We would see her many times at parties and I would try to be polite. Sometimes Richard would put Joan on our guest list for big parties. But the scene would always come back to my mind—and it still haunts me.

Maybe something good comes of everything. I know that what I witnessed at Joan's house influenced how I treated my children when I finally had them, showing them every day how much I loved them, never letting them have a doubt of how precious they were, never humiliating them in public. Joan had taught me a great lesson, but unfortunately at someone else's expense.

One place I always ran into Joan Crawford was at Hedda's. Hedda Hopper's parties were a must. Stars showed up in their best bib and tucker to please this queen of the press. Not to go might cause her to launch some nasty rumor. Joan Crawford was her special pet because Joan always dressed for the role of The Great Star and Hedda loved her for it.

Even though I dutifully showed up at Hedda's, prodded by Richard, she always knocked me in the column. She liked Richard and invariably plugged his various projects, but for me there was a barrage of barbs. Commenting about my Peter Pan collars, she wondered if there was something wrong with my neck. I took great pains to show up at her next party in a low-cut gown. Now she wrote, "What is June Allyson trying to prove?" Considering my lack of endowment, I wanted to phone her and say, "Obviously nothing." But under Richard's tutelage, I smiled as usual the next time we met.

I never acquired the frontage of Judy Garland or the bosomy Marilyn Monroe and never permitted the studio to fake it with falsies. But hips were as important as bosoms, and though I gnashed my teeth, the studio would often order a bit of padding sewn into my costumes to round out my hips.

I loved our Brentwood home. We could curl up in front of the fireplace, even if it had no fire in it, and Richard would sip a martini poured from the little pitcher Frank, the butler, brought in, as he spun dreams of directing great movies someday and maybe even producing. I would nibble on goodies—I didn't drink in those days—and tell him about my day at the studio. I was still just getting used to the new house when some strangers came in one day, accompanied by Richard. I thought he'd brought some guests home and I couldn't understand why he was showing them things like bathrooms. Wasn't that a bit tacky? When they were gone, I asked what that was all about.

"I just sold the house."

My heart beat like a trip-hammer. "Oh, Richard, how *could* you? I love this house. I'll never move. Never. Never." He grabbed me and mashed the hysterics out of me in a big rough bear hug that ultimately turned into a long evening of lovemaking.

The next day I sputtered all the way to Bel Air, grumbling about being thrown out of my house and deaf to his lecture on real estate values and the art of doubling your investment. He turned into a most impressive estate on Copa de Oro. There was a big iron gate and beyond it, half hidden in shrubbery, loomed a huge structure in a strange style. "English Tudor," said Richard. "It's ours."

I was standing like an orphan child before a feast. "Say something," he demanded. "Do you like it?"

"I don't know if I could live in it."

"But do you like it?"

"It's so big. And the yard is so big."

"It has about two acres of *grounds*. But do you *like* it, Flat-top?"

"Of course I like it. But it's just too grand." Richard didn't seem to think so. He played his old trick of musical walls and soon, after he'd ripped it apart and put it together again, the place was twice as beautiful. He had the walls covered in silks and tapestries.

I determined to have a finger in the decoration this time and I did it his way. Saying nothing to him, I kept ordering furniture that looked good to me at the furniture stores. He kept sending it back, saying "No, no, child. Early American furniture does not fit in an English Tudor house."

"Oh," I said. I hadn't known it was Early American. He began ordering beautiful old oaken pieces directly from England. And when everything was in place I couldn't imagine it any other way—it was indeed like living in an old English castle complete with swords, shields, armour, mugs, and even a wishing well outside. But no swimming pool this time—"Too dangerous for children," said Richard.

"Yes," I said happily. "Too dangerous for children."

But where were the children?

Everyone was happily having a baby, it seemed, except me. All my friends—Judy Garland, Dinah Shore, and Frances Bergen, the wife of Edgar Bergen, had babies. As the babies arrived, no one made a greater fuss than I. I haunted their nurseries. Judy would yell, "Hide the baby, here comes Junie."

The soulful-eyed Liza was born to Judy in March of 1946. Frances gave birth just two months later. I wanted desperately to have my own baby.

Someone said, "You can be a godmother," but that wasn't the same. You couldn't take the baby home with you after the christening. I tried to concentrate on my blossoming social life and the joy of being a hostess.

Ronald Reagan and his wife, Jane Wyman, were two of the most interesting new friends I acquired through marriage to Dick Powell. Jane and Dutch, as Richard called Ronnie Reagan, were products of the Warner Brothers lot, where Dick Powell had been under contract during the period he made his great musicals.

Ronnie and Jane and George and Julie Murphy were among our first dinner guests at our manse in lofty Bel Air, and over coffee and chocolate soufflé, I asked Ronnie if he got the nickname Dutch in sports. Ronnie broke into his wonderful grin and said in that amused, philosophical voice of his, "Junie, my dad took one look at me and said, 'With those fat round cheeks, he looks just like a little Dutchman.' The name stuck—or at least the diminutive Dutch."

Richard had a strong tie with Ronald Reagan because Ronnie had played the big city sidekick to Dick Powell's singing cowboy in the 1938 movie *The Cowboy from Brooklyn.* "That's one we'd both better forget," Ronnie said. Richard agreed—in public at least—but I happened to know that Richard kept many still photos from that movie, especially scenes in which he wore a cowboy suit with chaps that were gloriously Art Deco.

Ronnie and Richard were close buddies—a love of arguing politics drew them together just as a distaste for the same subject brought me and Jane Wyman together in a fortuitous blending of couples. We two couples made several trips together, including a political one to Washington, D.C. Richard was also old friends with Jane Wyman—they'd done *Gold Diggers of 1937* and *The Singing Marine* together. Richard had earned the right to call her "Button Nose" and she loved it.

At our Bel Air dinner Jane asked me to show her around the house so we could both get away from the men talking politics. I took Jane upstairs and showed her our separate bedroom suites. I am glad to say that Richard did not use his much, but he liked having a bedroom in masculine colors—brown and beige—and he would disappear there when he had to work on things requiring deep concentration. Other times we would look on the Dick suite as a sick bay where either of us could recover from a cold in muted brown and beige comfort. My bedroom suite was in a misty rose. And it had a niche for my collection of stuffed animals, witches, and, especially, Raggedy Ann dolls.

Back downstairs Jane Wyman and I joined the men, and Julie Murphy, around the fireplace. It was a riot to listen to

Ronnie, a staunch Democrat, trying to convert Richard while Richard argued just as hard to turn Ronnie into a Republican. I figured the only way to get into this conversation was to pop some basic questions at Ronnie.

He answered me carefully, methodically. When Ronnie got through explaining something to me, Jane Wyman leaned over and said, "Don't ask Ronnie what time it is because he will tell you how a watch is made."

It was true that he was very thorough, but he showed the same thoroughness in matters other than politics and he was interested in any number of things and always studying. He was a wine connoisseur and once after I asked some questions about wines, he sent me a book on the subject.

Jane Wyman seemed more upset with her husband's obsession with politics than I. I tried to make her laugh. "He'll outgrow it," I told her. To her it wasn't funny. But even more annoying to her was the fact that it took Ronnie so long to make up his mind about anything she asked him.

"But, Jane," I said, "that's Ronnie. He always wants to be sure of what he says and simply doesn't give snap opinions." I thought it was wonderful that Ronnie was so vitally interested in everything and was always studying a new subject, but I was not surprised when Jane and he were divorced in 1948, after eight years of marriage. Richard and I were heartsick over Ronnie and Jane but as Richard put it, "They just seemed to pass each other going in different directions."

Jane Wyman was one of the nicest persons I knew. A certain sad sweetness radiated from her large soulful eyes. That was why she was so convincing as the pathetic characters she played to perfection. She got her divorce from Ronnie and had her greatest triumph, the Academy Award for her role as a deaf mute in *Johnny Belinda*, in the same year. Richard said, "They would not have gotten a divorce had their careers not been going in opposite directions—hers up, his down." The movies had brought Jane Wyman and Ronald Reagan together—they starred together in *Brother Rat* before marrying in 1940—and the movies tore them apart.

Dick Powell, George Murphy and Ronnie Reagan were all deeply involved in the Screen Actors Guild and this also formed a bond between us three couples.

In 1946, George Murphy retired as president of the Screen Actors Guild and Ronald Reagan followed him into the presidency. We all celebrated over at the Reagans' and the fellows kidded me because I, too, had won an election that year—"Ideal American Girl of 1946."

Dick Powell was vice president of the Screen Actors Guild and could have moved up into the presidency but, unlike Ronnie, he did not want to. When asked, he said, "No, I just can't take that much time from business." Ronnie could and he made an effective Screen Actors Guild president, always trying to be fair. At dinner one night, Ronnie came up with what seemed like a great idea to me. He suggested that actors, like oil barons, have depletion allowances to help them with taxes. I don't know what George and Richard thought of it but I endorsed the idea enthusiastically. Eventually, however, Ronnie quit talking about it.

I was meeting other important and affable couples through Richard. There were the Firestones—Polly and Len. I used to say that Polly had brought me up because she took time to teach me the finer points of distinguishing between good taste and mediocre and plain bad.

Leonard, her husband, was the grandson of the original Harvey Firestone and he was part of the West Coast branch of the Firestone business. But tires were seldom mentioned, except in a humorous way—what Len wanted to talk about was sports, any kind of sports. He was part owner, with Gene Autry, of the Los Angeles baseball team and also a backer of our local football team, the Los Angeles Rams. He and Richard played golf together. Polly was Len's first wife—a novelty in itself, in Hollywood.

Then there were the Darts—Jane and Justin—as in Dart Industries. Justin was another sportsman. He had been a star football player at Northwestern, an All Big-Ten guard, and had married into the drugstore business. His first wife was Ruth Walgreen and he had eventually become general manager and director of Walgreen's.

Then he divorced and married the wife I knew, Jane, with whom he had three children—and I may deserve credit for having talked her into having a third one. When I met him, Justin Dart was president of the Rexall Drug Company, which then became part of Dart Industries, and I believe he was also a director of United Airlines. At our get-togethers we relaxed and talked of what was new in the world—outside of Hollywood—especially sports.

Justin and I had a running mock battle over my neatness. He thought it was hilarious that I was always trying to make everything look neat and he'd do anything to mess up me or my surroundings. Richard and I took a trip to Honolulu with the Darts and Justin drove me crazy throwing orange peelings and other trash through a transom into my room.

I said, "Justin, I'm going to kill you. You clean this all up if you want to stay healthy." But he just walked off, laughing.

Jane said to me once, "You and I always wonder what we talk about so long. It is just fun to be together and actually all the *girls* of our group are on the same wavelength."

The joke among our husbands was that they didn't need a detective to find their wives—our matching cars were a dead giveaway. Friends, too, tracked us down by our wild-looking Thunderbirds—hot pink for me, bright yellow for Jane. But if the Thunderbird was lavender, that meant Frances Bergen was somewhere around.

Frances and Edgar Bergen were right at the center of our

group. They were very dignified and never did corny things like bring Charlie McCarthy or Mortimer Snerd along to parties. In 1937 Edgar had received a funny acknowledgment for his work with his wooden dummy. The Academy Awards gave him a wooden Oscar, made especially for him. Later, we would tease him about it, threatening to take it back and turn it in for a *real* one. If you pressed him, Edgar would tell of his humble beginning with little blockheaded Charlie. Edgar said, "Charlie cost me $35 when I was in high school and paid me back by helping me work my way through college. I was studying medicine but I asked myself, 'Who would want to go to a doctor who talks to wooden dummies and thinks they talk back?'" Edgar gave full credit to Rudy Vallee for saving him from vaudeville and helping him get started in radio.

Edgar was born in Chicago, of Swedish parents, and he prided himself on his Swedish heritage and his mastery of the language. Once Edgar and Richard went to a bar in Sweden on a trip abroad.

Edgar said, "Let me handle it—I know the language." He turned to the bartender and explained in Swedish, "My friend wants a martini very dry, with a formula of nine to one." The waiter returned with ten martinis on a tray and proceeded to line them up in front of Richard.

I contributed at least one couple to The Group—Bonnie and Johnny Green. Back in my chorus line days, Bonnie was Bunnie Waters, a member of the Copa line when Jane Ball and I moonlighted there, and I followed Bunnie around like a puppy dog, just to look at her.

I was so delighted, when I got acquainted with the musical director at MGM, to learn that he was married to my old friend Bunnie Waters. She and Johnny had gotten married in 1943, the year I left New York.

I called him "Uncle Johnny." It was he who took the terror out of recording songs for me. I couldn't stand the sound of my own voice when we were recording a number—I was intimidated by it. Johnny talked with Kay Thompson, the MGM singing coach, and she came up with two cardboard coverings that I could put over my ears. Later for the cameras, I could sing as if I were really enjoying it.

Even in Hollywood, Bonnie was so beautiful, with blond hair and perfect classic features, that she could draw her hair back in a simple bun and turn every head as she entered a room. It helped that she was also statuesque—topping six feet. Together we looked like Mutt and Jeff. Any time I needed sympathy and quick advice, I called her. I used to say if I could have any face in Hollywood, I would choose Bonnie's.

In spite of her beauty, Bonnie was content to bask in the glory of Johnny's musical career. She had no desire to become a movie star.

Johnny's work as a composer—"I Cover the Waterfront" and "Body and Soul" were two of his classics—earned him an honorary doctorate in music. We had a running gag. He told me I'd have to call him Doctor from now on. I replied, "Only if you let me show you my appendix."

He said, "You can't see the appendix."

"You see? What do you know about medicine?"

George and Julie Murphy had been a famous dance team before I knew them. They started a square dance club and the charter members were the Len Firestones, the Edgar Bergens, the Justin Darts, and Richard and me. We wore square dance costumes and met at each other's houses, serving country-style food—especially ribs and country-fried chicken—on checkered tablecloths.

How we loved those hoe-downs, whirling to an authentic square dance band with plenty of fiddles, the women with fluffy skirts flying out into mushroom shapes, and the men sporting checkered shirts and kerchiefs. Richard, like the good Arkansas hillbilly he was, danced expertly and could call as well as dance up a country storm. But we hired a professional caller so Richard could just enjoy dancing.

Julie Murphy was my square dance teacher, but when it came to teaching me bridge—the group's other interest—that was another matter.

Julie had explained and explained and finally I was ready to play bridge with the group as her partner. Right off, I trumped her ace. So much for bridge, which I never played again.

7

JACK BENNY AND George Burns would both be invited to our parties and it would almost be a mistake to have them in the same room together. Jack would be there already and George Burns would put in a late appearance—probably purposely— and walk into the living room, flicking his cigar and pretending he was going to walk right by Jack Benny.

Then he'd sort of pause and half glance at Benny, flick and say, "Hi, Jack, how are things?" Jack would laugh so hard he would sometimes double up. "What happened?" we would ask each other.

We could never figure out what it was but we never stopped trying. I would wonder if it was something in George Burns' eyes, the way they twinkled. He always looked like he knew something you didn't know—and probably wouldn't find out.

Richard was very fond of George Burns and kept his favorite brand of cigars by the boxful. It didn't matter what others wanted to smoke, we only kept Burns' brand. That's the effect he had on people.

When Gracie Allen was still alive and came with him, she took no part in his constant story-telling, nor did he try to draw her into any gag. Gracie, whom I dearly loved, just wanted to sit around with the girls, talking about ordinary things like cooking and shopping—and anyone who tried to get her to be funny got a dirty look. But there were exceptions.

George liked to make the point that he *had* to marry Gracie because he owed her $200 and didn't know how else to pay it off. Once he added, "And I've been working it off ever since, right Gracie?"

Gracie, who was on her way to get her coat, turned to him and said, in her sweetest voice, "Oh really, George? I wasn't sure. I thought *I* was working it off." And she was until 1958, when she retired and let him work it off, solo.

Our guests would always say to Jack Benny, "Just do one thing. Just give your punch line when the stickup man says to you, 'Your money or your life.'" And Benny would wait a long time while they'd be keyed up with anticipation and finally Benny would say, "I'm thinking, I'm thinking." Jack Benny really did own a Maxwell car, the same one Mel Blanc, the sound effects genius, imitated trying to get up a hill. When friends asked, "How's your Maxwell?" Jack Benny would retort, "In fine voice, thanks." Everyone knew the Maxwell got better care than a baby.

It was amazing how much Richard and George had in common. George, as a child, had formed a singing group called "The Pee Wee Quartet." Richard had formed a kid musical group called "The Peter Pan Five."

"You see, I topped you," Richard would goad George Burns, "I had five to your four."

One night Judy Garland was with us when Richard and George Burns got into a wild exchange. George said, "I've played more places than you. Did you ever sing at the ferry, for the passengers coming off, and catch pennies before they hit the dock? And outside the subways and bus stations? Huh?"

"No, but I cornered the religious market—did you ever sing one night at the Presbyterian church and the next night at the

Jewish synagogue and the third night at the Episcopal church? Did you ever do that, my friend?"

"No, Dickie boy, I never thought of the religious market—I sang outside the Miller's Meat Market, though. Say, what kind of money did you pull down?"

"Good money, $15 from the Presbyterians on Sunday, $10 from the synagogue on Friday, and another ten spot from the Episcopalians on Wednesday."

"No, the Pee Wees were not in your league."

Judy Garland chimed in and said, "I owed my voice quality, my tremolo, to singing at a synagogue as a kid. My first agent didn't have the money to send me to a voice teacher so he sent me to the synagogue to copy what I heard and get emotion into my voice." Judy launched into an emotional Hebrew melody and there was not a whisper as she sang.

George loved to talk about his schooling—or lack of it—during his poverty-stricken days in the Lower East Side of New York. He claimed to have spent endless years in the fourth grade but he didn't mind a bit because the teacher, Miss Hollander, was young and pretty and besides, he had discovered show business. He was skipping school to sing wherever three people would stop to listen. Someone told him that Caruso had developed his great voice from eating garlic, so he'd load up on three or four cloves of garlic a day. "Whenever I skipped school, Miss Hollander would send my mother a thank-you note." George got a lot of mileage out of Miss Hollander. He would tell me or any other thin actress, "Kid, you'd better not stand sideways or Miss Hollander will mark you absent."

Richard tried to top George on the subject of grim determination. He had once been down to forty cents between jobs and he had lived on one ten-cent hamburger a day. On the fourth day, after he'd eaten his last hamburger, he had gotten a wire with a job offer.

"Did you give 'em a big kiss?" grinned Georgie between cigar puffs.

"Hell no," said Richard, "I told them if they had waited another day, I'd have taken another offer."

What they didn't know and what I didn't tell was the terrible effect poverty—and those very hamburgers—had on Richard's psyche. With all the money he was making and all the money I was earning and adding to the kitty—I never even knew how much—Richard still couldn't get over the effects of his early hand-to-mouth existence. We would go for a hamburger and Richard would stuff his pockets with a few packets of everything—ketchup, mustard, relish, mayonnaise, salt and pepper. I would scold him and make him put them back.

Richard would laugh and say, "It's a habit. Once poor, always poor. I can't get over saving against that last hamburger."

Judy Garland was one reason I wanted a grand piano. She would sing at everyone's party but mine and it was simply that I had no piano to accompany her. Richard could play piano and in a Hollywood crowd there were always several at every party who knew how. (Jack Lemmon not only played piano but composed songs.)

I told Richard, "I want a grand piano so bad. Can't you please work it into your decorating scheme? I'd be so happy and I'll take lessons and learn to play Sibelius."

"I doubt it," said Richard, "but it would be nice to have and if you want it, I'll get you the most beautiful one I can find."

He found one and I took enough lessons to get as far as Debussy's "Clair de Lune" and there I stopped. After the third time I had amazed my guests with "Clair de Lune," friends would tell Judy, "Oh God, Judy, just keep singing or she'll play 'Clair de Lune' again."

Once I caught the hostess fever there was no stopping me. I

would say I wanted to have a few friends in and Richard would say, "Fine, when?" And I'd set a date. Then I'd invite everyone I could think of. As the time approached, Richard would say, "Have you decided on the menu?"

I'd say, "No."

"You'd better think about it. How many people are you having?"

"A few."

"How few?"

"Is seventy-five all right?"

"Oh my God! What are you doing about entertainment?"

"Well, you know, I thought I'd leave that part for you."

"Oh God, and have you ordered flowers?"

"Flowers? I thought I'd just pick a few from the yard."

"You can't denude our yard. Oh, child, where is my clipboard?" Soon he would be making notes as fast as he could go. And the phones would be going and just in the nick of time he'd have it all together, including a small band for dancing. And I would get all the credit. Between the cooking and serving of my superb majordomo-butler and Richard's planning, I made a darn fine hostess, if I do say so myself.

Judy Garland was always the center of attention at any party she gave or attended and I would always be found tagging around in her shadow, even at my own parties. When she would sing, I would sit on the floor near her and just worship her. I was a worshiper of talent. But in the case of Judy, I would bask in her warmth, her sincerity, her generosity. Whatever she did, at that moment, she gave herself to it completely.

And like me, she could only love one man at a time. She was never a playgirl.

One evening Richard and I were sitting around our living room with Jack Benny, Ronald Colman, Judy Garland and Ronnie Reagan with Jane Wyman. Suddenly Judy pulled me to my feet and said, "Come on, everybody, we're going to play 'Guess

Who?' See if anybody can guess who we are. You first, Junie. Go, girl."

I thought quickly and stood there leaning my head to one side, pounding my ear on that side. Nobody guessed and I kept pounding the side of my head.

"Give up!" they yelled.

"Esther Williams," I said, and they laughed.

Then it was Judy's turn. She stood there looking very soulful, as if she was about to cry and she said, "And I'd like to thank the little man who drove me around the studio and the doctor, who borned me, and I want to thank the prop man. And I want to thank the man who brought me my tea . . ." And she went on and on but we could hardly hear for our laughter because, of course, everyone knew this must be Greer Garson accepting her Academy Award for her 1943 movie *Mrs. Miniver*.

Judy and I loved the Guess Who? game. I would stand wringing my hands and looking to heaven, and they would yell, "Margaret O'Brien."

And Judy would wipe tears from her eyes and be waving goodbye and that would be "June Allyson in *any* movie."

So then I'd fix Judy by dancing down the Yellow Brick Road clumsily while singing her Wizard song off key.

Joan Fontaine was one of Richard's favorite people and he always added her to the guest list any time he entertained. He admired Joan because she was a sharp businesswoman who invested in a diversity of things, just as Richard did—cattle, real estate, oil, even the stock market. She and Richard would go off in a corner and sound like a couple of executives at Merrill, Lynch. Joan admitted freely that she got some of her best business tips talking to businessmen at parties.

I had to learn how to be a hostess and I had to learn how to be a guest. Our Frank could make me look good in my own home but he could not follow me to other parties to teach me how to be a good guest.

Frances Bergen had become a friend so I felt particularly relaxed at her place, relaxed enough, on one occasion, to stand at her buffet table and clean up the whole platter of pâté de foi gras. It was imported and very delicious—and undoubtedly very expensive.

"Isn't this stuff yummy?" I would say to other guests who stopped to place a bit of it on a cracker and then move on. I didn't move on. I just stood there piling each cracker high until there were only bits left on the serving platter.

At this point, a distraught Frances materialized at my side, asking if she could see me in the other room. "June," she said, exasperated, "did you have to eat *all* of it? You didn't leave any for anybody else."

"Oh," I said, "don't you have any more? I thought you had gobs of it in the kitchen. I'm sorry. I'll send you some tomorrow."

"Tomorrow I can get some myself. What am I going to do now?" I offered to phone Frank, our butler, and have him bring some but she said, "It will be too late. The guests will have gone." I followed her around telling her how sorry I was and saying, "Why didn't you come over and just make me put the knife down?" She finally had to laugh and our friendship survived—but I noticed she never served pâté de fois gras again when I was around.

I was not the only one who committed social gaffes. At Bert Lahr's one night I watched in horror as Bert spilled his drink right down his mother-in-law's dress. The poor woman was most annoyed with Bert and let him know it. Bert pulled himself up and in his Cowardly Lion voice said, "It should have been molten lava." Then he leaped about acting brave, then scared, then brave, then scared, as he whined, "Uh, uh, uh, uh." The poor guests tried to cope with their laughter at Bert's antics, while showing sympathy for his victim.

Even Emily Post would have had trouble with that one.

As time went on, half the Hollywood colony was entertained

at our home—Humphrey Bogart and his "Baby," as he called Lauren; Papa Mayer, as well as his daughters Edie Goetz and Irene Mayer Selznick; the exquisite Merle Oberon; and Lana Turner with a husband or between husbands. Louella Parsons was always on hand with her husband, a doctor who always drank heavily throughout the evening. When it was time to leave, he would suddenly draw himself up and say with great dignity, "Well, I must go. I have to operate in the morning." It was all we could do to keep from laughing out loud because morning was just a few hours off and there was no way he was going to operate.

It was fun to venture out into Hollywood society as Mrs. Dick Powell. One evening we attended one of Mary Pickford's fabulous parties. I didn't realize that this had special significance. Nobody had told me that you hadn't arrived socially until you had been invited to Pickfair, the name her palatial estate had been given when she was married to Douglas Fairbanks.

When the big evening came, I threw on something and hopped into the car with Richard. He was amused that I could get ready quicker than any woman he'd ever known. It was true—the only thing I had to do was wash my hair. I wore no makeup and needed no lipstick because my lips are naturally pink. When we arrived at Pickfair, everyone was dressed to the hilt. In my Peter Pan dress I felt like the ugly duckling in a roomful of swans. But it didn't bother Mary Pickford, who made a big fuss over me. She had wanted to see with her own eyes, she said, this little girl who was being compared with her. "Yes," she said, "I can see myself in you and even your outfit makes you a worthy successor."

Richard told Mary Pickford how he had made me cut my hair and it had landed me the role that made me a star. Mary was delighted and told how she had cut off all her little-girl curls and this had forced the studio heads to give her a sophisticated role in *Coquette*.

"Did you save your hair?" she demanded.

"No," I said, surprised at the thought.

"You should have. All my curls were saved," she said, smiling. "They are part of movie history." Later I learned they were in a museum in Los Angeles.

I would like to say that after the Pickfair party, I always arrived wearing just the right fashion, but I'm afraid I can't. To a party at Claudette Colbert's I wore a three-quarter-length brown woolen skirt and white blouse. All the other women were in floor-length gowns, many shimmering with sequins.

Claudette decided to take me in hand and issue some fashion tips. She came over to lunch one day when neither of us had a film in the works. Instead of telling me how inappropriate I had looked, she said, "You know, June, you should dress up more."

I knew what she meant. I said, "But Claudette, Richard hates me in fancy clothes. I always wear plain clothes. They're me."

"Of course, dear. You don't have to wear fancy clothes to be more dressed up. You can wear what you are comfortable in and even a skirt and blouse to a party. But you go out and have a skirt and blouse made with an evening look. The difference is in the material. And the cut. A blouse can be an elegant evening blouse. A skirt can be an elegant evening skirt."

What Claudette taught me I use to this day—and once I have the right style I have it made in various colors.

As a dedicated fan of Claudette Colbert's, I was fortunate enough to be picked to co-star with her and Walter Pidgeon in *The Secret Heart*. While I was emoting as the mentally upset youngster trying to steal Claudette's fiancé away, I watched carefully and learned a lot from seeing how Claudette could switch from the light touch to deep compassion for the troubled girl and make it so convincing.

I found myself copying some of Claudette's ways. She had a habit of appealing to the Almighty in French and soon I, too, was going around saying *"Mon Dieu!"* Claudette never seemed to take herself too seriously and she talked freely about the ridiculous things she had to do in her early screen days—like take a bath in ass's milk in *The Sign of the Cross* and vamp it up on a barge in Cecil B. De Mille's *Cleopatra*.

Claudette's husband, Joel Pressman, a doctor, was a pilot just like Richard and sometimes we two couples would fly side by side in separate private planes en route to a dinner party, Claudette and I both hating every minute of it and saying we'd rather walk.

Once Richard took me to visit an old flame. Marion Davies, the fabulous mistress of the newspaper tycoon William Randolph Hearst, was somehow important in Richard's life. He might have had an affair with her years before he knew me. He had been her leading man in some of her movies. What had happened before me was none of my business and I never asked too many questions. But Marion had given Richard the most beautiful and expensive watch I had ever seen. It was an almost paper-thin pendant watch made entirely of lapis lazuli. The rim of the watch was set in a solid row of diamonds, and there were more diamonds in the hands. It was so feminine-looking that Richard never used it but kept it with his cufflink jewelry.

To my joy, Richard bought a delicate platinum chain and gave me the watch to wear around my neck. I made sure I wasn't wearing it on the day I was to meet Marion and her new husband, Captain Horace Brown. Marion caused a great stir in Hollywood by marrying just ten weeks after Hearst's funeral. When Marion's abrupt wedding was announced in 1951, Richard said, "This is amazing. She must have been terribly lonely. I heard this Captain Horace Brown was dating Marion's sister but suddenly he is married to Marion."

"Oh, Richard, you don't know anything about women," I said. "Maybe he was dating the sister all the time to be near Marion." Richard laughed. "You may have something," he said.

"You can't imagine how jealous Hearst was of Marion. She was always afraid she was being followed and I was always afraid I'd get shot." Richard had been a regular guest at Hearst's mountaintop castle, San Simeon. "I was always worried about making one false move," he said. "Guests were very careful to steer clear of romantic entanglements with Marion."

The trouble with San Simeon was—no cocktails allowed. "If a guest was found drinking," Richard said, "he was escorted out. Friendly but firm. He'd just be told that arrangements had been made for his departure and he'd never be invited back." All this trouble was taken just to keep Marion Davies from having a drink. Hearst spent all his time keeping her from liquor and she spent all her time scheming to get it.

As we drove to Marion's huge mansion, Richard told how once he had thought Marion was being very solicitous of a guest, escorting him to the dining room table but stopping at each statue along the way, as if to explain the art work. Then he realized someone had stashed a drink behind every statue for her. Mr. Hearst had looked at Marion very suspiciously as she sat down and gave every sign of being smashed.

When we were ushered into her presence, it almost broke my heart to see that she had been drinking. I could still see the beauty of that face—her eyes were enormous and very sad. But the Marion in the photographs with Richard—the ones he'd proudly shown me—no longer existed.

Richard and she laughed as they recalled their movies together—*Page Miss Glory* and *Hearts Divided*.

"My hair was curlier than yours was," Richard said.

"But mine was longer," laughed Marion.

"But not much," retorted Richard.

I could see the name "Norma Shearer" was still a dirty word to Marion and I could also see Richard signaling me not to say that Norma Shearer was also our friend.

Both ladies had been fighting to play Elizabeth Barrett

Browning, the poor invalid poetess who must escape her tyrannical father to marry Robert. Marion had enlisted Hearst's help and Shearer had gone to her husband, Irving Thalberg, a top power at MGM.

"When Mayer gave in to Thalberg, there was nothing I could do but *walk* and it broke my heart," Marion said. She was close to tears even years later. "A-ha," Richard said, determined to keep it light. "But if you hadn't taken that walk to Warners then you'd never have gotten to act with me, and wouldn't you be sorry?"

"Very sorry," Marion said, and she was laughing again and asking her husband to pour another drink.

From then on, we would keep in touch with Marion by letter—but it was always the Captain who penned the notes for her.

Fans bring joy as well as terror. Once I was shivering with cold on the set, wondering if I was going to come down with pneumonia, or at least the flu, when a package arrived. By strange coincidence, it was a hand-sewn felt jacket from a sailor in the Pacific. I was shooting *Two Girls and a Sailor* at the time with Van Johnson. Gratefully I huddled in the warm felt, and as a result of some unknown fan's act of love, I didn't get sick. For years I used that jacket and kept it in my dressing room for luck. I bless that unknown sailor who is my fan and I hope he is reading this today so he can see how meaningful his act was.

On the other hand, when Richard and I toured together to promote the first movie to star both of us—*The Reformer and the Redhead*—I was not prepared for such violence. Before I knew what was happening, someone had ripped out the sleeve of my beloved mink coat and made off with it. And that was not the worst. I suddenly realized someone had cut a big swatch of my hair. All in all, I was left looking pretty pitiful.

Van Johnson and Charles Boyer were just two special friends

who had a lot of trouble with women fans trying to tear their clothes off for souvenirs—or maybe to see what their heroes really looked like. Once Charles Boyer came away from a premiere saying women were getting stronger or he was getting weaker. It had been all he could do to hang on to the coat over his arm.

There are two kinds of fans—the ones who follow a single star around and the ones who are not selective but collect any object or autograph from almost any star who comes along. A fan we called Alley Baba—because he slipped around in Bel Air alleys—belonged to the voracious second type. He was always going through our trash cans in search of souvenirs. He would scurry home after a raid on some star's garbage and each item would be carefully tagged and labeled.

Among his treasures, Judy Garland told me, was a Kewpie doll found in Wallace Beery's backyard and a paperback book of advice from Mickey Rooney's trash can—on the subject of marriage.

I have a fan who collects everything about my life, and through the years he has become one of my best friends—Ronnie Dayton. I met him when my brother graduated from Culver Military Academy. He knew I would be attending and came to get my autograph. He did nothing in particular that day to indicate to me that he would become my shadow and a delightful part of my life, and I was aware of him only as a member of the large group that accumulated around me during the course of that festive day at the academy. Later he became a stand-in for Frankie Avalon and this would make it easier for him to spend time with me. He sent cards on every occasion. I invited him to dinner occasionally. Getting used to my brand of cooking, he would answer my invitations to dinner with "Only if you promise to burn it." Even today, as I write this book, I have note after note written to myself and saying, "Ask Ronnie."

8

HARD AS SINGING and dancing were, movie acting came easy to me. Some actors really had to struggle to memorize lines and I felt sorry for them. I was lucky. I could look at a script for twenty minutes and almost have the whole thing. Or I could take ten pages and read them and then you could give me a cue and I'd give you every line that followed.

I was told I had a photographic memory. Whatever the gift is called, I see pictures as I read a script. I see myself walking through it. I see myself saying the lines and becoming the character so it's very easy for me to memorize.

Judy Garland was another one with a so-called photographic memory. People would be worried about her because she hadn't studied the script. Then she would read it through and amaze everyone by having all the lines. And behave like a real pro.

Usually one take was all I needed to get a thing right, but there were times I had to repeat a scene five and ten times. There are some sadistic directors who put actors through endless takes just to show they can lord it over a star.

One story that made the rounds concerned Olivia de Havilland when she was filming *The Heiress*. Over and over again, director William Wyler kept her repeating a scene descending a staircase and he wouldn't tell her what she was doing wrong.

She was getting tired and finally, on the thirty-seventh take, she dropped her fan out of exhaustion and Wyler yelled, "Great! That's it." In this case, the director hadn't known what he wanted, either, until he saw it.

But it isn't always the director who is to blame. In *The Bride Goes Wild* in 1947, Van Johnson and I drove our director, Norman Taurog, crazy. In the scene we were shooting, Van Johnson and I were supposed to be falling in love and saying words that had nothing to do with the way we felt.

There's an undercurrent—the dialogue played against the scene. He says, "I had a friend who got his finger caught in the car." I say, "I had an aunt once who fell off the roof and broke her clavicle." Van is supposed to say, "That's too bad." But when I told about my aunt's clavicle, he said, "Oh my God, did it hurt?" That broke me up and Van had all kinds of snide remarks about the anatomy of my aunt.

We couldn't stop laughing over the word "clavicle." Poor Norman Taurog was getting angrier, and the angrier he got, the funnier *that* seemed. Norman glared and then he started to laugh, too. He threw up his hands and said, "All right, everybody go home. We'll never get anything done today." The next morning, Taurog wouldn't even let me speak to Van Johnson off-camera. He refused to give us a run-through before shooting. He sent me off the set while Van said his first line. Then he sent Van off the set while I gave my reply. Then Van spoke his next line to the empty air, and so did I. It was certainly an extreme measure because in a close-up, you are interacting with your scene partner. All I had for this scene was the dialogue director off-camera, cuing me with Van's lines. As soon as we got through the clavicle scene we were all right, but even today I can't hear that word without grinning.

One night Van and I had attended an acting seminar at

MGM and left in our separate cars. Van got into a terrible accident that left him with serious facial scars. I hoped Van would get plastic surgery to remove the deep scars on his forehead, but he told me, "No, I don't want them removed. This is now part of my character. Let people see reality."

Van and I have always tried to spend Christmases and birthdays together. He is the kind of friend who loves you whether you're up or down. Although Van chose Evie Wynn and I chose Richard, some friends refused to believe we hadn't married each other. One Halloween eve, after Richard and I had children, I took them to Van's house to play with Van and Evie's daughter, Schuyler, and Evie's sons, Keenan, Jr., and Ned Wynn. We were passing out candy whenever the trick-or-treaters rang the bell, and at one point Van and I opened the door together. "See," said one of the teenagers at the door, "I *told* you they were married in real life, too."

People wondered why Van Johnson would marry the wife of his best friend, Keenan Wynn, when so many younger girls were panting for a date with him. I was surprised that he married at all—he was a confirmed bachelor. But as long as he was marrying, I was not surprised that he chose a woman with warmth and maturity. Van had been a guest at her home and had seen how caring Evie Wynn could be. Though the triangle precipitated a painful upheaval, something good did come of it—a lovely daughter, Schuyler.

I remember one birthday, after Van was married to Evie Wynn, when she brought me a present from Van—a miniature painting of a clown with a birdcage on his hat and an umbrella over the bird.

Another marriage that surprised the movie colony was Peter Lawford's to JFK's sister, Patricia Kennedy. We all thought he would marry Sharman Douglas, the daughter of the former Ambassador to the Court of St. James's. Sharman had rented an apartment in Brentwood a block away from Peter Lawford's house. For a time they were inseparable. I seem to recall that I either introduced them or was there when they first met. Sharman was my friend. I had met her through the Firestones.

Sharman and Peter kept protesting they were "just good friends" but I knew they really cared. I was with them once at Ciro's and they mentioned that this was the seventh day in a row that they had eaten there. They were sharing a sandwich, but this didn't mean cutting it in half. He would take a bite, then he would hold it while she took a bite. They were gazing into each other's eyes the whole time.

Working with Peter Lawford was like going to a party. He made a game of whatever he did. He was funny and witty and he used many strange Briticisms for things that he knew would crack us up.

When I worked with Peter on *Good News* in 1947, it was our second time around; we had already appeared in *Two Sisters from Boston* together in 1945. In *Good News*, Peter plays an American football hero who is about to flunk out if he can't pass his French test. It was my job to teach him enough French to get by.

Everything about the movie was unbelievable. No one made any effort to change Peter's British accent to American. For that matter, my French accent was atrocious and his was superb—he spent hours teaching me how to teach him French. Peter said, "This is the most ridiculous part I've ever had or hope to have." But at the end of the movie, all was well and I got my man—didn't I always?

And he was still wearing his little velvet slippers.

When Richard and I got together with our friends Jimmy and Gloria Stewart, Richard kidded Jimmy and me about the string of hit movies that had made us the reigning romantic team in Hollywood. As Gloria put it, "June is Jimmy's perfect wife—in movies—and I'm his imperfect wife." Richard referred to our "husband-and-wife relationship," and once rose to introduce Jimmy at a banquet saying—"And now, let me introduce my wife's husband—Jimmy Stewart." At the same banquet Richard said in front of our whole table, "Junie here must be a good wife. Jimmy Stewart has married her three times." Jimmy sure did—in *The Stratton Story*, in *The Glenn Miller Story*, and again the next year in the impressive *Strategic Air Command*. I said, "Yeah, he married me but he couldn't make it stick." Jimmy and Richard chuckled when they compared notes about their "helpless" wives and how they had to fix everything around the house or it would stay broken forever.

Well, of course they could fix things, I told Gloria. Richard had been paid by the chore as a kid. And Jimmy Stewart had gotten degrees in engineering and architecture—I should hope he could fix a leaky faucet after all that.

I knew Jimmy Stewart before he married Gloria. With my cooking, it's a good thing he didn't marry me. The poor dear weighed only 154 pounds before he was married and he was all of 6 feet 2 or 3 inches tall. Jimmy hated being photographed when he was out with a girl and he seldom took his dates to nightclubs. Instead, he fed them steak that he grilled himself in his own backyard. If they didn't like that and wanted the limelight, they were not for him.

As a bachelor, Jimmy had lived two doors from Greta Garbo and he would talk of his plans to drop in on her. He said he would tunnel from his place into her backyard, where he would rise from the ground and say, "This is so unexpected."

Gloria was the perfect choice for him. They were so suited to each other—both tall and slim and dignified and both with the same wry sense of humor.

Jimmy's humor frequently featured his housekeeper, whom he swore handed his dates their stoles or other wraps at midnight, letting them know in this *subtle* way that it was time to go.

He even blamed his late marriage—at age forty-one—on her. He claimed she had read all his mail first and kept him from seeing anything of a romantic nature. Why hadn't he fired her? He had a quick answer for that one—she was a great judge of scripts and told him which ones he needn't bother to read. "You just couldn't fire a person like that," he told Richard and me. "And anyway, she didn't choose to go."

Jimmy Stewart was so relaxed between scenes, I wouldn't know if he was asleep or awake. But when you needed him, he'd jump right up and be all ready to go right through the scene. I never knew anyone like him.

One morning he came in and was sitting in his chair and he said, "You know, June, I never do my exercises at home. I wait till I get to the studio. You don't mind if I do them now, do you?"

I wondered if he was getting ready to stand on his head. I said, "No, I'd like to see what kind of exercises you do."

He started wiggling his fingers.

I said, "Is that all?"

"That's it. If I did any more, I wouldn't weigh as much as I do now."

Jimmy knew I was the most gullible person in the world and he was always finding a new way to put me on.

In The Stratton Story we were always laughing at the antics of Frank Morgan, who plays the over-the-hill manager who first discovers the young ballplayer.

The venerable Frank Morgan always called me a brat. One day he came on the set slightly tipsy. The director went over to quiet him down, saying, "Shhh, June Allyson is in the middle of a scene so you have to hush."

Frank Morgan boomed out, "What for? She can't act anyway."

Another time the white-thatched actor loudly avowed that

he had no use for actors and no faith in them—"not since it was an actor who shot Lincoln."

Jimmy Stewart was certainly different from any other actor I knew, including Richard. Jimmy did not want to see himself on the silver screen. He didn't want to look at rushes and he didn't go to see the finished picture. He said he'd just embarrass himself by going to our gala premieres.

When Richard and I acted together in *The Reformer and the Redhead*, he studied and analyzed every aspect of the production—we discussed his performance, how camera work could have been improved, lighting, angles at which a sequence had been shot. He said he was in training to produce movies himself someday.

I worked harder acting with Richard than with any other co-star. I was afraid the public would refuse to believe I was anyone but what I was in real life—his wife.

If Richard hadn't been in *Reformer*, I doubt that I would have accepted the role. There were live lions running around and I was constantly terrified on the set. With my childhood phobia about cats, I died a thousand deaths working with those two lions. One of them got loose on the set and—just my luck—it headed straight for me. The trainer spoke quietly, saying, "Don't move, June." As if I could.

The thing about *The Three Musketeers* that shocks people is that I wanted out of the picture. I never felt comfortable being in a period piece. I thought I was only convincing as the girl next door in blouse and skirt or the perfect wife in apron and skirt, the roles that I'd played now for five years. I looked at myself in my sweeping robes and was not convinced that anyone was going to believe me as Lady Constance. I was sure Papa Mayer would see it my way and probably be relieved to get me out of a totally unsuitable role. After all, the filming was just starting and it wasn't too late.

"No, Junie," said Papa Mayer firmly. I was sitting in the chair beside his desk, feeling miserable. "No, no. You will finish the picture."

"Yes, sir," I said. "I just wanted you to know I look ridiculous."

"I have seen and you look fine. Now go back to work."

"Yes, sir," I said, getting up and walking the longest mile to his door. The film was one of MGM's biggest grossers, which shows what I knew about casting.

For Gene Kelly and me, *The Three Musketeers* was a reunion. He had been the choreographer for *Best Foot Forward* on Broadway.

Gene and Richard had a long history, too. When Richard was on tour in the early '30's, Gene Kelly sent him a fan letter asking if he could please have his picture made with the crooner. Gene was a part-time dancing teacher who had developed good muscles as a ditch digger in Pennsylvania while waiting for his big chance. Richard had just arrived at his hotel from a long trip and was exhausted. He was not in the mood for having his picture made with a small-time dance teacher, but he pulled himself together and told the bellboy to have the fellow come up. When Richard visited me on *The Three Musketeers* set, he and Gene Kelly joked about the change in circumstances.

Lana Turner was always very uptight and unsure before a scene, but the minute they said, "Action," she sprang to life. A big scene in *Musketeers* finds us together—she as the evil Lady de Winter, safely in prison at last, and I, of course, as the personification of goodness, the sweet Lady Constance. And she is pleading with me to bring her a knife so she can kill herself. But what she really wants to do is kill me so that she can escape.

Lana did the scene without makeup, and she built so beautifully to the point where she is crying real tears that she had me mesmerized. If it had been for real, I would have given her the knife. That's the kind of actress Lana was.

Little Women was also a period movie, but this time I was playing a character who hated the clumsy long dresses as much as I. Jo wanted to wear pants like the men and climb trees and be free and unrestrained. I played the role with enthusiasm when it called for Jo to burn her dress, leaning back into the fireplace, or to spill tea down the front of it or, better still, to tear her skirts as she picked them up and leaped over a fence.

Jo also wanted to be the world's greatest writer, and I could relate to that—I had once wanted to be the world's greatest poet, a goal I had shared with Judy Garland.

I loved eating in the studio commissary with the rest of my *Little Women* co-stars. All the "sisters" would troop down together in our nightclothes or hoopskirts to get our nourishment—Elizabeth Taylor, Janet Leigh, Margaret O'Brien and me. Much of our talk revolved around Papa Mayer.

Elizabeth could not stand him, she said. She recalled that once, when she was a little girl, she had told L. B. Mayer, "Go to hell!" and had run out of his office because he had "talked mean" to her and her mother for daring to bother him. Someone called Elizabeth on the phone immediately to tell her to go back in and apologize but she refused and hung up. She said it was Mr. Mayer who should apologize. We laughed but we shivered at her defiance of the little god. It seemed to us a miracle that she was still at MGM.

No matter what people said about the Metro-Goldwyn-Mayer mogul, everyone admitted he had certainly been brainy to rise from junk dealer to the most powerful studio chief in Hollywood and the highest-salaried person in America. His first job had been to help his father find bits of junk with a horse and wagon in Canada. By a lucky break, young Louis got into the nickelodeon business on an investment of $50. He never rested until he owned a studio, but he never seemed to be very happy. We never saw his wife and we heard she was an invalid.

Directors learned not to challenge me. I was not the kind of actress who rose to a challenge. I would retreat from it. So they knew they must approach me gently. Pat me on the head and I will cry for a director or do anything else he requests. But scream at me and I freeze up. If a director screamed at another star, I disappeared. I would hide in my dressing room until peace returned. It was soon known among directors that the only way to get a good performance out of me, if they were dissatisfied with the way I was doing a scene, was to take me aside and quietly explain what they were trying to do, how they saw the emotion they wanted me to register. They had to suggest, not demand.

I was not a Method actor nor did I improve with a lot of rehearsals. If any kind of an emotional scene involving anger or crying were rehearsed, I would only walk through it, though this was sometimes unfair to the other actor in the scene, who needed help in knowing what I was going to do. But I couldn't help it. To do my best acting, I had to know the time was now, in order to give a natural reaction. I acted by reacting.

I really felt it was my life and my world when I was in a particular movie. Sometimes I would still be sniffling and feeling sad after I got home at night. But if it was not an emotional scene I could leave it at the studio and go home, hardly remembering that I had to be on the set the next day.

The hardest I ever cried was in the scene in *Little Women* when I realize our little sister is doomed to die. Margaret O'Brien tells me she doesn't mind dying and tries to comfort me as she lies on her deathbed, telling me not to be sad.

I cried so hard I had to be sent home. I got into my car still blubbering and continued to cry for hours.

June
Allyson

Best Foot Forward—we stopped the show every night, singing "The Three Bs." I belted the barrelhouse; Nancy Walker (right), the boogie woogie; and Erlene Schools (center), handled the blues.

I met Dick Powell when he came backstage one night with Joan Blondell, his wife. I never dreamed that one day I would be married to him. *(From the motion picture* Model Wife, *courtesy of Universal Pictures.)*

Jane Wyman worked with Richard in his early films, and, as Mrs. Ronald Reagan, she became a great friend of ours. Once we even took a trip together as a foursome.

The future President, whom I called Ronnie and Richard called Dutch, was Dick Powell's sidekick in the 1938 movie **Cowboy from Brooklyn**. Ronnie was a frequent guest at our house, where he argued politics with Richard. *(Copyright © 1938 Warner Bros. Pictures, Inc. Renewed 1966 by United Artists Television, Inc. All rights reserved.)*

Judy Garland told me it was okay to date David Rose (far left), from whom she was getting a divorce, but Papa Mayer, head of MGM, said it was not all right with him. We double dated with Gene Kelly and Betsy Blair anyway, often picnicking on the MGM back lot. That's Peter Lawford with us.

I loved to co-star with Van Johnson. As they said at MGM, Van flew so many missions over my dressing room they lost count. Papa Mayer tried to play matchmaker, even providing a limousine for important dates. *(From the MGM release* Two Girls and a Sailor, *© 1944 Loew's Inc. Renewed 1971 by Metro-Goldwyn-Mayer Inc.)*

Another Hollywood "romance." Peter Lawford was enormous fun to be with, but it was never the serious courtship Papa Mayer encouraged—after his plans for Van Johnson and me fell through. *(From the MGM release* Two Sisters from Boston, *© 1946 Loew's Inc. Renewed 1973 by Metro-Goldwyn-Mayer Inc.)*

A joyful wedding day. Dick Powell was a hard man to lead to the altar, but when I did, it was the happiest occasion, with Papa Mayer giving me away at Johnny and Bonnie Green's house.

Welcome to instant motherhood. Soon after the wedding, Richard sent me to Joan Blondell's house to get Ellen, his daughter by Joan. His son Norman also lived with us part of the time. I loved them both and was happy to have them and to see how they adored their father.

No sooner would I get used to one house than Richard would move us to another—this time to Bel Air. But I loved it. It was English Tudor.

Margaret O'Brien (far left) and I were known as The Town Criers because any time a role called for a lot of tears, one of us got it. When she died in **Little Women**, I couldn't turn the tears off. A blond Elizabeth Taylor is on the left and Janet Leigh and Peter Lawford are on the right. *(From the MGM release* Little Women, © 1948 Loew's Inc. Renewed 1975 by Metro-Goldwyn-Mayer Inc.*)*

I didn't want to do **The Three Musketeers** because I hated period costumes. But I didn't hate Gene Kelly. I'd known him on Broadway, too. *(From the MGM release, © 1948 Loew's Inc. Renewed 1975 by Metro-Goldwyn-Mayer Inc.)*

Baby Pamela—our first—at her christening. Claudette Colbert was her godmother, and Regis Toomey (left) was godfather for both our children.

I played Jimmy Stewart's wife so often that Dick Powell once rose at a banquet and introduced him as "My wife's husband." *(From the MGM release, The Stratton Story, © 1949 Loew's Inc. Renewed 1976 by Metro-Goldwyn-Mayer Inc.)*

Too Young to Kiss—and dressed for the role when Richard brought Pammy and Ellen, my stepdaughter, to the set to visit me. You can see why Richard often said he had "three girls to raise." *(Courtesy of Metro-Goldwyn-Mayer Inc.)*

With Bill Holden in **Executive Suite**. Bill was powerful at Paramount and was supposed to have set up everything for Dick Powell to direct a movie there, but it fell through. It was RKO and Howard Hughes who eventually granted Richard's wish to become a director. *(From the MGM release, © 1954 Loew's Inc. Renewed 1981 by Metro-Goldwyn-Mayer Film Co.)*

Alan Ladd and I fell in love while filming **The McConnell Story**. It was as if our lives had run on parallel courses. There were terrible tragedies ahead for both of us. (© 1955 *Warner Bros. Inc.*)

The good life at Mandeville—with Pammy, Richard and Ricky. In the background, above the lake, is the guest house where my brother Arthur Peters lived while he went to college and later medical school.

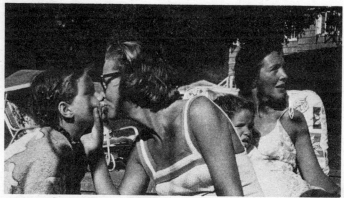

Nancy Reagan and I would visit each other and go swimming with our children, Pammy and Patty. Strangely, Pammy was the child who ended up working at the White House and Patty ended up in show business as a songwriter-actress.

Richard learned that he had cancer, but he never knew it was terminal; I insisted he not be told. This is our last photograph together. *(Los Angeles Herald Examiner)*

Judy Garland, bless her, tried to keep me busy after Richard's death, when I simply fell apart. Judy (right), Carolyn Jones (left) and I held a press conference to raise funds for the families of the children killed in the bombing of a Birmingham, Alabama, church in September 1963. Behind us are our daughters, Pamela Powell (left) and Liza Minnelli. *(UPI)*

During the bad years that followed Richard's death, when I hid with a book and a bottle of wine, my children were wonderful to me. Thank you, Ricky and Pam. *(John Engstead)*

Life today—David Ashrow, my new husband (left), and I decided to do a play together, **My Daughter, Your Son**. With Bob Moak, director (right). *(Ron Jones, 1980)*

Van Johnson and I remain loving friends after all these years. Today he is known as the King of the Supper Theaters. Here we are at the Fiesta Dinner Playhouse in San Antonio. *(Ron Jones, 1980)*

Margaret O'Brien today (far right). I had a reunion with dear Maggie on a cruise in the Caribbean with my husband, David. Maggie is very happy today—and it shows. And I am very happy today—and it shows.

Welcome to Shangri-la. Dr. David and I live on a mountain and the world looks beautiful again. This is the balcony outside our bedroom. *(Bill Delaney)*

Little Women brought me the compliment that I most cherish. Naturally, as an actress, one receives a lot of compliments, but nothing has ever thrilled me more than what Elizabeth Taylor said to me. We were all sitting on the floor of my dressing room when I noticed that Elizabeth seemed to be studying me and suddenly this fantastic world-class beauty said, "Oh, I wish I looked like you! That's the way I want to look." It gave me strength for the next twenty years.

Career and parties and friends were great, but I wanted a baby. I couldn't understand why we weren't having babies. Richard went with me to see a doctor about it and the doctor confirmed that because of my childhood accident, I might never conceive. The doctor said my pelvis, which had been broken, was not quite right. "But you're still very young by nature's clock, and miracles happen every day. And then, of course, there's adoption."

I must have looked as tragic as I was feeling because the doctor said again, "Even though it seems impossible you will ever be pregnant, miracles do happen."

In the car, I burst out in tears. "Miracles," I blubbered. "Miracles are things that happen to other people. They only happen in movies."

We were still sitting in the parking lot and Richard had his arms around me, comforting me. "There, there," he said, rocking me. "Little one, would you like to adopt a baby?"

I leaped out of his arms. "Oh, Richard, could I? Could I?"

"Of course," he said, "if having a baby means that much to you."

"Oh, Richard, miracles *do* happen and it's just happened to me!"

"Why didn't you tell me you wanted to adopt a baby?"

"I was afraid to. Why didn't you say something?"

"I didn't think you were cut out for motherhood." He

groaned in mock horror. "Here goes—now I'll have two kids to raise."

I had no problem with the idea of adopting children. Many of our friends had done so—Ronnie Reagan and Jane Wyman had adopted a little boy, Michael, and George and Gracie Burns were there for reassurance with their adopted two—Ronnie and Sandra.

August 10, 1948. It is a date engraved on my heart. The first time I set eyes on Pam and held her in my arms. I was in the middle of *Little Women*. Richard had been able to stay home to be there when the adoption agency delivered our brand-new, two-month-old baby. After all, he said, how would it look to say the baby was delivered to the butler?

"Yeah," I said, "they'd probably turn around and take him back."

"Over Frank's dead body," said Richard. "That man is as eager for that child to arrive as we are."

All day, every hour on the hour, Richard called to say the adoption lady had not yet arrived.

"Oh, I'm so worried," I said. "All the way from Tennessee. I hope everything's all right. I hope they haven't changed their mind at the last minute."

"Relax, darling. I'll call you the minute they're here and in an hour if they're not here."

I was in my dressing room when the call came. The baby had arrived at last. "Richard, don't move. I'm on my way." I ran out of the sound stage in costume. I didn't tell anyone I was leaving because I knew they would try to stop me from disrupting the shooting schedule. I drove as fast as I could, feeling an excitement and anticipation I had never experienced before—call it adoptive expectant motherhood. I ran into the house and up the stairs—and the nurse was on her way down, holding the baby.

I stopped and gasped. "Can I hold her?"

The nurse smiled. "Of course—you're her mother." And I

just melted. I looked down at that tiny face and I could hardly breathe. She was beautiful. That night I didn't sleep. I sat looking at my baby as she slept in her crib.

In the days that followed, I was terrified when I fed her her bottle, afraid she would choke. The nurse we had hired assured me that all was well and that Pammy was behaving just like any other baby, crying no more and no less, gasping no more and no less. At night I would watch her breathe and I would listen. And I did something bad, but out of love—and fear: when I couldn't hear her, I pinched her. I was ashamed but relieved to hear her respond with annoyance or a cry of pain.

I thought of Claudette Colbert and how dear she had been to me ever since *The Secret Heart* two years previously, and I knew I wanted her to be Pammy's godmother and someday teach her whatever she needed to know, as she had taught me. And Regis Toomey, a great character actor and friend, consented to be godfather.

Claudette brought Pammy's christening gown back from Paris and it was magnificent, richly decorated with lace. The first thing Pammy did on the way to the christening was throw up all over it.

"We have to go home," I told Richard. "It has to be washed."

"Are you out of your mind? Claudette will understand."

"*You* don't understand. It's a Paris original. Claudette must never know. Turn around. *Please*." He groaned but turned around and rushed us back home. A maid washed and ironed the christening gown and we hurried back to the church, where Claudette awaited us. She was wearing a lovely string of real pearls and Pammy pulled them and broke the strand—pearls all over the place.

Everyone rejoiced that I finally had a baby of my own so I would stay out of their nurseries and quit mooning over their little ones. Judy Garland complained that I'd just missed having the baby on her birthday by a week. "You're lagging behind again," she said. Judy was referring to a running gag between us that had started at a party we'd both attended. Judy and I were singing a song together. Not to entertain the crowd but just for ourselves. She was such a perfectionist, however, that it was bothering her that I seemed to be dragging a bit behind her beat.

She turned to me and said, "Junie, keep up. Don't you realize you're lagging behind?"

"Yeah, I know," I said, "but I sing quite differently than you do."

She looked at me with that pixie face and said, "Yeah. Quite!"

When Pammy arrived Judy was still needling me. "Your timing is still off and you're still dragging," she said. My birthday is June 10 and you have to get a baby with a birthday a week later."

When Pammy was two and a half, there was a congressional investigation of the baby-adoption racket and it was charged that some agencies were running a black market in babies and collecting a lot of money from stars and other wealthy people under the guise of "transportation costs."

The Tennessee adoption agency from whom we had obtained Pamela was one of those under fire, and the state of Tennessee was making angry noises about coming to take her and other babies back. The federal government was involved because the children had been taken over state lines.

Some stars refused to discuss the adoption procedure by which they had gotten their babies. Richard was accused, in some newspaper accounts, of having paid one million dollars for Pammy. He *did* discuss it. He was livid with rage. He said, "I adopted the child in court legally two and a half years ago. If they come to get my daughter, they will have to bring a very large cannon."

For many years we hid from Pammy any talk of the storm that had raged around her head that might have carried her away. But we never hid from her the fact that she was "adopinated," as she called it. Instead of a bedtime story she would say, "Mommy, tell me again the story of how you adopinated me."

When Pammy was almost two, we decided it was time for her to have a little brother, and we went to the same agency in Tennessee to find him. There he was, and he was beautiful, and we were assured that soon—after the usual lapse of time for paperwork and investigations—he would be ours.

I was delighted to hear from MGM that they wanted me to dance in a movie with Fred Astaire. I wanted to call every girlfriend from the old Bronx days. I wanted to ring bells. I wanted to shout it from the top of the famous HOLLYWOOD hillside sign.

The name of the picture was *Royal Wedding*. I had just started to rehearse with my idol and it felt so good gliding over the floor with his masterful touch guiding me. And suddenly I didn't know what was happening—I felt weak. I felt nauseated. I felt faint.

I was in awe of Astaire—but not that much. I went directly to my doctor. And from his office I called Fred Astaire excitedly and said, "Fred, I want you to be the first to know—I'm pregnant."

There was a stunned silence. Then a horrified voice said, "Who *is* this?"

What to do about the little boy we were adopting? We had seen and already loved him, and how did we know the baby I was carrying would be a boy? Richard was discussing our dilemma with a producer friend who said, "Let me adopt him. You'd make us so happy and we'll be good to him."

Richard helped me let go. It hurt, but we let the other couple

121

have our darling adopted-to-be. We always wondered if the little boy we would see growing up ever knew we were almost his parents.

Naturally the doctor decreed that I would have to drop out of the movie because it would be risky for me to do the strenuous dancing required. I couldn't even shed a tear. I had gotten the one thing I wanted more than to dance with Astaire.

However, I did secretly wish that I had been able to spend just a little more time with him.

I had barely gotten acquainted with Fred Astaire. I told him about seeing him seventeen times in The Gay Divorcee, of course, and he looked at me with that wry smile, his eyes crinkling up. I wasn't sure he believed me, but then I told him I had crashed Broadway and even gotten to Hollywood on his training—and then he threw back his head and laughed.

Gloria Stewart, Jimmy's wife, was also pregnant while I was carrying Ricky. One day Richard and I were driving along the shopping area of Beverly Hills, when, tripping across the street, ignoring all traffic, came Gloria.

I was trying to yell at her to get out of the traffic when she leaned into the car with the most dazed, happy and euphoric expression and said, "Hey, I'm going to have twins," and floated off again into the traffic.

Richard was starring in the movie The Tall Target with Adolphe Menjou, who played the suave villain, and both men waited out the last days of my pregnancy together. Menjou was especially interested in the time of birth. Astrology was his big passion and he was busy checking Ricky's horoscope. "While you're at it, find out for me what the heavens say about the stock market," Richard could not resist teasing him. Menjou wore a fine gold watch—he said it was a gift from his best friend—and it was inscribed: To the man I most admire—Adolphe Menjou, from Adolphe Menjou. He was such an elegant man that he had no compunction about having his chauffeur drive him down to the unemployment office between pictures to pick up his check. He would arrive there impeccably dressed in top hat, morning coat and cane.

I carried Ricky all in front of me. And every old wives' tale proved wrong. All predictions were that he would be a girl. If you were heavy in *back*, that meant you were carrying a boy.

And then came the acid test—some girlfriends, laughing, hung my wedding ring from a string and held it over my stomach as I lay on the couch, waiting to see if it would swing back and forth or in a circle. "Definitely a girl," they said.

"Wrong," I said, "and his name is Herman."

When I went to the hospital, I knew I was nervous because when it came to signing myself in, I couldn't remember my name. I turned around and whispered in Richard's ear, "I can't remember my name."

"June," he said, not even acting surprised.

"Oh, that's right—June Dick Powell." And that's what I wrote and what appears on the hospital records.

That was the easy part. Then came the hard part. Eighteen hours of labor. Problems developed and they had to do some cutting. And just when they decided it still wasn't going to work and they would have to do an emergency caesarean, my baby pushed forth into the world.

But I knew something was wrong. Where was the cry? Why wasn't my baby howling like all babies do? "Oh God," I prayed, "don't let this happen to my baby." I saw the doctors turning the baby back and forth and slapping him over and over.

And finally there was that tiny little sound of a cry and I gasped with relief and a mighty joy filled me. "He's fine, June. You've got yourself a fine boy and, gracious, he looks just like Dick Powell."

I looked at the baby and he looked like a shrunken squash—

the ugliest child ever born. So this was what newborn babies looked like? Well, I loved him anyway. "That's my Herman," I chortled. "Hi, Herman." It was Christmas Eve.

Richard and my friends had been going through agony in the waiting room, knowing I was having big trouble inside. They were expecting to see a prostrate form wheeled out of the delivery room. Instead, I came ripping through, sitting up and yelling, "Merry Christmas, everyone! I've got a boy!" I spied Richard and yelled, "Hey, Richard, I won my bet!"

I had bet I would give Richard a baby for Christmas even though the doctor said it was due in mid-January. As soon as they got me to my room, I ordered two big club sandwiches, polished them off and chortled, "Just send the bill to Richard. Hey, Richard, I won the bet. Where's my money?"

He pulled out a quarter and gave it to me. "I have something else, too," he said.

"What? What? I *love* surprises."

He was pulling out a porcelain box and slipping something on my finger—a brand-new wedding ring, similar to the old one but gem encrusted. "Now you don't have to wear the plain old wedding band anymore," he said, kissing me.

"No, no," I said. "I'll wear them both." And I did.

Richard was almost out of his mind with happiness. "I can't believe it. I'm forty years old and my wife gave me a son. The one thing that I thought we would never have." After Richard finally left that night, he went directly to the George Murphys', where he and I had been invited to spend Christmas Eve. Afterward George told me Richard had come in, sat down, said, "It's a boy," and keeled over sound asleep.

Even when I was ready to go home, Ricky still had to stay in the hospital in an incubator—but at least he had made it! Not a present under the tree had been opened without me, and when I got home it was the happiest unwrapping session I'd ever known.

Richard told two-and-a-half-year-old Pammy that her biggest present was yet to come—a baby brother who would be wrapped in a blanket. He assured her that the baby was hers and before anyone could see him, they would have to get permission from her. Pammy was so happy about her new possession that she completely forgot to be jealous.

Of course, I didn't name him Herman. I had known all along that if he were a boy, he would be called Richard. Where had the name Herman come from? friends asked. "Oh, I thought everyone knew," I said. "Herman was my co-starring lion last year in *The Reformer and the Redhead*. And another Herman was a marvelous acting seal I once met."

Eventually I remembered to ask Richard what Adolphe Menjou had said about baby Ricky's future as written in the stars. After much study and work with a chart, Menjou frowned, shook his head and said he was sorry Ricky's horoscope was not as lucky as his own, which foresaw twelve years of great financial success upcoming. The eerie thing about this prediction was that Adolphe Menjou was to die exactly twelve years later.

Richard Diamond, the tough guy Dick Powell played on the screen—and sometimes in life—simply dissolved when it came to his children. He cried when Pammy arrived in her baby blanket and he cried at the birth of Ricky and he almost cried when I made fumbling attempts to discipline a child.

For example, once Ricky was having a temper tantrum after some member of the household staff wouldn't let him do something. I slapped Ricky to stop the tantrum and it did. But by accident the slap had opened a cold sore on his lip and it bled a little. Richard came on the scene, saw the blood and reacted as if I had struck *him*. I felt terrible, as though I should be taken to the execution chamber immediately. I was so shaken I could barely explain to Richard about the cold sore and show him the little sore.

We had made such a fuss over how special Pammy was, being "adopinated" and all that, that toddler Ricky wanted to be adopted too. He seemed to feel very strongly on the subject. He was almost broken-hearted when we tried to explain that it wasn't necessary.

So we said all right, he could be adopinated, too, and we arranged with our favorite minister, the Reverend Casey, to perform a little ceremony while all the rest of the family watched. And sure enough, Ricky felt very good that he had been chosen, too.

It was sad to realize that one person's happiness was another person's tragedy. Judy Garland would call me in the middle of the night and tell me she needed someone to talk to, and I would arrive at her place and just sit listening.

In a strange way, I had been a part of her studio problem, though not at all responsible.

It all began with my becoming pregnant at the beginning of my movie with Fred Astaire, *Royal Wedding*, and having to be replaced. Judy was invited to take the part, even though she was in such an exhausted and depressed condition that she had been hospitalized several times and had spoken of suicide.

Judy had no choice but to say yes, even though she was only in the second week of what was supposed to be six a months' rest period. If she refused the offer, the studio could suspend her and wouldn't have to pay her salary. "Can you imagine," Judy recalled, "they told me I was making twice as much as the President of the United States and I still could barely make ends meet."

So Judy had stepped into my dancing shoes in *Royal Wedding* and tried to start learning seven dance routines immediately, as well as her songs and dialogue. She couldn't take it. She couldn't sleep or concentrate. She started having migraine headaches again and was back on pills.

One morning her system ground to a halt and she couldn't even get out of bed. She thought this was it, that she had had a stroke. Instead of sympathy, Judy received a telegram from the studio telling her that her contract was terminated for failing to work on a movie in progress. "In other words, I was fired," Judy said sadly. "Do you know what that's like?"

I tried to tell her that I certainly did, and that I had been fired from musicals on Broadway, but she brushed that aside. "Huh—that was nothing! You were just a kid. That was just like growing pains. You didn't have a family to support and a whole goddamned entourage of servants and a house."

I had to agree she was right, but then I tried again to tell her she needed someone special to look after her finances like Richard had so that she wouldn't have money problems all the time. "Hah—you don't know any more about money than *I* do," she said. "So look who's talking. And let's wait and see what happens to your money, Junie face. You may be in for a surprise. I figure better live it up and use it, because who knows what others are doing with it, anyway."

"No, Judy," I said, almost shocked that I was giving advice to my idol. "You need a competent, ethical company to invest your money wisely and put you on a budget—"

"Stop, Junie—you just said a dirty word. I don't want to hear any more about any damn budgets. Do you want a drink?"

"No, thank you."

And Judy was back to her sad recital of how distraught she had been at being cast off by MGM. She had stumbled into the bathroom, locked the door and given herself a slight cut on the neck with a fragment of broken glass, then had stopped herself as she realized she did not want to die. "Everything I do is so damn *public*," she said. "The blood was hardly dry before it was plastered in newspapers all over the world."

Judy had humbled herself and gone to see Papa Mayer to explain that she was dead broke and at least needed a loan from the studio to survive. He had made a phone call and had told her sadly that the loan had been denied. She had gotten up in a daze from her chair, feeling absolutely lost and abandoned, and Mayer had been so upset by the action of his superiors that he had personally lent her a few thousand dollars.

"But wasn't that nice of him, Judy? At least he cared."

"I don't know what nice is anymore. He's the one who fired me in the first place, wasn't he? That was conscience money. Oh, don't listen to me, Junie. I'm just bitter." She tried to smile but it came out a grimace. "After all, he gave me my first watch, didn't he?" Judy stared into the distance and said, "That's life. One person's disaster is another person's luck." We talked then of how Judy's firing had given Jane Powell her big chance when she followed Judy and me into *Royal Wedding.*

For Judy, the year 1951 saw the end of one era and the beginning of another. It marked the end of her marriage to Vincente Minnelli and the beginning of her dramatic marriage to Sidney Luft. As Judy told me so many times, "I can live without money but I can't live without love."

9

Happy as we were at Bel Air, Richard would talk of his dream of the simple life, and he would lapse into his Arkansas accent. "Someday I'm gittin' me a little ole farm whar I kin take mah shoes off. I'll have me a little ole cow and raise me the best sweet corn you ever flopped your lips over."

We would laugh and talk about raising our kids on a postage-stamp-sized farm, far from the studios. And how Pammy, now four, and Ricky, pushing two, would have all the animals to play with that I had always dreamed of—goats and rabbits and chickens. "And I can milk the cow," I told him.

One day we were driving around just to relax when Richard said, "Let me show you a nice area." He drove to Mandeville Canyon. The road curved round and round as we made our way up the mountain.

"It's beautiful," I said. "Lovely view."

"I hope I can find the place," he said.

Eventually he turned into a long, long driveway that wound past a lovely lake over a bridge and ended up at some sort of private resort or public park. Finally he stopped the car. "How would you like to live here? Would this be too isolated for you?"

"Heavens no!" I said, starting to like the idea. "It's a nice community. How many people live here?"

"Just us, Junie. It's our—sixty-eight acres."

I was in a state of happy shock. The huge stone building was the main house, and all around were outbuildings—guest house, stables, corrals, buildings for the live-in help. It was hardly the kind of place where you would take off your shoes and just loaf. At least Richard couldn't, and when he got through gutting and building, it was even more elegant. And upstairs he created a special wing for the children to live in and make all the noise they wanted. And a separate dining room for them. And a suite for their nannies.

Mandeville was such a busy complex I was confused.

I didn't know who was working and who was just stopping by to visit. "How nice of you to come. Would you like a cup of coffee?" I asked a couple of young men who came to the door. They would, and after coffee and conversation they thanked me and asked if they could see the bathroom Mr. Powell had sent them up from the barns to fix. Richard accused me of being overly friendly with the help, but I just couldn't bring myself to demand, "Who are you and what do you want?"

Richard gutted and renovated the guest house. Even the caretaker had a darling little house. Soon there were thirty black Angus cattle ranging in the fields, and 5,000 chickens in the hen yard and dogs barking and thirty sheep grazing, and turkeys and pheasants—and in the stable, horses for riding.

Somehow Hedda Hopper managed to track me down for an interview. I was outside to welcome her when she arrived. The children were playing around me on the lawn. With hardly a hello to me, Hedda looked at the children and said, "Oh, I forget—which one is yours?"

I was furious, but I answered sweetly, "What do you mean, which one is mine? They're *both* mine." The children stopped playing and looked at me. I hoped Hedda would let it go. But there was no stopping her. "Oh, I know that," she said irritably. "I mean which one is adopted?"

I looked at Hedda and I looked at the two upturned faces. I laughed and said, "You know something? I can't remember." It was my shining hour. And Hedda had it in for me even more after that. The next time she called she rudely asked if my bosoms were real. I was tempted to retort, "Yes, aren't yours?" But what I actually said in my intimidated state was "Yes, ma'am."

Evenings would often find the language of politics spoken at Mandeville as Richard and Ronald Colman and Ronald Reagan and his buddy George Murphy gathered around the fireplace or on the porch. The voices got louder and louder as the arguments heated up and past and present Presidents and their policies were attacked and defended.

The main goal, from what I could hear, was still to shift Ronnie Reagan into the Republican party. But why this was so important or why this was anyone else's business I couldn't understand. Richard and Ronnie also loved to talk about their small-town background, and Richard was proud that his hometown folks in Hope, Arkansas, had sent him a prize-winning watermelon of some 195 pounds—he proudly showed the picture to Ronnie, saying, "It's gooder than snuff and ain't half as dusty."

After Ronnie's divorce from Jane Wyman we remained friendly with both of them. We continued to entertain both Ronnie and Jane but never at the same function. We were delighted when Ronnie brought Nancy Davis along to dinner one evening. Richard and I felt he had been alone long enough and we wanted to see him happy and settled down.

In a private moment, I eventually enthused to Nancy, "Oh, you've got to marry Ronnie. I can see how he looks at you, and he's wonderful—you've just got to marry him." Nancy smiled and I realized she didn't need any urging.

One night Ronnie took Nancy Davis to a party and a gossip columnist wrote, "She never took her eyes off him all evening." When Ronnie was running for President of the United States years later, reporters started saying the same thing—"She never took her eyes off him all through his speech"—and hinting that Nancy did this for effect. Wrong. That's the way it's always been with them—at our house, at their house and in public.

How casual the first meeting of Ronnie and Nancy had been. It was a blind date, arranged by director Mervyn Le Roy. It was in 1951, and each explained there would only be time for a short dinner. They ended up talking half the night and dated again the next night and the next.

I do not know whether it was Richard or Nancy and her staunchly Republican family who finally switched Ronnie's allegiance to the Republican party. I only know Richard took full credit for it and chortled with glee over the conversion. I remember the big event—but not the exact time. Richard, as usual, was haranguing Ronnie about his politics when Ronnie suddenly said, "Hold on, I've switched. You don't have to gnaw at me anymore. I'm a Republican." Richard turned to me and said, in a low voice which Ronnie may or may not have heard, "What have I done? The son of a bitch will probably end up running for President someday—and making it."

One night Richard and I were having dinner with Ronnie and Nancy in their home. The other couple invited was Elizabeth Taylor and her fiancé, Eddie Fisher. I thought it was very brave and nice of Nancy and Ronnie to have invited them because they were being regarded as renegades and outcasts in the movie colony. Mike Todd had been killed in the crash of the plane named for her—*Lucky Liz*—and Eddie was still sitting out his divorce from Debbie Reynolds. Debbie had been Elizabeth's best friend.

The room was crackling with emotion at the Reagans' that night. Richard had co-starred with Debbie Reynolds just a few years before in *Susan Slept Here*, and considered her a good friend, and I had co-starred with Elizabeth Taylor in *Little Women* and considered her a good friend. Thanks to all the tension, for the entire evening I kept calling Elizabeth Debbie. I'd say, "Oh, I mean *Liz*." Elizabeth said, "Oh, that's all right." But it wasn't. The next time I made the slip she snapped, "Why don't you call me George? Just call me *George*."

Elizabeth was clinging to Eddie and looking at him with the same lovesick eyes I had seen before when she was dating Mike Todd. "I still love her and don't want to hurt her," Liz said about Debbie Reynolds that night. "But this is life and I have to go on living. I didn't intend to fall in love with Eddie, but I have and there's just nothing I can do about it." She looked at Eddie again with those steaming violet eyes. Eddie, too, said he hated to hurt Debbie, but he insisted the marriage had been rocky before Elizabeth was in the picture. Liz was saying she was tired of being the Scarlet Lady because of Debbie, but that after all, Debbie and Eddie had been married only three years and Elizabeth and Eddie were going to be together forever. Eddie was even of the same faith as Mike Todd—Jewish—and Eddie had been Mike's best friend. It was almost as if Mike Todd still lived—through Eddie.

The Mandeville years for me were really "the top of the mountain," the height of happiness. We were a happy family together on the boat or at the ranch. Richard seldom used a real name—Pammy answered to My Special Girl or Special Girl; Ricky was plain Speedy. Wherever we went in those happy days, Richard and I wanted to take the children, too. When we went to Sun Valley to ski, we took the kids, and when we went to Europe, where I was on location, we took the kids. Evenings, just for a ride, we took the kids. Sometimes Richard took Ricky out yachting on the *Sapphire Sea*, successor to the *Santana*, while I cooled my heels on shore. One night there was a great storm, something on the boat broke, and they found themselves adrift on the ocean. I died a thousand deaths till they phoned from someplace that they were safe.

We had celebrations for everything—maybe to make up for the fact that we didn't have seasons and snow to break up the year. Birthdays were big. Christmas was very big. The Fourth of July was spectacular, with Richard lighting the firecrackers and the kids swinging sparklers around. Birthdays were religiously observed. Pammy was proud that she almost shared her birthday with Judy Garland, who was born June 10, and later she would be thrilled to know that Paul McCartney was a true June 18 "share."

Movie industry families make a big thing about exchanging Christmas gifts. I went with a gang of friends to deliver gifts to other friends. Pammy was known as "the Perle Mesta of Mandeville Canyon" at age seven—she'd hop out of the car with little packages and invite people to stop by the house for Christmas cheer. Richard's gifts to the children were so elaborate they wouldn't fit in the house. He built Ricky a baseball diamond on the property and Pammy got a riding ring with bleachers on one side and jumps to take her horse over. No wonder she was soon winning ribbons. I cherish the music boxes Pammy has given me through the years since she was a child—music boxes on every theme and design—clowns, roses, jewels, and even one with a copy of Sir Thomas Lawrence's "Pinkie."

Rick was more like his father, giving me gifts that he personally found practical—a can opener, a lamp, a deep, dark, persimmon ceramic kettle (which did indeed look good on the stove), and a set of stemmed, silver-rimmed glasses.

Richard's gift to me one year was a new linoleum for a room I never went into—the kitchen—in a color I detested, when he eventually led me in to see it. But since Frank had obviously picked it and Frank was the one who had to look at it, I gulped and said, "Beautiful."

Easter time was special and celebrated wherever we were,

even on shipboard. I never gave prizes for finding the most eggs—I didn't believe in making one child feel good at the expense of the others. Halloweens, Pam and Ricky and I would get dressed up for trick or treating. I never let them go out alone at night, but I didn't want to make them fearful, so I went along, wearing a costume that rivaled theirs. One Halloween at Mandeville, when Pam was about five or six and Ricky was three or four, we hit the jackpot. Our butler Frank drove us down to the end of the canyon and waited there as we went up and down and in and out of the houses with our trick or treating. We got to Gregory Peck's and the kids rang the bell. Greg himself answered the door and said, "Come in, come in." He had a foyer simply full of bowls of trick or treat candy and bubble gum and all things to delight a child. It was the most lavish display we had encountered, and the kids just stood there looking at it all, wondering what to take. Greg chuckled and said, "Go to it, children. Try some of everything." I stood back and they happily started tossing things into their large paper bags. Greg noticed I wasn't dipping in, and he said, "Hey, this little one isn't getting anything." He started tossing chocolates and bubble gum into my paper bag.

"Oh, Greg, come on now," I said. He peered down at me and said, "Oh, my God, it's you." He lifted the battered hat of my tramp outfit and roared.

We went on to another house, this time Robert Mitchum's, and again we were received with grand hospitality from the head of the house. "Come on in," he said. The Mitchum family was having dinner on trays in front of the fireplace and Bob said to all of us, "Just help yourselves." He returned to his tray. Ricky did not hesitate to walk right over and help himself to a baked potato that was swimming in butter and sour cream on someone's tray. I was mortified, but before I could open my mouth, he had popped it into his bag. Bob just stood there watching me in my tramp's costume, trying to fish out the greasy mess of potato. Disgustedly he said, "Let the kid have the potato." I slunk out behind the kids, hoping that his eyesight was as poor as Gregory Peck's, and that he didn't know who I was. I sure as heck wasn't about to tell him.

Candice Bergen and her mother, Frances, were both important in Pammy's life. Pammy would go swimming at the Bergen house before we got our swimming pool installed at Mandeville and Frances would bring Candy when she came to visit us. Though Candy was older, she took a liking to Pammy and they played well together. One day Frannie and I were sitting at her poolside talking while Candy splashed in the water. Frances had told her not to go into the deep end.

But suddenly I looked and she was gone. I raced to the water and swam to the deep end, where she was floundering under water. I got her out, doubled her over and started hitting her on the back to get the water out. She quickly revived but did not cry even though she was badly shaken. "Thank God you were here!" Frances said. She was a much poorer swimmer than I and wasn't sure she could have saved her child. After that Candice seemed more precious to both of us.

For a moment, once, I thought I was raising a couple of alcoholics. First it was little four-year-old Pammy drinking the dregs of cocktails left behind by the guests as they moved in to dinner. Then it was Ricky at six, learning to make himself cherry Cokes with cherry cordial from the bar. Richard looked at his tipsy son and said, "What next, June? Check your baby books and give me a clue on what comes next."

What came next was a contempt for toys. Ricky was taking model planes and cars and placing them in the middle of the road to see how long it would take for a car to run over them.

"When I was a kid, I cherished my toys. I got one new toy a year," Richard said. Pammy, at least, did not destroy her toys. She simply gave them away. When little children came to visit and took a liking to a toy, Pammy said, "You can have it." Once a child expressed delight over everything she spied and walked out with her arms loaded. I didn't stop her.

I fretted over what this was doing to Pammy's values, but I did nothing. "Well, she's certainly not selfish," I told myself. "That's a plus." But Richard said, "By God, I'm going to teach these kids some respect for their possessions!" He finally blew up when he saw Ricky open a box and toss it down with a sneer—"Aw, I've got *three* of these!"

"That does it," said Richard. He decreed that each child could pick only a few toys to keep of their Christmas haul and the rest would be sent to hospitals and charities.

I longed to stay home with the children and just be a mother, but Richard pointed out that once you lose your momentum in movies it is difficult to get back in—I would become one of those wives we felt sorry for, the ones with nothing to do but cling to their husbands. Often they were jealous of their husbands' careers, became nags, and made themselves and everyone around them miserable. The answer was to put together a large staff to run the house and make Mandeville feel like a home at all times. It didn't always work that way. One governess slept in the trees and we had to get rid of her soon—Richard, of course, doing the firing. One had food fetishes and insisted on growing her own vegies in her room. She didn't last long. One took the job thinking she'd get to go on a trip and see the world, traveling with us. When our travel plans weren't extensive enough to suit her, she quit.

The prize package was the governess we eventually nicknamed Awful Nanny. I was much impressed when I saw a gold star on Pammy's collar. "Nanny put it there 'cause I was good," Pammy said. "If you get a gold star you can go on a walk with Nanny."

"Isn't that nice," I said, as Nanny and Pammy beamed. Months later I would learn the rest of the story. While Pammy got the walking privileges, Ricky would be locked in a closet. For some reason, Nanny didn't like Ricky. Ricky certainly didn't like Nanny—it was about this time he developed a habit of biting people. He bit everyone—nurses in doctors' offices were in mortal fear when he was brought in for shots. The household help suffered much more. As one maid explained to a new girl, "You treat him like a snapping turtle—mostly you just leave him alone."

Awful Nanny insisted that Pammy eat everything on her plate at each meal or it would reappear at the next. I discovered this when I opened Pammy's desk and found it full of spoiled food. Strangely, I was too frightened of Awful Nanny to face her, and instead I conspired with Pammy. We went running back and forth to the bathroom and flushed all the bits of reeking food down the toilet. Before Awful Nanny came back to the nursery, I said reassuringly to Pammy, "Don't worry, darling. Don't ever eat anything you don't want to. I'll come in here every day and clean out your desk."

I went back downstairs realizing that in Pammy's mind, her nanny was more powerful than her mother. Hadn't we both acted scared that Nanny would catch us? I struggled for the courage to censure Awful Nanny and lost.

It was Frances Bergen who finally brought about the downfall of Awful Nanny. Richard and I went on a trip, and we asked all our friends to stop in, when they were in the neighborhood, to check on the children and give them the feeling of normalcy. When our friends went away, we did the same with their children—popped in to say hello. But this time, when I got back, Frances Bergen called me, perturbed. "I don't like to interfere and I don't know what happened, but I came into the house and I heard Pammy crying very hard. I went upstairs and found her leaning against the wall and screaming, 'I want my mommy! I want my mommy!' I think you ought to check out what happened."

Pam seemed frightened and wouldn't tell me anything. I went to Awful Nanny. She looked at me coldly and said, "I do not have to discuss my discipline with anyone but the children." Over and over she refused to discuss it.

That did it. I said, "You will either discuss it with me or you are fired."

She said, "I will hand in my resignation, Mrs. Powell, and I always give a three-month notice."

"Well, I am giving you a three-minute notice. I want you out of here." Was this *me* talking? She said, "I can't do it that fast and besides I have no place to go." I said, "I'll help you pack and Frank will drive you to a hotel." I gave her a month's salary and she was out in an hour. The irony was that when we were entertained by a prominent Hollywood family, a week or so later, there was Awful Nanny, smiling at us with her sinister little smile as she came in with their children to say goodnight. Richard and I looked at each other. I hadn't the heart to say anything. "Maybe she'll be different in their household," I told Richard on the way back. But I doubted it.

Jimmy Cagney looked in on us regularly at Mandeville. Once he stopped by for breakfast, and suddenly a little apparition appeared, dripping water from the top of his boots. Ricky was soggy from his cowboy hat to his gun holsters, hanging to his knees. He stood with terrified eyes and said, "I'm sorry, I falled in." He looked ridiculous.

"Into what?" I asked, unable to imagine. "The wawa in the lake," said Ricky. Jimmy Cagney laughed until tears came, but I shook like a leaf. If I hadn't taught both children to swim before moving to Mandeville, Ricky could easily have drowned, because the water was very deep. "Well, now that you've had your swim, you'd better change clothes," I said, hiding my emotion.

After the Awful Nanny incident, Frank became more important than ever. Frank could do anything—he could discipline the children in a nice way, help them with their homework and even take a lot of their abuse without caving in. Ricky had listened to his father firing servants, and so whenever he was displeased with Frank's discipline, he would say to him, "You're fired!" Frank would tell us he had been fired by Ricky, and we would make a big fuss over rehiring Frank again. I guess we wanted Ricky to feel he had some power around the house—but not too much. Ricky preferred to bring his problems to Frank and not to his nanny. One day when he was three or four, his problem was that he wanted shiny shoes for a very important friend's party. He kept complaining to Frank that he couldn't get his shoes shiny enough.

"For that you need elbow grease," Frank told him and sent him back to his room to try again. Soon Ricky was back, saying he had to be driven to the drugstore. "Do you have your allowance?" Frank asked him.

"Yes," said Ricky, flashing his fifty cents.

"Okay," said Frank. "I have some time right now before dinner, if we hurry." Off they went, and Frank, as usual, stayed well away as Ricky conducted his business.

After looking around a bit, Ricky sought out a clerk and said, "Where's the elbow grease?" This time Ricky had had it. When he got Frank out of the store he said, "You're fired—and this time I mean it."

Ricky's shopping was indeed picturesque, and one time there was no one to fire since he'd gotten his inspiration from a TV ad. He bought a tooth product he had heard extolled and tried it as soon as he got home. He was disgusted. It didn't have the foam, the bubble and the peppermint taste. "It's yucki and I want my money back," he said.

"Let me see it," I said. "You're a little ahead of yourself," I explained, hoping I could keep the laughter down. "This is to keep your dentures in."

Ricky loved shopping for greeting cards for every occasion,

and Frank would never interfere with the selections he made. I got a birthday card from Ricky which said on the cover, "With deepest sympathy," and a get-well card at the hospital once that said, "To my favorite aunt." When Pammy pointed out his mistakes and asked how he happened to choose such a card, he said, "I don't care what it says *outside*, I like what it says *inside*."

Pammy loved animals. Ricky loved mechanical things. He puttered with glue and model airplane parts. She puttered with canaries and parakeets. When Timmy, the cat, broke open her bird cage, Pammy cried as she discovered that the population of nine feathered friends had been cut down to six. Once she had a pet lamb that followed her around and one day it disappeared. Then lamb chops appeared at the dinner table a few nights later and she asked her daddy if it was her lamb. I could see him wrestling with the problem of what to say. Truth won and he said simply, "Yes, it is." Pam threw her lamb chop across the room and ran out of the house.

Richard went out to find her and explain about farming, but I could not help but side with her. It was one of the few times he had acted like a tough rancher instead of a doting father. "I want them to know the realities of life," he told me later.

"But I don't understand, either," I said.

"Well, you're a lost cause," he said, shaking his head. "You'll never learn the realities of life."

After Pammy started school, I took three-and-a-half-year-old Ricky to the studio with me. He loved it and tried to be helpful. He heard me calling each morning for breakfast to be served in my dressing room, and one morning he grabbed the phone and said *he* would order breakfast. I told him what to dial and he said, "My mommee would like to have for breakfast—" and he went through the list of things he had heard me order and hung up.

"Ricky," I said, "you didn't tell them where to send the breakfast."

"Oh."

"You have to dial them again and say *who you are*," and I carefully emphasized each word. "And say, 'Hello.'" Again I helped him dial and this time he said, "Hello, who you are," and hung up.

Ricky was about five when he ran away from home. He didn't think anyone was treating him right, nobody would listen, nobody would buy him what he wanted, so he was leaving. "I'm packing," he told me.

"I'll help you," I said. I got everything he called for and he piled it all on his wagon—underwear, candy, T-shirts, a loaf of bread, a quart of chocolate milk, his dog Tinker Bell, and a few toys. He did not have to pack his cowboy hat and two guns because he was already wearing them. He kept looking back as he trudged along the drive until he was out of sight. I waited outside, twenty minutes or more, hoping he would turn around and come back, but finally I could stand it no longer. I ran to Frank, tears streaming down my face. "Please take the car and go find Ricky. He's more stubborn than I am and I think he really did run away."

"No, no, Mrs. Powell. He'll be all right. He's probably just behind the bushes somewhere. Do you want to go with me?"

"No, I'd better not. Please hurry, Frank. I'm so worried." How I wanted to get into that car with Frank! But I didn't, and that was one of my better decisions. Frank found him a full mile away, at the end of the driveway, outside our gate at Mandeville Canyon Road. He sat with him and they talked about life— when you're grown up you can do what you want to, but until then . . . Pretty soon Frank was back and lifting the wagon out of the car. "Hi," I said to Ricky, who was still sitting in the car.

"Hi," he said. He climbed out and he and Frank started carrying his things back in. Nothing was said about where he'd been, but soon he perked up and started running around and playing happily with Tinker Bell.

It's hard to rear children who are absolutely unspoiled when there are at least nine people around the house taking care of four people and when other children and too many adults stop them to ask with some awe, "Oh, is Dick Powell really your father?" or "Is your mother June Allyson?"

By now, servants and staff people were falling over each other. We had a long list of live-in help—a laundress and foreman who were married to each other; a gardener and assistant gardener; an upstairs maid and downstairs maid; a nanny or governess; a cook; a secretary for me; the chauffeur; and, presiding over everyone, Frank, the butler and majordomo.

Nobody shopped. Everything came by phone order. Staples from Premier Market. Vegetables were delivered three times a week by Johnny, the vegetable man, driving a blue truck. Helms Bakery came three times a week, ready or not. Meat was brought from our own lockers—Frank could phone. The pool man arrived like clockwork. There was even a lake man to look after the lake and check the fish.

Still Richard wasn't satisfied. He launched himself into TV production and scored a great coup when he formed Four Star Productions with David Niven and Charles Boyer. Richard's only complaint about Four Star was the time it took to drive to the studio. His solution was to add a heliport in a pasture near the lake. He took the helicopter while his chauffeur drove to the office to be available during the day and evening—taking him wherever else he was going, and eventually home.

And, of course, the chauffeur drove him to the helicopter in the pasture in the Lincoln Continental, each morning, where the private pilot waited. I felt very democratic as I continued to drive myself.

Now that Richard was a TV big shot we could afford the luxury of screenings at home. Down would come a huge automatic screen at the end of our living room at Mandeville and Richard would show one of his movies before it was released. We would sit on sofas and chairs and on the floor and watch the show. The kids, of course, had a great time with the big movie screen at birthday parties. I tried not to act hurt that they never seemed to want any of my movies to show to their friends, but only Disney or anything with horses, like *My Friend Flicka* or *National Velvet*. But my day finally came. "Oh, Richard, the kids want me to get *The Reformer and the Redhead* for the birthday party. They want to see their parents acting in a movie together—the Dick and June team." After a short chat with Pam, Richard came back to me and said, "Sorry, honey, I've got bad news for you. It's not the Dick and June team they want, it's the Herman and Caesar."

It was, of course, a letdown, but the incident gave us a phrase that became traditional in our family. We have Pammy to thank for it. In the movie, I am the daughter of the zookeeper and have taken the gentle lion, Herman, home with me. Richard, who is dating me, is terrified and starts walking on furniture to get away from him, ending up sliding along the piano keys on his bottom. Pammy, seeing that, screamed out, "Oh, look, Daddy can play the pee panny with his bee bottom, too."

After that, whenever we wanted to say that someone was showing off, we'd say, "Hey, quit playing the pee panny with your bee bottom."

Four Star brought all segments of our family closer together. First it was my half brother, Arthur Peters. With incredible generosity, Richard gave him the guest house at Mandeville and sent him to college and medical school, fulfilling my childhood dream, vicariously, of becoming a doctor. Earlier, Richard had sent Arthur to Culver, an exclusive private school, when his son Norman had not wanted to go.

Then my mother wanted to live near us, too. My darling Richard said let her come, and he gave my stepfather a good job at Four Star, in transportation and maintenance. Then Norman was launched on a Four Star career by his father. He started at the bottom and became an assistant director, showing talent and promise at an early age.

RICHARD

Eventually Norman Powell would become a producer—as his father was—but he would never have an interest in the acting end of show business. Richard's daughter Ellen also lived with us at Mandeville. I can admit now that I was a better mother to Ellen later than I was at first. I wasn't old enough to understand her and her problems, and for this I am sorry.

Richard would call me his oldest child and say he had three children. Perhaps what made it so difficult to be a real mother to Ellen was that we were so different in our approach to life. She had seen a lot of disappointment and had an aura of sadness about her. I was the Pollyanna, trying to keep everything happy and upbeat. She needed sympathy and help. Had she needed a playmate sister, I would have been ideal. But the ranch was a great place for Ellen to find herself. She loved every kind of animal, and was phenomenally intuitive about them. She always knew when a foal was about to be born and would run out of the house to the stable to wait. She sat up all night in the rain helping a horse in the pasture. This girl, who was so reticent and never showed her feelings—which was one of the reasons I couldn't help more and didn't understand her—cried silent tears when an animal was in pain.

Pam started going to the office with Richard at the age of eight, sitting sagely at his business conferences. He would come home and tell me, "If she were twenty years older, she would have been closing the deal. She's turning into a sharp little businesslady, and she even gave me a few ideas on how to save money."

"Spare me the details," I said, "and please quit calling her Papa Mayer."

Ricky was more like me—shy inside but hiding it with bravado. We'd generally say yes to any idea right off so everyone would love us and then I'd say, "Richard, please help me out of this." Richard and Pammy were cautious and would say no to a new idea and have to be convinced slowly—much better in the long run. As for appearance, Ricky was the image of his father, although his personality was more like mine, while petite Pammy grew more and more like a carbon copy of me, even though she had Richard's personality.

I'm sure Pammy must have known more about my movie earnings than I did. Only after my MGM contract ran out and Richard took complete charge of my business affairs did I start to earn what was considered big money in those days—like $100,000 a picture. But it had little meaning for me because I never saw the money and I didn't even ask Richard how much it was. It went into a common pot with Richard's money and he worked with his friend, Morgan, of the A. Morgan Maree company, figuring out investments for the excess above living costs.

I remember once being so surprised to read that I had received $125,000 for a movie and another time that I had received $50,000 for a three-minute segment of Our Town. I'd come a long way from the coldwater flat in the Bronx, when I'd march down to the corner bathhouse with my soap and towel to take a bath.

Richard spoiled me with bathrooms that were not just bathrooms but spacious suites that included a dressing room with a connecting door. I loved my dressing room so much I spent hours puttering around there, reading, arranging my clothes, making phone calls.

Around the ranch, Richard wore old clothes when he went riding. He had contempt for those "Hollywood cowboys" who dress up in fancy riding clothes—the kind he himself had had to wear in his early singing-cowboy days. His wardrobe included about fifty suits at all times—all very conservative and each in a slightly different color or texture. Best of all, he loved to wear sports jackets and slacks. I padded around the house in blue jeans and flat shoes and my heart sang as I surveyed our home, gazing with contentment at the exposed beams, the braided rug, the wood paneling, the huge stone fireplace. A few dogs followed me companionably. The children tumbled about the lawn. What more could any human being want?

I resisted all efforts to turn me into a cowgirl.

Every time I tried to learn to ride—maybe two times—the horse did something completely unreasonable. Like breaking into a gallop without my permission or riding under a low branch to wipe me off its back completely.

But finally Pammy, who was growing into a fine little horsewoman, received a horse that was more to my liking. Well, it wasn't a horse exactly; it was between a horse and a Shetland in size—a Welsh pony. Now I would learn to ride a horse and make my children proud.

By sheerest accident, however, the stable helper, who had saddled the creature, did not properly tighten the lines and I knew nothing about checking the harness. As I tried to throw myself into the saddle, I ended up sliding saddle and all under the belly of the horse, coming up on the other side, still clinging to the saddle.

Little Ricky did not see the humor of it and started to cry. Thereafter he seemed to prefer the stability of his red wagon to horses. As for me, I never went near another horse until I had to practically co-star with one in a movie called *Stranger in My Arms*. Other than horses, the movie starred Jeff Chandler, who was an old friend of Richard's. Jeff and Richard had played gangster roles together in *Johnny O'Clock*. I told Richard, "Yeah, great casting. *Me* they give a horse and *you* they give a gun. I'll hold your gun, you ride 'um horses."

Richard, my splendid horseman husband, started to explain how I should handle the horse and overcome my fear of horses.

"Stop," I said. "The problem has been solved."

"Oh great, Junie, you're riding a horse now?"

"No. I'm riding a stuffed horse, dummy!"

Richard let out a cowboy yell—"Yee-hah! What about Jeff?"

"Oh," I said, "he's riding one too."

This struck Richard as even funnier—the star of *Broken*

Arrow and *Taza, Son of Cochise*, who was as fine a horseman as any Indian, being stuck on a mechanical stuffed horse.

There was an unfortunate accident at the Mandeville ranch involving Van Johnson's daughter, Schuyler, who had come over for a little horseback riding. Schuyler was on Pam's favorite horse, Bright Eyes, a feisty creature who had one blue eye and one brown one. Bright Eyes bucked, and Schuyler fell off and broke her collarbone. Richard was upset, not only because of Schuyler's injury but because Van might be angry. But Van had too much class for that, and this was when Richard saw he was not just a fair-weather friend.

Horseback riding was not the only thing that could be hazardous. Once after a party everyone was trapped in a rain-in. Some guests left in time but I told the rest, "You'd better stay or you'll be washed down the mountain. There's plenty of room." They were still singing and talking and laughing and in no mood to go home. For three days all of us were family, and Richard and I were the den parents. As the tropical storm continued, we laughed and sang and held barbecues on an inside porch, watched favorite programs on TV all day and entertained ourselves and each other by night.

Jane Wyman, it turned out, had a lovely voice and sang a solo. Rita Hayworth danced to records. Richard gave an impromptu concert using the piano and various instruments, but brought down the house with his virtuoso number on the kazoo. Judy Garland and I were the clowns, doing duets and purposely wrecking each other's important songs. Van Johnson did a soft-shoe dance, and once he and I did a hammy portrayal of my life with Richard, Van doing the role of June Allyson about to cry, I being a tough Richard, laying down the law.

Rita Hayworth emerged as a real friend and not the "princess" people had bowed to as a result of her marriage to Ali Khan. Rita said that marriage to a prince had not left her wealthy—she'd had to go back to Columbia to beg for her old job after the divorce. She hadn't had to beg very hard. She said

Harry Cohn had told her, "You're still the Love Goddess of Hollywood, and we're glad to have you back." I told Rita I was terribly jealous because she had danced in two movies with my idol, Fred Astaire, and she smiled happily as she remembered the experience. Then someone prevailed on her to get up and show us how she'd peeled her gloves off in *Gilda*. Rita said she should be jealous of me because I sang in my own pictures, while her songs had been dubbed in *Gilda*. I recall hearing that it was the voice of Anita Ellis.

Judy was still calling me, off and on, to come help her get through the lonely nights. Her fortunes, as usual, were up and down and so was her private life. She and Sid Luft had had a lovely baby, Lorna, in November of 1952, but that did not keep the marriage from being shaky.

I was happy for Judy when she made a comeback in *A Star Is Born* and became the leading contender for that year's Oscar. March 1955 found her in the hospital with two exciting things to think about—the upcoming Academy Awards and her second baby with Sid. Baby Joey arrived the day before the Oscar ceremonies. I was sure Judy would win and told her so. Everyone—including me—had helped make her hospital room beautiful for the TV cameras. Then I'd gone home to watch the Oscar show on TV. When I left Judy's room, studio hairdressers and make-up experts had arrived and were busily doing their magic tricks as she sat up in bed.

The moment finally came when the nominees were called out, including "Judy Garland for *A Star Is Born*." I was praying and Judy was on her fluffed-up hospital pillows praying when the envelope was opened. "And the winner is Grace Kelly for *Country Girl*." Judy said it was so cold-blooded that it was almost funny—the TV crew immediately rolled up their wires and unplugged her and disappeared within five minutes. "Not even with an 'I'm sorry,'" Judy said. "To them it was just a job and I had wasted their time."

Judy was almost two people because she could pull herself

out of depression, put on a happy act and be the life of the party. Sometimes she lectured me. "Never never take pills to wake you up or put you to sleep because pretty soon you won't know whether you're awake or asleep," she said. Pills and alcohol were obviously taking their toll on Judy, but actually it was much more a drug problem with uppers and downers than it was alcohol—she drank very little.

Richard began to complain. He felt quite rightly that it was dangerous for me to be driving on the highway alone at all hours. But I couldn't desert Judy. She looked vulnerable sitting in the big chair in her living room, all curled up like a lost little girl waiting for someone to find her. Finally Richard put his foot down and said I couldn't go running to Judy anymore. I tried talking on the phone with her for hours, deep into the night, but I felt I had let her down.

Merle Oberon invited us to dinner. She was known to be one of the most elegant and proper hostesses, and her invitations were like a royal command. I was ready early and waiting for Richard. I had on a white satin sheath, floor length. In order to keep a single wrinkle from forming before Richard saw me, I stood on the large enclosed porch and idly looked out toward the pool. It was getting dark when I realized there was something going on down there in the pool. Walking closer, I could hardly believe what I saw. It was a very busy pool with black Angus cows milling around. I hurried into the house and called up to Richard, "You'd better come down." He said, "Honey, I'll get down as soon as I finish getting dressed."

"You'd better hurry down here now. We have black Angus swimming in the pool."

"June, you're not a bit funny."

"I'm not but wait till you see the black Angus."

He came running down the stairs in his black tie and dinner jacket. We got the servants to help and we all grabbed sticks and tried to prod the cows out of the pool by making them walk up planks. By the time we got them out, we were both wet from head to toe. After chasing the cows back to their fields, we were coated with dirt.

"Great," I panted. "Now we can run get dressed again."

"No, we can't. First I have to fix this fence. Run get me a hammer. Get me nails, the big ones. Get me wire. I'll guard the cows so they don't get out again. You'll find the—"

"No," I said, "I'll guard the cows. You get the nails. You find, you carry." Afterward, we rushed to the house, changed clothes, and arrived at Merle Oberon's just as everyone was finishing dinner. We adjourned with them to the drawing room for coffee and liqueurs. Richard had already told me, "Honey, you better be the one to make the explanations. It would sound too ridiculous coming from me." I was ready before I entered the room, and I started right away, breathlessly saying, "You will never believe what happened to us. We had to get the cows out of the swimming pool and mend the fence and we were all covered with mud and we had to change of course and I'm so sorry. And please forgive us." There was a deafening silence. Every pair of eyes was trained on us, and it was as if I could hear their voices saying, "Sure you did" as their minds came up with the more reasonable explanation, "They probably had a fight." Merle had not suggested that the butler bring us our plates. We didn't dare look hungry and drank many cups of coffee. Merle did not invite us again.

The most lavish party I ever gave was for Curt Jurgens, the German star. I wanted to introduce him to the movie colony since he would be starring in *The Enemy Below*, which Richard was directing in 1957. Robert Mitchum, Curt's co-star, would also be an honored guest. It would be a sit-down dinner for 150 at Mandeville Canyon. The thing was amazing for the sheer logistics. Everything had to be trucked up the hill. Abbey Rents trucked in a tent big enough to seat 150 and accommodate an orchestra and dance floor. Food came from Chasen's and Romanoff's—thousands of dollars' worth. Flowers were trucked in from Harry Findlay's Flower Fashions—thousands of dollars' worth. Liquor had to be trucked up by the load to supply six bars, as well as supply the waiters, who would walk among the guests with trays of drinks and hors d'oeuvres. A dozen electricians trucked fancy lighting up the mountain.

All the trees were decorated with hundreds of Japanese lanterns. Torches were installed in the ground with pink, blue and red lights. Sound engineers set up an elaborate system for the band. After dinner, dancing would continue at the side of the pool and on the grand porch some distance away. The porch band would play quiet romantic music. The large orchestra would really swing.

There were relay teams of busboys who walked the trays from the heating tables in the house out to the tent. Dozens of kitchen staff served the food and would handle the enormous cleanup job. We figured it took a hundred people in all to put on the party. Dozens of attendants were on duty to handle valet parking. The attendants waved chauffeurs up and down the roads to safe parking places. Chauffeur-driven limousines picked up the guests as they got out of their cars and drove them up the dark winding roads of the mountain to the house—it was much too great a distance to walk. I asked Richard why a field couldn't be used so the guests could walk to the house from their cars. "It isn't done," he said. "That would be gauche." He looked shocked.

The evening started with a disaster. Joan Crawford arrived with four escorts. It was a stunning entrance, I'll admit, but this was a sit-down dinner and we had made *one* place card for *one* Crawford escort. I wanted to swat her, but instead I smiled sweetly and ran for Frank to rearrange the table and make way for the queen and her court. It was almost unbelievable that

Joan would do this to me, for she prided herself on her elegance and good manners.

The party had an embarrassing postscript some months later at the Oscar ceremonies. I don't know how it happened, except that I must have been born with a tipsy angel looking after me— or maybe with the curse of the leprechauns. Curt's movie, *The Enemy Below*, was nominated in the cinematography category for an Academy Award. By coincidence, I was slated to present the award for that category. My shining moment arrived.

All eyes were on me. I would have been more thrilled had my Richard been nominated for his directing of this film, but no matter. I opened my mouth to announce the name of the winning movie, enunciating each word distinctly—"*The . . . Enema . . . Below.*" It brought down the house.

DOWNHILL ALL THE WAY

10

IT WAS A movie that started us sliding down the side of the mountain—slowly at first and then like debris in an avalanche.

Richard didn't recognize the danger signals. To him it seemed that Howard Hughes was taking him to the top of the mountain at last—everything was now within his grasp. He was finally going to produce and direct a superspectacular, *The Conqueror.*

Somewhere along the line I had become aware that Richard was having many meetings with Howard Hughes, the owner of RKO. But these were not the usual meeting of executives in an office during the course of a working day. Oh, no. These were strange meetings in the dead of night. The phone would ring. Richard would jump up and get ready. A car would arrive and Richard would go rolling off into the night.

"Just once let me go along," I pleaded.

"Sorry, Flattop, can't be done."

"Why, Richard, why?"

"Mr. Hughes just doesn't do business that way."

"Why does it have to be night—and so late?"

"I guess he likes the night."

"Well, doesn't he know you have a wife who doesn't like to be left alone?"

"You're not alone. You've got a houseful of servants."

"I *am* alone. Why does he have to see you at night?"

"We discuss business. RKO business."

"I know he's RKO, Richard. That doesn't explain anything."

"I've given my word not to discuss it, but maybe someday, honey, I can tell you. Now be a good girl—you know you never pry."

"I know. But you tell him you've got a wife who's getting plenty mad. You hear?"

Richard grinned and kissed me. "Oh, sure. Of course I'll give Mr. Hughes your message." And the car came and off he went. It was true that I didn't pry into Richard's business. If he didn't offer to tell me, I didn't ask questions. It was not my affair.

One day Richard came home and said, "I want all the servants off the premises tonight. They get the night off. Howard Hughes is coming to the house."

"Oh, good—I get to meet him."

"Oh, no you don't. You'll wait in your room and I'll let you know when it's safe to come out."

As night came on I said, "Can I sit here at least until we know if he's coming?"

"Of course," Richard said. "It's your home."

"Thanks for reminding me. I was starting to wonder."

We had an entrance at Mandeville Canyon Road—an iron gate that was kept locked and controlled by security. Since everyone was dismissed that night, Richard controlled the gate from the switch in the house. There was almost a mile of driveway brightly lit by a winding row of lampposts. The whole driveway was ablaze with these lights the evening Howard Hughes came to call.

Finally the buzzer sounded and Richard talked to the gate

from the control box. He came over to me at the fireplace and said, "We have to turn off all the lights outside and all the lights inside except for one light inside the door. It's to be unlocked."

He went around flicking off lights and turning off the drive lights and then left the front door ajar. He returned to the speaker and said it was clear to come up.

"Okay, Junie," he said, "now please, honey, go to your room. You've got to get out of here. You can feel your way."

I said, "Nope."

"What?"

"I just want to look at him and then I'll go to my room."

He could have picked me up and carried me, of course, but he didn't and we were still quibbling when three or four well-dressed men entered the house, sort of ignored me and proceeded to check out the rooms as if expecting an assassin to jump out. One of them went to the door, motioned, and in came—I don't know what I expected, but this wasn't it. It looked like they had brought their gardener. Howard Hughes was a tall, very thin man who seemed to be extremely shy. He reminded me of Jimmy Stewart, though Jimmy would never wear such garb.

I can tell you exactly what the mystery man had on, even with only one light burning. He had on a tattered gray sweat shirt and tattered gray, never-been-pressed white ducks, no socks, and *completely* worn-out tennis shoes. I use the word completely in the strictest sense. The shoes were ragged.

Richard introduced me saying, "Mr. Hughes, this is my wife, June."

In a quiet, high voice—very high pitched for a man—he said, "How do you do, ma'am?"

And with that, I put out my hand and started pumping his hand up and down, saying, "How do you do, sir?" Then I excused myself and felt my way up to my room in total darkness.

I suddenly realized Richard hadn't told me whether I could put the light on inside the room. Should I yell downstairs? No, I decided, I'd just lie across the bed and wait in the dark like a good little soldier. And the good little soldier fell asleep. The meeting went on for hours. I didn't know what they talked about and Richard didn't volunteer anything. He did, however, have a complaint about my behavior.

It seems that somehow I had done a terrible thing when I'd been introduced to Howard Hughes. "You touched him," said Richard reproachfully. "Nobody touches Mr. Hughes. He doesn't like to be touched."

"Oh, big deal," I said, most annoyed. "Put it on my tombstone: SHE TOUCHED HOWARD HUGHES." After all I'd put up with for this man's visit, here was the thanks I got. Richard wasn't laughing. "You just don't understand," he said. Later I would read that aides had to wear white gloves to touch Howard Hughes—he was that terrified of germs.

Not till later did I learn that Howard Hughes wanted to name Richard acting boss of RKO, with Richard running the studio. He made him an offer. Richard talked about how he would manage the studio, the kind of movies he'd make and the conditions under which he could work. There were other meetings after that at other places, and Richard seriously considered the job of studio chief but decided he would rather produce and direct an occasional movie for RKO and have time for his other enterprises.

By the time I learned about the offer, it had already leaked from RKO. Richard was a very good man with a secret. But one thing I did know. In Richard's mind, all good things came from RKO and Howard Hughes. They'd let him play tough guys and direct a thriller, *Split Second*, in 1952. He had tried other studios and they had turned him down. The Paramount rebuff had hurt the most because his friend William Holden supposedly had clout there and had set it all up for Richard.

Richard didn't even blame Howard Hughes for calling him away from his directorial chores on *The Caine Mutiny*, which led to the only fiasco of Richard's career. He had a yen to play Captain Queeg, the cruel and paranoiac skipper of the *Caine*; it was, Richard said, the only role he ever begged for. *The Caine Mutiny* was going to be produced as a movie, and Richard went to see Stanley Kramer at Columbia Pictures, who was casting. "No way," said Kramer. "It's useless." Kramer had his heart set on Humphrey Bogart for the role, but then theatrical producer Paul Gregory phoned Richard and said he'd heard about Richard's wish to play Queeg and offered him a chance to play the role onstage in *The Caine Mutiny Court Martial* with a company that would be touring for twenty weeks, all over the country, and then opening on Broadway.

I told Richard if he took it I was divorcing him, because I wasn't seeing enough of him as it was. He turned it down and then Gregory asked him how he'd like to direct the play instead, get it ready for Broadway. It would be an all-Hollywood cast with Henry Fonda as Lieutenant Keefer, the good guy, and Lloyd Nolan as Captain Queeg, the bad guy who rolls steel balls around in his hand when he gets nervous.

Richard would have his name on a Broadway playbill for the first time as a director without even having to go to New York. All rehearsals would be in Hollywood and the play would open in Santa Barbara, where I could be in the audience opening night. I gave my seal of approval and was excited for Richard. He was looking forward to directing Henry Fonda. Fonda still had to be consulted on whether he would approve Richard as director. Richard had never before directed onstage and had only one film-directing credit, *Split Second*.

Paul Gregory phoned Fonda, who was in New York, and Hank said Richard was fine. "All that fun and they pay money too," Richard said.

One week before the play opened, Howard Hughes called

for Richard and wanted him immediately to go into his role in the movie *Susan Slept Here*. Richard did not argue or ask for time. He told Paul Gregory that he had to leave, but assured him that the performances were set and he really wasn't needed anymore. Richard left five days before the opening. The headline in a trade paper said HUGHES PULLS POWELL OFF 'CAINE' LEGITER. Paul Gregory was furious and made Charles Laughton, the co-producer, the director for the last week—giving him the full credit on the marquee. Richard was furious and eventually filed suit for the loss of his credit. *Caine Mutiny* went on to be a great hit.

As Christmas 1953 approached, Richard was at his best—excited and absorbed by the colossal movie he was to direct for Hughes—the multimillion-dollar saga of the great Genghis Khan, *The Conqueror*. Shooting would take place in North Africa, with either Marlon Brando or Yul Brynner as the Mongol warrior who leads his hordes across Asia in the thirteenth century. Everything Richard touched was turning to gold, and he was like a dynamo, busy with Four Star, his TV series, TV movies, and the feature movie that he and the ebullient Debbie Reynolds starred in, *Susan Slept Here*, which became a box-office smash.

Richard was predicting that Debbie would be a great star. I had nothing against Debbie but it didn't help my ego any to read my husband's funny quote in the gossip columns: "If this keeps up, June will begin to look too old to me."

"I was just kidding, Junie face," said Richard as I waved the paper at him. "Come, my child bride," and he coaxed me into bed, where he proved he still loved me more than ever.

I begged Richard to cut down on work and take a vacation. He was noncommital. "Well, what would be your idea of a good rest spot," I pressed. "My idea of a vacation," he said, "is to rest *quietly* in the shade of a blonde," and he was looking at me with bedroom eyes.

"Oh, Richard," I said disgustedly, pretending I was going to punch him in the nose.

As soon as Christmas was over, he was completely lost to me and the children as he prepared for his biggest challenge. He described *The Conqueror* as a "violent love story in the midst of an epic military conquest." Hughes was giving him carte blanche. "Dick, this one's all yours," he said. "Just make it the biggest spectacular ever. Get the biggest stars. Don't worry about the money." I told Richard, "If I get a divorce, I'm naming Howard Hughes as co-respondent. You didn't have time for me before this and now I swear you're married to a movie."

"You're right, Junie face, but just remember—it's only a short marriage and then I'll be back to you full time."

"But why can't you let other people do things? Why are you picking the actors? I thought you believed in delegating authority."

"I do," he said, "but this is different. I'm known as an actor. How would other actors feel if I didn't give them the courtesy of a personal interview?"

"I don't know how they'd feel. I just know how *I* feel. Left out. Anyway, what I say makes sense because even the casting office told you not to worry about it—let them handle at least the minor roles."

"I know, I know," he said, "but I have to do it my way. This is the most important movie in my career. Millions of dollars are involved and I have to justify Howard's faith in me."

Day after grueling day, Richard interviewed and screened an army of actors and extras and when he was through, he had seen 2,000 people. He came home daily and said, "Let me sit here in silence. Just let me eat without talking." It was not to be—we couldn't get through a meal anymore without a major interruption. The phone would ring and it would be someone important and Frank would tell him who it was and he'd say, "Oh, yes, let me talk to him." There were daily news breaks and reporters calling for details. The star would not be Brando or Brynner. Instead, the star signed was big John Wayne. "He'll be a terrific Genghis Khan," said Richard. Richard was calling me on the phone, virtually the only means of communication left to us now. "John looks like a conqueror, and I swear, with that head-gear, he takes on a Mongol look. But his accent is *horrible*." Richard imitated him, saying, "Whar's mah horse, Abdool?"

Susan Hayward was to be Duke's leading lady. "The right chemistry," said Richard on the phone. "Something happens between them. It will work. She's not trained in harem-type dancing, but we can have someone give her a few lessons on location."

Location was a crucial matter on a picture of this magnitude. Richard wanted terrain that looked like the Gobi Desert without going to Mongolia. It was a red letter day for Richard when he flew out with RKO scouts, in March 1954, and came back saying they would not have to film in Africa, after all. "St. George, Utah, is a dead ringer for the Gobi," Richard reported to me. "The same red sand—fantastic rock formations. It won't be hard to clear away any signs of civilization."

"And it's close enough for me to visit," I chirped. But I was talking to myself.

The day Richard and his stars flew to Utah to start shooting was full of bad omens. The wind seemed to be trying to tell them something and driving them away. The chartered plane carrying Richard, John Wayne, Susan Hayward and a dozen other top actors almost crashed, and they landed only to find that their tent city was in shambles, destroyed by a fifty-five-mile-per-hour gale. But shooting had to start the next morning because Richard had another problem—Susan Hayward was getting a divorce and they had to film her while they could get her. She would be flying back and forth to Hollywood as needed by the lawyers. Richard kept men working through the night and he began shooting on schedule.

He did not sound perturbed as he phoned me to say he had arrived safely and all was going well. It was I who called him back later to say, "Richard, why do I have to learn these things from the newspapers? You could be dead."

"What things, what dead?"

"Here's the paper and I'm reading the headline on this big story: GALE WRECKS BIG UTAH LOCATION SET FOR RKO'S 'THE CONQUEROR.' And your plane made a dangerous landing."

"Yes, there was a little high wind trouble but nothing to worry you about, Junie pie. You just relax."

"Richard, I love you. I'm coming there to be near you." This time he couldn't ignore me.

"I love you too, honey. Sure, come on. I'm lonely without you. This is a terrible, remote desert. You'll make it fun. And Junie face, will you do one more thing? Bring Ellen, Pam, and Rick. It should be educational for the kids."

My little 450-mile safari started, with me at the wheel, and, safely packed away, little objects from home to make Richard's room look friendlier, especially framed photographs of all the children.

How Richard could have said he was lonely in the midst of all that chaos, I'll never know. Most of the town of St. George was in costume, acting as extras. And Indians from a nearby reservation made excellent Tatar and Mongol horsemen. They were paid $12 a day if they rode, $10 if they walked and $4 on days they didn't work. The school had been turned into a wardrobe center, makeup department and cafeteria.

When I arrived, they had just had another disaster. Pedro Armendariz had fallen from his horse and three teeth had been knocked out. Those could easily be replaced, but what was worse from a pictorial standpoint was that his lips and face were swollen and banged up. Richard, an expert at coping, said, "We'll write in a fight scene immediately and that will explain the battered face."

I could hardly believe people could work in heat that hovered between 110 and 120 degrees. But obviously they could, and between takes men still pursued the dancing girls, who looked almost naked in their flesh-colored body stockings. Richard was riding way up high on his camera boom, and from far down below he looked like an MD with the surgical mask he wore over his nose and mouth to keep the sand out when the wind started to blow.

The red sand was like a plague—it got into everything and clung to the skin. Our food was invariably full of it and someone nicknamed it Utah chili powder. Richard had outdoor showers installed to rinse it off.

One day, the nerves of the actors were particularly frayed; they were in agony from the heat, and I realized that *The Conqueror* company was close to rebellion. At that instant, from high in the air, Richard started singing a song, "I Only Have Eyes for You," way off-key, just as he did at home when he wanted to break the tension and make us laugh. His timing was inspired. Suddenly everybody was laughing. And then he boomed, "You see, the heat's getting to me, too, so let's all get together and give it another try. Okay? *Action.*"

The next time tension mounted, he put up his hands and spoke the magic words, "God is Love." From his perch atop the giant boom, Richard used a loudspeaker to direct the actors and extras—he'd give the signal and giant battle scenes would begin as Mongols clashed with Tatars in hand-to-hand combat or with flights of arrows.

John Wayne looked so alien, so fierce, it was hard to believe he was good old lovable, easygoing John. No matter how hot it must have been for him in his heavy costume and thick makeup, he never lost his sense of humor. When one of the most dangerous parts of the battle was about to be shot, Richard told John, "Well, pal, here's where we separate the men from the boys."

John rumbled back, "I just hope we don't separate the men from the horses."

It was a miracle that men and riders survived. The script called for an unprecedented stunt—a simultaneous fall of six mounted horses. They did it and not a single stunt rider was hurt by his own horse or the other horses galloping by.

After the day's shooting, Richard and I together with John Wayne, Agnes Moorehead and Susan Hayward would relax over a cold drink. Richard told us how he'd made his first good impression on Howard Hughes when he was directing *Split Second*. He would let the paychecks sit uncashed for seventeen weeks. "I knew money was the only way to get his attention," Richard chuckled. "*Contempt* for money, that is. And sure enough, he phoned to ask me what was wrong. I told him. The script was being nibbled to death and changed without my being permitted to have any say. Hughes asked for my ideas and immediately phoned the writer to work directly with me. *Then* I picked up my checks, the movie was a hit and Hughes started cultivating me."

In private, Richard confided to me that he was very worried about *The Conqueror*. The cost of the production was soaring, and Hughes indicated that he was not so happy about it after all. The spend-what-you-need-days were over, and when costs rose to $3.5 million and then to $4 million, Hughes ordered, "Start shaving." It was impossible—the movie was supporting a whole town, St. George—which wasn't cheap. Richard dreaded the call, but he knew he had to level with Hughes. Hughes did not even ask for an itemization of the additional costs. He simply asked, "Does Wayne like it?" Richard said, "Yes."

"Susan like it?"

"Yes."

"Well, do *you* like it?"

"Hell, yes!"

"Then hop to it and if it's not good, I'll take the full blame. Maybe we'll even start a new trend—Mongolian westerns."

Susan Hayward confided in me. "You'll have to excuse me, honey," she said. "It's a terrible time. I'm divorcing Jess Barker and we're in a bitter custody fight over the twins. Some days I feel so low I hate to even get up." I tried to comfort her. I did not foresee that after the movie and the bitter court scenes, Susan would become so depressed that she would attempt to kill herself.

Susan and I compared notes on how we had gotten to Hollywood and Susan said she had been brought to test for the role of Scarlett O'Hara in Gone With the Wind and had failed that. She had gone on to get two Academy Award nominations only to lose out there too.

"You deserve an Oscar for this movie on survival alone," I said.

She was beautiful and seductive in her flimsy costumes and could hold attention even against six-foot-four Wayne. Their shots had them rolling on the sands together—hot bodies against hot sands. It was a provocative scene at the time, but it doesn't look so sexy to me when I see it now, after the mysterious deaths of so many of the stars and crew involved in the filming of The Conqueror.

I could not stay full time on the desert location because I had a new movie of my own to go into, The McConnell Story, co-starring Alan Ladd. I had to hurry back.

If it hadn't been for that movie commitment—had I stayed longer on location with Richard—I might not be alive today, nor my children.

But all the death and suffering would be in the future. What annoyed me when Richard finally came in from the heat and the devastation of the desert location was that he still could not slow down and I saw less of him than ever.

167

He was involved in every phase of the spectacular, the cutting, the reshooting of scenes, the musical score. And tons of red sand and rock that had been trucked in were put to constant use. In a phone conversation I overheard, Richard said that the production cost was now hovering around $6 million.

I could feel the tension around him. He had to succeed.

He now had to plan a nationwide campaign that would assure *The Conqueror* the blockbuster status essential to earning out. Otherwise it would be considered a failure, and that was one word Richard could not stand.

I do not know the bottom line of profit for the movie, but Richard eventually mentioned in my hearing that the movie had grossed $18 million.

11

I HAD BEEN warned about working with Alan Ladd.

Sue, Alan's wife, was also his agent and manager and never left the camera area, I was told. She watched every scene and every shot—and all shots had to favor Alan, even to the detriment of his leading lady.

I had said I didn't worry about those things—I just concentrated totally on the person I was involved with in the scene and let the professional cameramen handle the rest. If the wanted the back of my head, so be it.

And then I was given the final warning. Alan was a very cold and distant man, they said.

Again I said, "Don't worry. I'm there to do a job, not hold a tea party."

I gathered from my first day of working with Alan Ladd that everything I had been told was true. Sue was indeed giving all kinds of suggestions and orders and Alan wasn't opening his mouth. I noticed that he had some nasty bruises. She said he had fallen in the shower and cut his head. I couldn't imagine a shower causing that much damage. I fought back the urge to say something funny. Sue did his talking and he merely listened impassively.

Once she was off the set I clowned around with everyone just to see if I could make Alan laugh. He certainly looked like he needed cheering up, but he regarded me as if I were some kind of strange creature—not at all what he had expected—and he wasn't sure whether this was good or bad.

At home nothing had changed or improved. Richard was still muttering about the problems on *The Conqueror*—when he was home—or talking on the telephone.

When I was passing Alan one day at rehearsal, I stumbled over my own feet—maybe by accident, maybe for fun—and Alan grabbed me. "Hey, small fry," he said, looking down at me. "One accident-prone person in a movie is enough." He laughed for the first time since I'd met him. He had been holding me in his arms and now he let go, self-consciously. The rehearsal resumed. At the next break, he showed up in my dressing room. "May I come in?"

"Only if you stumble in," I said.

He chuckled. "Stumble in? You're lucky if I don't fall in." Now we were both laughing and bubbling with things to say that might seem like trivia to other people but that showed how alike we were. "Do you want to hear something ironic?" he said. "Here I am playing the flying ace and I don't fly."

"You mean you don't fly your own plane like Richard does?"

"I mean I've never even been in a goddamn plane."

"But you're getting into a plane in this movie."

"Yes. But it never leaves the ground, and even so, just being in it panics me and makes me want to throw up."

"I can't believe it."

"That I'm such a coward?"

"No, that we're so much alike. Richard has to practically throw a bag over my head to get me on a plane. And practically the greatest misery I ever felt was each time he bought a new plane that I would have to set foot in."

Our film was a wartime love story. Captain Joseph McConnell was the first triple jet ace in the Korean War. I played his wife, who lived in mortal fear that something terrible would happen to Joe but hid her fears as she followed him from camp to camp to be near him, throughout his career.

His early life had been a study in frustration, yearning to be a pilot while having to settle for being a navigator in World War II. He lived for the day he would fly. Finally he got his wings. It was ironic that some of the finest movie scenes ever shot show Alan waging dog fights with MIGs across vapor-streaked skies and yet he never left the ground.

His life comes to an unhappy ending, just as our personal love story would. In the movie, McConnell meets death in a test flight of the new F-86 as his plane screams across the sky. And there am I, full of tearful resignation.

But my own tears would come later. All through the shooting, Alan would make me laugh as he made fun of his fear of flying.

"Let's get this crate off the ground—but nothing over two inches," he said, giving me a funny little look as he'd climb into the cockpit, firmly anchored to the ground.

"But how do you travel?" I once asked him. "How did you get to Europe? How did you get to New York?"

"Cars, trains, boats," he said. "It's easier to avoid planes than people think." Richard was away beating the drums for The Conqueror, and Alan would make some excuse to Sue so we could dine in our dressing rooms after shooting.

"I'm so glad I'm doing this movie. I have someone at home who picks all my movies," Alan told me. "I have her to thank."

"I have someone at home who picks all my movies. He reads all my scripts."

"I have a superstition," Alan said. "I never read a script until I'm signed for it. What's your excuse?"

"Just lazy, I guess."

We burst into laughter. We concluded that was the reason we failed to win Academy Awards—we needed new script readers.

"But don't forget the popularity polls," I reminded him. That set us off again as we regaled each other with the other kinds of rewards we'd received that showed that somebody out there must like us—we'd both won Number 1 spots in the fans' poll of 1950 for favorite actor and actress.

"Do you suppose the Academy Awards people should consult the public?" Alan asked, half serious.

"What!" I said. "And ruin everything!"

More laughter. When we were together, life held no sting and everything was happy and hilarious.

We each had someone at home who guided our careers and who was considerably older than we.

Each of us was suffering in that relationship, but for exactly opposite reasons—I because I wasn't getting enough attention and Alan because he was getting too much.

"I can't call my soul my own," Alan said. "I must tell where I am every minute."

"I may as well not have a husband," I said. "I'm married to a telephone."

"I never know when I'll have a free minute to call my own."

"I never know when I'll have a husband to call my own. He's getting home so late these days I have to show the children pictures of their father so they won't forget him."

"But I guess they're doing it for us."

"Oh sure, they're doing it for us."

We talked of the early years of breaking into movies. He'd once tried blackening his hair with mascara to look like an Italian boxer. "Sue told me to look Italian," he said.

"Did you get the part?"

"Hell, no. It was the hottest day of the year when I tested and the mascara and sweat were running down my face. And you know who got the part?"

"No. Who?"

"Blond boy William Holden."

"It figures. What was the movie?"

"*Golden Boy.*"

Everything he mentioned seemed to have a counterpart in my life. My marriage to Richard involved two children, the girl older than the boy, and two children out of the past. So did his. My marriage involved a ranch and a procession of houses. So did his. Our ranch had riding horses, cattle, and 5,000 chickens. His ranch also had 5,000 chickens, prize black Angus and riding horses, but he also had thirty-six pigs, a herd of rabbits and seventeen boxer dogs. Plus that he raised racehorses and one was a winner.

"I'm scared of horses," I said.

"That's all right," he assured me. "You teach me how to get on a plane that really leaves the ground and I'll teach you how to get on a horse."

"And stay there?"

"And stay there."

"No thanks," I said.

Alan once said that I reminded him very much of his first love. I assumed she was dead and asked no questions. Only later was I shocked to read that I resembled his first wife, Midge. I saw a picture of her in a book and indeed there was a resemblance. The son they called Laddie was Alan's son with Midge. I thought he was Sue's child by a previous marriage, just as Carol Lee was.

Alan's previous marriage had been a well-kept secret, just as Richard's to Mildred had been, in order to preserve the Hollywood fantasy of romantic availability. Midge died of diabetes at the age of thirty-five or forty, loyally concealing to the end that she'd been the wife of a screen idol.

"It's hard to be a completely honest person in Hollywood," Alan said. "Right from the beginning we have to start lying for the sake of the studio biography."

I nodded in agreement. "Mine says I was born in a little town in New York State that no longer exists—you can't get phonier than that." Alan said, "At least my name is real—Alan Walbridge Ladd." He spoke of his horror of "soup and sheep"—his diet as a child in Hot Springs, Arkansas. "I can't eat vichyssoise to this day. Cold or hot, it's still potato soup to me and I hate it."

"Beans," I said. "*Beans.*"

"What do you mean, beans?"

"I can't eat them. I ate enough beans in childhood to last a lifetime. When I'm served chili, which I love, I try to eat around the beans."

"A real job." He smiled. "Not easy. We couldn't afford beans. We could only afford free potatoes from the potato field and cheap cuts of mutton." His father was a traveling man who seemed to be mostly away from home until one memorable day when Alan was four. His father was just arriving or leaving when he fell over on the floor—dead of a heart attack. "My dad was of Scottish heritage, how about yours?" he asked.

"Dutch," I said. "You're talking to Kathryn Ann Eleanor Frances van Geisman." I felt safe telling Alan about my early hardships and heartbreaks. We looked at each other with deeply felt sympathy. He was the first person who really understood. It was as if our lives had run on parallel paths. He had been a great swimmer. I had been a great swimmer. My prowess had been the result of correcting my back injury. His had been the result of proving that though small, he could do anything anyone else could do—and better. "I was almost ready to compete in the Olympics, in 1932," he said.

"What kept you from going ahead?"

"I dived in once and hit my head a really serious blow."

"I got hit on the head too," I said. "This is too much." We gave each other concern and tenderness without any kind of pressure. I was falling in love with Alan but I knew there was nothing we could ever do about it. We would lounge in my dressing room with the music up high—not because we liked it that way but to keep anyone from overhearing us. We played the game of "What if?" a lot, speculating what "would have" happened had we met in New York when I was on the stage—or if he had been on the MGM set when I arrived in 1943—or if I had been a little kid in his neighborhood when he was growing up. We created a whole life together in our reveries.

"You know, I was a pretty tough little kid before that tree branch," I said. "There was a little boy that wouldn't stop tormenting me so I knocked him out with my fist." I gave Alan a little rabbit punch. "What about that, huh? Get tough with me, will ya!"

He grabbed my arms and held me. "You're talking to a pretty tough customer, so you better be careful. This bully kept pushing my face in the water fountain. I was about twelve and it was a new school and already he'd stuck me with the nickname of Tiny and everyone in class started calling me that."

"That wouldn't bother me."

"Well, it bothered me. Especially when he shoved my face in the fountain. So I took a punch at him. And suddenly there were two of him."

"He knocked you dizzy?"

"No, Junie, he was identical twins. And now they both were coming at me with their fists."

"So you ran between them."

"So I took them both on and I knocked them both out." He was looking deep into my eyes, and the green intensity of them was making me dizzy. So was his voice, rich and vibrant. "I told you I was a tough kid. Do you want to fight?" And suddenly he was kissing me. And I wasn't even fighting back.

We knew that our happiness was on borrowed time. Sue Ladd was busy getting ready for a wedding at their Holmby Hills house; Carol Lee, her daughter, was to wed Richard Anderson, a young actor, on January 22, 1955. "I'm seldom alone," Alan told me. "You can't imagine what this does to a man—the lack of privacy. That's why I go to the ranch alone whenever I can." Luckily he had his working hours free. Sue had hung around the set for only a couple of days, watching and making suggestions on lighting or his interpretation of a scene.

Alan and I teased each other about our past movie partners. "I heard all about your big romance with Van Johnson," he said. "Never happened," I replied, "but I heard all about your big romance with Veronica Lake."

"Never happened, she was happily married and had a new baby. And besides she had one flaw. She wasn't wacky like you. Poor Veronica. They could never settle on the right name for her at Paramount. She was the daughter of a Danish sailor, and her name was Constance Ockleman. They changed it to Constance Keane but that didn't help either. As soon as they settled on Veronica Lake, though, she created a sensation."

"It's a beautiful name," I agreed, "and so is her one-eyed hairdo."

"Sure is. But so many Rosie the Riveters copied it that the government actually asked her to pull her hair back, to cut down on machine accidents in war plants."

Alan was indeed accident-prone. Two years before our movie, he had gone to his ranch during the shooting of *Botany*

Bay and a horse he was trying to help out of a ditch bit him. Then in his next movie, *The Iron Mistress*, he insisted on doing his own stunts and broke his hand when he punched concrete by mistake during a fake fight. He smashed his hand filming *Hell Below Zero* and two fingernails had to be removed and took their time growing back. A few months before our movie, he slipped and broke a rib while taking a shower. "What about those scars on your forehead?" I asked. "Automobile," he said. "Windshield." He didn't elaborate.

When we were acting together in *The McConnell Story* there was no sign that Alan was drinking. Afterward I would hear the rumors of heavy drinking, but even then no one ever said that Alan Ladd drank during working hours. He was ever the professional.

We rarely spoke of our spouses except to acknowledge in a bittersweet way that they had helped us enormously. Sue had found him jobs and gotten his career into high gear, and Richard had been my trusted mentor. We could never hurt them—ever. I did once ask Alan, "Didn't Sue give up her acting career to become your agent?"

"Not really. She had already become an agent when she met me. She devoted herself to my career and hardly had time for any other client. We used to ride around with every kind of costume in the car, looking for parts to test for." He told me how they'd first met. She was just starting her agenting business and needed potential movie actors to represent. She heard two voices in a radio play that sounded interesting—one of a young man and one of an old codger. She called the radio station and left word for both men to stop by. Only Alan Ladd showed up. "Where is the other man—the old man?" she asked. "That's me, too," said Alan, going into his elderly cackle. Alan was a natural mimic and could imitate almost any accent. That was another thing we had in common. I could pick up any accent, too, and we would carry on hilarious conversations, each of us using a different dialect and pretending not to understand the other.

"How can you always be so cheerful?" Alan asked me this repeatedly.

"I'm not," I assured him. "Sometimes I go off and just sit brooding. Or read my favorite cynic, Oscar Wilde—you know, 'that little tent of blue, which prisoners call the sky.'"

"*The Ballad of Reading Gaol*," he said. "Tell me more." I quoted:

> Yet each man kills the thing he loves,
> By each let this be heard.
> Some do it with a bitter look,
> Some with a flattering word.

"Oh yes," he said, "the cruelty of words." He leaned over. "So we won't use words." And I felt his lips on mine. "Now that I've found you," he said, "I'll never have to feel so lonely again. I'll know that somewhere there is one person who has seen the world as I see it and understands." He looked so lost. I lapsed into my Italian accent—"Hey, ah Tony, what's a thees understands? You sick ah sometin?" But I knew that the same thing applied to me, and that wherever Alan was I would always feel an invisible tie to him from now on. "Hey, ah Tony, looks a thees step. You wanna have a little accident? I poosh you over." He laughed and pretended to lose his balance.

We clung to every minute we could have together and played our "What if?" game. "How would it feel to wake up next to you?" Alan asked me. "You wouldn't like it," I told him. "I sleep in flannel pajamas." He chuckled. "Crazy but cozy." We sat thinking about it. He was leaning back and I had my head on his shoulder. "You know something," he said. "You've taken the place of sleeping pills. Since I've been working with you I don't even need anything to put me to sleep."

"Oh, great," I said. "I put you to sleep. I'm honored."

"Cut it out. I'm serious. Falling asleep is a real serious problem with me. I have to take sleeping pills, but somehow I haven't needed any during this movie." He leaned further back, surveying the ceiling. "Maybe there *is* something to this happiness people are always yammering about."

"Yeah. Just might be," I said.

"And accidents. Hey, have you noticed I haven't had a single accident since I've been working on this picture?"

"Knock on wood," I said. "But you better let me check you over for any bumps, cuts or bruises." I pretended to be a monkey grooming another monkey. "Okay, that does it." He grabbed me and pretended he was going to give me the spanking of my life. We were like puppies, wrestling, growling at each other, then marching off, the best of buddies, arms around each other. Even on the set we walked that way, knowing perfectly well that we were setting tongues wagging. It was just as Rhett had sassed Scarlett—"Frankly, my dear, I don't give a damn." Trouble was, we didn't know where to go from here— we knew too well that the answer was *nowhere*.

As Richard had once done, Alan would sing to me. When we were alone he would break into some Gilbert and Sullivan. He had played the lead in his high school production of *The Mikado*. "What do you like to sing when you're not singing for money?" he asked. He was surprised when I didn't launch into some cute modern number but instead sang him "Clair de Lune," using lyrics I had written for it. "It's beautiful," he said. "What do you call it?"

" 'I Remember.' "

" 'I Remember.' And now I'll remember, too. I wish you'd record it, just for me. A single record."

"It wouldn't be wise."

"Oh, you're right. I guess it wouldn't be wise."

One day I couldn't resist sharing a comment little Ricky had made when his father and I had coaxed him to go to nursery school. Four-year-old Ricky had protested he didn't want to go, and when we pressed him to tell us why he was dead set against it, he said he didn't want to be a nurse—he wanted to be a football player.

"What is your dream?" Alan asked me. "What would you really like to do?"

"That's easy," I said. "Just give up acting and stay home and be an ordinary housewife and mother. I almost made it."

"I can't believe it," he said. "That sounds so wonderful. I admire the way you don't get involved in the business end of acting."

"Business," I scoffed, "what's that? I don't even know what I'm making on this movie. I let Richard handle all that."

"He's a lucky man," said Alan.

"I'm lucky, too." I suddenly felt protective about Richard.

"I know," Alan said.

"What's your dream?" I asked him. I was sure it would be something about handling his own career, but that wasn't it at all. "To play Lawrence of Arabia. Did you ever read his book *The Seven Pillars of Wisdom?*"

"No," I said. "I never was clear on what Lawrence did in Arabia."

"Just united the Arabs. Just helped them revolt against the cruel Turks, who were on Germany's side in World War One. Just disrupted the German shipping lines—Germany's railroad from Berlin to Baghdad. Just helped in his own way to win World War One. That's all."

"Oh."

"And do you know how tall Lawrence was?"

"No."

"Five foot three. I'm inches taller."

"We small people have to stick together," I said. He greeted this crack with a look of smoldering fury. "I'm not *small*. I *hate* the word. It's hounded me all my life and it's completely wrong when applied to me. I'm average height—five feet five." It was the first time I'd seen him lose control.

"I'm sorry, Alan," I said. He immediately calmed down. "Can I amend that to 'We giants have to stick together'?" Now Alan looked contrite. "Forgive me for blowing up, but you don't know what this word has done to my life. Just for the record, I'm *slight*. I will agree to that. That's what I am, slight of build. But I shouldn't blow off steam at you."

"What are friends for?" I asked.

"I know you must have heard about actresses standing in ditches for close-ups with me."

"Yes, but you know how gossips are."

"It happens to be true. But people were wrong in thinking I ordered it because of vanity. It was always the directors and photographers—they wanted to make me look tougher or more romantic and it's been twisted into something personal about me—"

"I understand how you feel," I said—and I could.

"I'm so glad you're so dainty and slight," he said. "It's just great to stand there and look down at you and know you're not in a ditch."

"Thanks," I said. "I'm suddenly gladder, too, though my height has given me a few problems in the past."

"Mine are endless," he said. "Last year in *Saskatchewan* Shelley Winters never quit bitching about the fact they put her in a little ditch for a close-up. And in *The Great Gatsby* they did even worse." He paused for breath and I was determined to lighten his mood. "Oh—more girl trouble?" I teased. "No, it was all the men. They teamed me with a whole roster of tall men like Howard Da Silva and Macdonald Carey and Barry Sullivan, so they built a slanting platform and covered it with carpeting like the rest of the room and I had to stand on that. And I felt like a fool, I'll tell you, standing above them like a preacher and having to walk on a slant." I had to laugh—it was so funny, thinking of Alan walking on the slant. Now Alan was laughing too. "I'm so glad I got that out of my system. I can see how amusing it is, now, but at the time it made me feel like a child propped up for a damned photograph."

It felt like being married—that special awareness two people develop when they feel that they belong together. Eventually he said, "You know people are talking about us."

"Yes, I know."

"Well, I think I am in love with you." And I said, "I think I'm in love with you, too, but I belong to Richard and you belong to Sue and I know we'd never want to hurt them." I suggested we both tell our mates before they heard rumors that we were running around seeing each other off the set. I said I thought we ought to tell them this was just a warm, loving friendship that would not turn into a clandestine love affair.

I don't know who talked, but the gossipmongers started writing about us. One item said, "Tense 'Good Mornings' on the McConnell Story set—the Alan Ladds and the Dick Powells are having their problems." A big exposé story was headed LADD, POWELL RIFTS DENIED.

Sue called Richard and said, "Don't you know that Alan is in love with your wife, June?" Richard said, "Isn't everybody?" To demonstrate that there was nothing to the gossip items, the four of us went to Trader Vic's for dinner. Richard was full of his subject—promotional themes for The Conqueror; the kind of man Genghis Khan had been when he set out to conquer the world—and Alan and I were full of our subject—the adventure of filming the great flying ace and the tender love story in his life. Then Sue or somebody brought up the latest divorce story to hit the papers—I think it was Susan Hayward and her custody case involving the twins. There was some cryptic and rather tense talk about how tragic it was for a man and woman to have to fight over children. This led to a general discussion of marriage and Sue said how terrible it was that marriages could break up over an outsider. I should have bitten my tongue but it just popped out—"*I do not believe that anybody can take a husband away from his wife or a wife away from her husband unless they want to go.*" It was like I had thrown a cake of ice onto the table and the ice just sat there the rest of the evening. I think I went home and threw up.

Richard and I were invited to the Ladds' home in Holmby Hills for a Christmas party, and Alan didn't come out of his room. Sue said he wasn't feeling well. So immediately I said, "Oh, can I go in and see him?" Sue said coolly, "No, I don't think so." He didn't come out all evening and I realized it had been a mistake to go there.

Richard and I had a little tiff in a restaurant one night and everyone assumed it was about Alan Ladd. It was about Ellen. Louella Parsons phoned both Richard and me to get our versions of what happened. Under the heading LITTLE SPAT, Louella wrote, "When I reached June, she said: 'Dick and I had a little quarrel, but it certainly had nothing to do with Alan Ladd. Our little quarrel had to do with a small family problem, which will iron itself out very soon.'"

When Louella reached Richard, he was shrewd enough to make sure he got his current film mentioned first—"The only problem I have is to try and find Howard Hughes to show him the finished print of *The Conqueror*. There is also another problem—my daughter Ellen flunked her grades at Westlake School and I have to go and see the dean."

Richard and I were expected to attend Carol Lee's wedding at the Alan Ladds' and I was getting nervous about being there with Sue. There had been so much gossip about Alan and me by now that there was no way I could back out. If I stayed away, there would really be something for the wagging tongues. And what would I tell Richard? I realized Sue was trapped, too, and there was no way she could recall the invitation. It was expected to be the biggest Hollywood wedding of the season, and it was, but unfortunately the marriage would scarcely last out the year.

Alan warned me, "Sue is very jealous of you. Whatever you do, don't look at me while I'm escorting Carol Lee up the aisle or when I come back down the aisle. Because if I see you looking at me, I won't be able to hide my feelings about you."

When Alan walked with Carol Lee to the altar I didn't look up. But during his walk back down the aisle with Sue, I looked up too soon—right into Alan's eyes. The expression on his face tore me apart with its love and conflict. Sue was looking at me too and her look was a stab of steel. I wished that I could get up and run but I knew that this day every move I made was being audited by the guests as well as the press. I managed to get up, smile, make polite conversation, and dance with Richard under the outdoor lanterns.

According to Beverly Linet's biography of Alan Ladd, "Alan couldn't take his eyes off Mrs. June Allyson Powell the entire evening, although he did his best not to be obvious. Sue, of course, noticed. She and June smiled graciously at each other, and Sue resisted the obvious temptation to shove her rival into the swimming pool." Biographer Linet also mentions the quote attributed to Sue which was repeated to me later and which eventually found its way into The Saturday Evening Post. Likening me to a pesky bug, Sue was quoted as saying, "I'd like to drown her in a teaspoon of water."

As soon as I could, I escaped to the safety of home, and if Richard had heard anything, he was kind enough not to say so.

My buddy, Judy Garland, called me to ask, "What's all this I read in the papers about a hot romance between you and Alan

Ladd?" Judy was sympathetic, and the only thing she really wanted to know was "Where do you meet?" I explained to her that this was one love story that was being played out almost exclusively in our dressing rooms at work.

"Does Sue still hang around the set?" Judy wanted to know.

"Well, she didn't for a long time but now she often brings Alan his lunch. Then he always comes over to my dressing room and shares it with me."

Judy warned me of an obvious danger that Alan and I hadn't even thought about—Sue could walk in on us at any time.

Luckily, when Sue did confront me on the set, I was not in Alan's room nor he in mine. When I heard Sue Ladd's high heels clicking in a fast staccato toward my dressing room one day, I was with my secretary, who had brought my lunch in from the ranch. "Oh, my God," the secretary said, looking out the door. "It's Sue Ladd and she's brought a witness."

Sue said, "We have to talk." She was all wound up in her subject, which concerned me and how I was enticing her husband and stealing him away. I tried to assure her that there was nothing sexual and said, "Do you think Richard would stand by for a minute and put up with anything like that?"

I could see that she wasn't impressed. I continued, "Sue, now just hold it! First of all, you must be aware that there has been nothing going on between me and Alan in the physical way you think there has. I love Alan dearly and he loves me dearly and we are friends. And I've already talked to Richard. And I think you are a very lucky lady. You have a man who respects and idolizes you and I think you would be very foolish to spoil it."

I had run out of steam. We stood looking at each other and she said, "Humpf, that isn't the way *I* hear it," and stalked out. Richard received a phone call from Sue that night—"Do you know that right this minute Alan and your wife are in a restaurant having dinner together?"

Richard said calmly, "That's strange because right now I'm sitting and looking at my wife, Sue. Would you like me to put her on?" The conversation ended abruptly.

Now Richard turned to me and said, "Would you like to talk about this, June?" When he said June and not a nickname, I knew it was serious.

"Yes," I said, hesitating. "I guess so."

"Do you love him?"

"Not the way I love you."

Richard said, "You never love two people the same way." There was a pause during which neither of us spoke, and then he continued: "Are you going to walk out on me, June?"

"No. Not if you want me."

"Do you love Alan?" he asked again.

"Yes," I said. "I can't help it but I do. But I'm not having an affair. I mean the kind they're talking about."

"I trust you. Do you love me?"

"You know I do," I said, "only you're always going away without me and you never come home from the office on time and you haven't any time for me."

He was rocking me against his shoulder now. "I know, I know," he said. "But you have to understand that I'm trying to build something for the future and someday we'll have all that time together you're always talking about. And be young enough to enjoy it." He described the ultimate dream house that he was going to build for us at Newport Beach. He would design it and this time I could be completely in charge of the décor.

"That's no problem," I said. "It'll be New England all the way."

"Fine, that's settled," he said, getting up. "Now take my hand." He led me into the bedroom and made love to me until we felt again the same passion for each other that we had felt the first time we made love. "I'm glad you said what you did," he whispered to me when we woke up the next morning in my bedroom. "Just remember, little one, I will never let you go."

A few days later Alan Ladd packed his clothes and moved out of his house. The press didn't know where he was but I knew he was at Rancho Santa Fe.

Alan phoned. "I left home," he said.

"Oh, Alan," I said. "I'm so sad."

"Did you tell Dick we're in love?"

"Yes."

"What did he say?"

"He asked me if I wanted a divorce."

"Oh. And what did he say?"

"I said if there were no Richard Powell and if there were no Sue Ladd, then everything would be different. And if there were no Pammy and Ricky and no Ladd children. Oh, Alan, I said I wouldn't do anything. I hope I haven't hurt you too much."

"Of course not. You've brought a little joy and sunshine. I'll just have to work this out somehow. I hope I haven't hurt you."

"Of course not. And I always will love you in a special way." Soon the gossip columnists were reporting a big reconciliation, with Sue rushing to Santa Fe to join her husband for a second honeymoon.

Sue was telling reporters by phone that the word "divorce" had never been mentioned and it had only been a trial separation. Of this breakup in the Ladd marriage, Beverly Linet says, "Whatever it was, Alan played the role of the repentant husband admirably. . . . But Alan's smile appeared forced in the photographs, and the light, as they say, was gone from his eyes. That once-expressive, vulnerable face was now more a waxen mask. Alan Ladd would never quite look—or be—the same again."

I tried to get over Alan Ladd. I tried to seem as carefree as usual, but a lot of laughter was now gone from my life. I realized *I* would not be the same without him. One day he sent a gift to me. It was a record of "Autumn Leaves." When I missed him now, and that was most of the time, I would closet myself and play it over and over. How, I wondered, would I ever get this gentle and sensitive man out of my system?

After the precious time we stole together while working on *The McConnell Story*, our romance consisted of sometimes hurried, sometimes long and loving phone conversations. It was our only link. On the phone he would speak the three words that echoed in my heart: "I miss you."

"Oh, Alan, I miss you, too," I said. "Please be happy." He promised to try. He was having trouble sleeping again and the old pattern of accidents was back. On his next picture, *Frisco Bay*, he caught his foot on the ropes of a boat and was almost thrown overboard. He was robbed while traveling on the Orient Express—the thief even took his evening clothes. He caught chicken pox and had a serious bout of flu. There were rumors of heavy drinking and a weight problem.

I wanted to scold him over the phone but I restrained myself. It was more important that he hear happy things like "Hey, ah Tony, you fallin' off boat? You wanna send me a pickcha?" When Richard answered the phone, he and Alan would have long conversations and I didn't pry into what was said. Sometimes Richard would be there when I talked to Alan and I would put Richard on and we would have a three-way conversation.

The last time I saw him was at a big party that Grace Kelly threw. Grace was in the reception line with her parents—it was a formal party. She had already met Prince Rainier and would marry him in 1956. Grace made the mistake of seating us at the same table as Lloyd Nolan, mistakenly but understandably assuming that Dick and Lloyd were friends from working on *The Caine Mutiny Court Martial*. Grace didn't know that Richard was in the middle of a bitter battle to reinstate his directing credit for *Caine* and that he had tried to get an injunction to stop Lloyd Nolan and the rest of the cast from opening at the Plymouth Theater in New York. It was not the liveliest table at the party.

Richard had excused himself from our table to escape for a while, leaving me to handle the social amenities. I thought, What am I going to say to get myself in trouble this time? And I could hardly wait for Richard to get back and take over. I said, "Oh, there's Richard," and I swiveled around with a big welcoming smile. Only it wasn't Richard, it was Alan and Sue, obviously heading toward their seats.

My tipsy guardian angel had done it again—it looked like I was expecting Alan and was greeting him. Oh, what a terrible moment. Sue said something to Alan, and he looked a little sick. Without coming a step closer, they turned and walked out of the party and never returned.

Alan still called frequently, usually late at night. Richard would turn off the light and go to sleep and I would sit on the floor of my dressing room and talk to Alan. When I got tired, I'd lie on my stomach, still holding the phone and listening to Alan. He was a lonely, desolate man. We still played the "What If?" game—just dreaming about what it would be like *if*. We both knew it had worked out the way it had to. Nothing else would have been right. He said, "You're lucky to have a man like Richard who is wise and full of understanding."

Time did not make us forget. I missed Alan's calls when I went on location in Europe. Sharman Douglas helped me get over the blues in London with a round of parties, including one where she introduced me to her friend Princess Margaret. I had just completed *Interlude* in Germany with Rossano Brazzi. London was hectic but fun.

Sharman gave a dinner party for me at Les Ambassadeurs. Lawrence Harvey sat next to me and told me he was going to marry Margaret Leighton. The next morning, seeing me off at

Heathrow Airport, Sharman said, "Oh, I hate to see you go." I said, "You don't have to see me go. Get on this plane with me." We laughed at the preposterous idea, but when I said, "Come on, I dare you," Sharman had her passport out of her purse and we were getting on the plane together. As we settled down, I said, "Why don't you take your coat off? Aren't you hot?"

"Very," she said, "but I have only my nightgown on."

I was so glad when my dear friend Carolyn "Sissy" Jones co-starred with Alan in a United Artists' movie, *The Man in a Net*, in 1959. Through her, I could feel closer to Alan. And her husband, Aaron Spelling, became a writer and producer for Alan, just as he had been for Richard. The word on Alan was that he had come down with a painful case of shingles because of his nerves.

I knew that more and more Alan was finding his lovely home in Holmby Hills a depressing place to be, and when it started closing in on him, he fled and phoned us to say he was alone at his ranch in Hidden Valley, Alsulana. It was the night of November 1, 1962, and he spoke a long time with Richard.

He was urging Richard to drive out there. I did not ask whether the invitation included me. All I know is that the conversation went on interminably. The next day came the news that Alan had been found in a pool of his own blood, his gun beside him, a bullet hole next to his heart. He was near death and a .38 caliber bullet would have to be removed.

Richard was beside himself with grief because he had not gone out to Hidden Valley as Alan had begged. Stories were flying thick and fast. Every newspaper edition had a new version: Alan had stumbled over his gun. Alan had heard a burglar and was stalking him.

Eventually Alan would add yet another version. "It was a silly accident. . . . I tripped over one of the dogs in the dark. . . ."

I was so sad and I would have been sadder could I have seen ahead.

12

HOWARD HUGHES had continued to be very important in Richard's life—and in mine, by osmosis. I continued to resent the inordinate amount of time Richard spent away from me in conference with Hughes and working on Hughes' projects, but once I had reason to bless him for saving my Richard's life.

Richard woke up in the middle of the night, telling me he was in great pain. It seemed to be all over his stomach area. And no wonder. His appendix had burst. I called our doctor—who was also Bogie's doctor—and he came immediately and sent for an ambulance.

They operated immediately but gangrene had already set in and they weren't sure they could save him. Paralytic ileitis followed—I believe that's what they called it. Anyway, everything had stopped moving in his intestine and he would soon be dead.

Howard Hughes sent his personal doctor, and Richard went back for corrective surgery. They split him from one end to the other. Again he hovered between life and death. The happiest sound to me was when I put my head down on his tummy and heard a faint gurgling sound.

As soon as he could get back to work, Richard was again patterning himself after the multimillionaire Hughes, savoring the feeling of power—changing lives, discovering and molding new talent and spreading opportunity and wealth wherever he went.

Richard enjoyed building his empire. He gave breaks to many budding actors and beamed with pride as they became rich and famous. Peter Falk gained fame overnight in *The Price of Tomatoes*, a Four Star movie, and Richard put Steve McQueen in *Wanted, Dead or Alive*. He saw the potential of a different-looking face—Telly Savalas—and helped him escape from his chores as news director at ABC by giving him starring roles.

One day Richard showed me some film on David Janssen, who had been a child actor and then had graduated to minor adult roles. Richard said, "That's the guy I'd like to have take over the Richard Diamond role that I used to do on radio."

I said, "Richard, he isn't at all the right type."

So then Richard knew he'd made the right choice. David Janssen did take over and he was brilliant in it.

Richard would say that he had discovered Mary Tyler Moore. He used her voice and legs as the unseen character "Sam." And that got her started.

Richard was helping my old friends keep busy too. Mickey Rooney was still changing marriage partners like a game of musical chairs and consequently had accumulated some alimony problems. Richard showed Mickey in a new dimension as a lonely seaman in *Somebody's Waiting*. Other producers suddenly wanted Mickey's talents, too.

Milton Berle, who didn't need the money, Richard cast as a blackjack dealer in *Doyle Against the House*. And his friend Jack Carson, who usually played only a supporting role as a pest clown, was given the starring role as a beatnik in *Who Killed Julie Greer?*

Richard was gaining a reputation for innovative casting. As for me, I was not rescued from being Goody Two Shoes until José

Ferrer chose me to play his wicked, wicked wife in the movie *The Shrike*, for which I am eternally grateful. A shrike is a bird, and the female of the species preys upon the male and destroys him.

I loved the role and I loved acting with the great Academy Award-winning actor.

We filmed two endings for *The Shrike*. In the original story, the wife gets her husband out of the mental institution by a ruse, and you know he is going to continue to be her victim and that he is doomed.

That ending was shown at sneak previews. The audience was distressed and would not believe that June Allyson could be so cruel.

When the studio first told José Ferrer that he should change the ending, I wanted him to fight and stick by the ending with artistic integrity, but he just laughed and said goodnaturedly, "You can't fight city hall."

So the second ending was filmed showing me reforming and saying at last I understood and was going to make up to my poor husband for all the abuse he has suffered in the past.

And so there I was—back to Goody Two Shoes.

It was Richard who got Kim Novak together with Harry Cohn of Columbia Pictures, who made her a star. He used to tell me, "Junie, I have found a girl who is just like you—same type, same voice." So I looked forward to meeting a girl who was just like me—the girl next door.

In came a creature of loveliness, all blond and misty—and all curves. I told Richard, "If that's another girl next door, I'm the boy next door."

Richard's wheeling and dealing on TV boggled my mind. At one point Four Star was buying the stock ownership of Marterto Productions—which owned, among other things, ninety episodes of Danny Thomas' hit series *Make Room for Daddy*—for $1,800,000. Richard, figuring in his little notebook, assured me that the first $1,300,000 would quickly be earned back in reruns of Danny's show. *Time* magazine called Richard "one of the major—and sharpest—businessmen in U.S. television." Richard was quoted as saying, "I won't be satisfied until we're the biggest—and we will be." *Time* called him "a millionaire many times over."

Richard loved his money games, and his favorite phrase was, "Nobody loses, everybody wins." He liked deals that were advantageous to all concerned, and he liked to involve our friends. He got Len Firestone to take over the distributing of Four Star's series, opening a new office for syndication. He even involved me. "You're one of my new talents, baby," he said to me, grinning. "The public is going to love seeing you every week with your own show."

"Are you crazy, Richard?" I protested. "I can't act in a new movie every week."

"Of course you can't, Junie face. I'm talking about an anthology, with you as the host. I refuse to call you 'hostess,' like in a nightclub. Every week a different story with a different set of actors, but you will introduce it. And when you like a story, you'll be the star of it, now and then. But of course you'll appear in the first segment as the kick-off and of course we'll call it— guess what?—*The June Allyson Show*." I stared at him speechless. "Say something, honey. I've wanted this for you. Are you happy?"

"I'm terrified. Are you sure you want me?"

"Would I put you in it if I wasn't sure you could handle it? Are you happy, Monkeyface?"

"Oh, Richard, you dummy. Now I can be a part of it and have an excuse to go to Four Star to have lunch with you. Of course I'm happy." I grabbed him and kissed him. He put on his tough detective face. "Stick with me kid," he said, "and I'll make you a star yet."

The show, produced by Dupont, was a success. I stuck with it for fifty-seven installments. Many important stars appeared in the plays, which ranged from tear-jerkers to comedy—Ginger Rogers, Bette Davis, Joseph Cotten, Jane Powell. I also used stars I had acted with in movies—David Niven and Rossano Brazzi. The play that excited the most comment was *Silent Panic*, in which Harpo Marx made a rare appearance, playing a deaf mute. He still wouldn't talk on camera.

Richard had his own anthology series and he appeared in every third segment of *The Dick Powell Show*. There were many series at Four Star—*Richard Diamond*, *The David Niven Show*, *Robert Taylor's Detectives*, *The Gertrude Berg Show*, *Dick Powell's Zane Grey Theatre*, *The Rifleman*, *Johnny Ringo*, *Trackdown*, *Stage Seven*, *Hey Jeannie!* and *Wanted—Dead or Alive*.

I could never understand Richard's hunger for money. He made no bones about it. He was always out to turn a profit. If someone liked our house, he would say, "You want to buy it?"

"Don't listen to him," I would quickly interrupt. "He's just trying to be funny."

"It's only funny depending on the offer," Richard said with a wink. If friends even looked like they were taking Richard seriously, I would go into my speech. "I love this house. It is my dream house. I will never move. Period." But Richard was restless at Mandeville Canyon. I could see it coming when he walked out of my bedroom one morning and came dashing back muttering, "Christ, if I ever live in a house where I can go out of my room in my shorts without running into a maid, I'll be goddamn happy."

I will never know why Richard sold Mandeville. Maybe it was just sand in his shoes and he had to move along. The reason he gave me and himself was that he had too much responsibility at Mandeville. "It's interfering with my career. I can't produce and direct and act and wonder what's happening in the barns."

"Get rid of the cattle—get rid of the horses," I said. "Quit the farming and just let it be our home."

"I can't," he said. "It's a tax problem. You wouldn't understand. Believe me, if I do what you say, with sixty-eight acres, the taxes would zoom."

"I thought you were going to sell some land. You talked about a subdivision. Sell the land and we can live in the big house. I'm not moving."

But it seemed I was. All by himself Richard had found a place we were to call Alpine after the street on which it was located in Beverly Hills. It was long and sleek, had lots of glass and I hated it on sight. It broke my heart when Richard sold Mandeville.

"Where can I put my braided rugs?" I wailed.

"You can't," said Richard. "They don't belong in a contemporary home and they'll have to stay at Mandeville."

"Where are my exposed beams?" I wailed again. "I feel closed in. I don't feel natural. I feel like I'm in a prison."

"You'll get adjusted," Richard said, surprised that I did not appreciate the sleek lines, the showcase curved glass enclosing lovely plants, the showcase patio. "Wait till we get all the new contemporary furniture in here. You'll love it."

"Never."

Everything good had to be left behind—not only my beloved rug, which had been specially made and was said to be the largest braided rug in the country. Also left was the old English hunt table in the shape of a horseshoe. And we left most of our comfortable British furniture at Mandeville and started a whole new life with bad feelings.

Now Richard went in for contemporary things to blend with the beige and orange of the living room at Alpine. I had always had a soft-peach bedroom. Now it was a garish yellow. Chintz was a bad word now and printed patterns were gone. Solids were the rule, and straight lines.

I clung to the one soft touch I added which Richard did not

dare throw out of the living room—the crocheted throw that his mother had made. I kept it on the sofa in front of the fireplace. Somehow it softened the effect of that orange rug. (And I have it to this day across the back of the sofa in my family room.)

Richard consoled me. "Don't worry, Junie face, pretty soon you won't have to look at Alpine anymore. I'm finally ready to build our ultimate dream house—the retirement house."

"You're retiring?"

"Not exactly. I can delegate more authority. You know we've been talking about building our forever house on that land at Newport Beach? I am seriously at work on the plans now. I'll show them to you. And we'll sell this house and move to our vacation house at Newport Beach while we supervise construction on the new place."

Where was love? Where was tenderness? Where was Richard? He was never there. He was late. He was sorry but he wouldn't be home early enough—just go ahead and have dinner without him.

"Why? What's the matter, Richard?"

"Oh, trouble at the studio. We're going to have a late story conference. We're ordering in some food." Or he was packing a bag. "Where are you going, Richard? Why didn't you call me?"

"It was unexpected. I'll be back in a couple of days. Just take messages for me. I have a deal to look into in Dallas."

"You don't make movies in Dallas."

"This isn't movies. This is oil."

"Why can't you take me with you? I'm lonely."

"You're needed here. There's so much to do in this house. Or you can read scripts, find something you like."

"I hate scripts. I hate this house. It's a modern museum. It is not a home. I'm not going to be here when you get back— sometime."

He hugged me. "Now, now, honey, be a good girl. Don't

give me any more trouble than I have and I'll take you to Mexico one day." He kissed me and was halfway out the door.

"Yeah, but by that time I'll be in a coffin. You going to hitch it to your car? Hey!" I realized I was shouting at the wall. I wasn't sure that I wanted to be Richard's "third child" anymore. I was tired of having him end arguments by saying, "Go to your room and think it over and come back when you see the light." He was always right and I was always wrong. Women friends thought I was crazy. "You're lucky to have a man who takes care of everything," they'd say.

I didn't think there was any other woman—and still don't—but it was becoming a hollow marriage with love on the run and phone calls destroying every intimate moment.

I deliberately picked fights, knowing how they'd end. "Are you sure you have time between phone calls?" I said one night with nasty sweetness as he marched me along to the bedroom, picking me up and carrying me when I tried to fight him off. I detested telephones. They were ruining my marriage. In every restaurant a phone was automatically brought to Richard's table now. At home, Frank would bring the phone and Richard would wheel and deal through dinner. Sometimes I would get up and stalk to my room. When he hung up he would come and get me. Something snapped when he had a phone installed right at the dining table. "Tacky, tacky," I said.

"I need it," he said. "It's the way I do my work."

"Don't you have an office?"

"I'm trying to accommodate you," he said. "It's your objections to my working at my office that make me bring my office home with me."

"Well, that just makes it right then, doesn't it? You're home but you don't have to talk to me. You talk to the phone."

"I talk to people who have business with me. I don't see why I have to justify it."

"Oh fine, fine—but I don't have to listen to it." In the end he stopped coming and getting me when I'd march to my room during phone conferences. My anger would smolder all evening. The next morning I'd attempt reconciliation in vain.

"Richard," I begged, "let's just get aboard the *Sapphire Sea* and take off for Mexico, like you always promised. How about it? Please? We'll take the kids."

"As usual, Junie, you have picked the worst possible time to be bothering me with vacations. Try me next year. Now I have to go to Europe." I was furious and he wasn't even doing anything to soothe me or kid me out of it. I gulped and said, "If you really intend to be away from home that much, it's silly for us to stay married. I think we should get a divorce."

I couldn't have been more shocked when he agreed with me. I'd only been bluffing, but he said, "If that's what you want." I was sickened by what was happening but powerless to stop it. "I don't even know how to go about it," I said. "What do I do?"

He looked up from his notes and said, "You get yourself a lawyer, of course, and *he* will tell you what to do. I haven't got the time."

I thought, How rude, and silently watched him get up and take his notes with him. "I have to pack. I'm going to Europe with David Niven on Four Star business, so please save your other complaints till I get back."

I thought, We'll see about that. He hadn't even invited me to go along.

The next day I called his office and asked for the name of the best divorce lawyer in town. I'm sure they thought I wanted it for a friend. They told me it was Jerry Ciesler.

I called Giesler's office but couldn't get past the secretary, who wanted to know what I wanted to talk to him about and what my name was. Feeling vulnerable and exposed, I finally said, "Tell him this is Mrs. Dick Powell, the Third, and it is urgent."

In a moment he was on the phone and inviting me to come

and have lunch with him so that we could talk about my problem. I was grateful to him for making it easier for me, and I did indeed tell him in a dignified way that I wanted a divorce, and that Richard seemed not to care one way or the other, having told me to do whatever I wanted.

I was very proud that I hadn't cried. Actually I was in a sort of fog and just went through the motions of signing this and that and answering all kinds of questions. What did I want? he asked. I didn't know. I didn't really know if I wanted anything from Richard. "The children," he said. "What do you want for the children?"

"I don't know," I said, speaking through my fog.

"What did you earn during your years of marriage, and what did Richard earn?"

"I don't know."

"I'm sorry. Let's simplify that. First, what did you, *personally*, earn in your years at MGM?"

"I don't know."

"You don't *know?*" He looked horrified. "*Who* knows?"

"Richard knows. He took care of everything."

"*You* don't know?"

"Well, I remember I started at $125 a week and then it went up to $150 and Richard took over and I never paid much attention, but he got all kinds of raises and I know I was the number one star in the fan magazine polls year after year."

"But that's all you know?"

"Well, he did say that with TV, movies and all, I went over the million-dollar mark a couple of years—maybe that was just one year—but anyway, he said I deserved an extra bag of jelly beans for that."

His lips twitched in what might have passed as a little smile.

"That's very nice, but nobody told you what you were earning?"

"Well, Richard might have told me but I never paid attention because he was investing my money with his and we were going to retire some day and just sail around on our boat—the *Sapphire Sea*, you know."

He sighed and wrote that down. "The *Sapphire Sea*. That's an asset, you know. That could be sold."

"Oh no."

"Why not?"

"Richard couldn't live without his boat."

Jerry Giesler looked at me strangely. "I think I'd just better get in touch with your husband's lawyer and work this out with him. And I presume your husband's office will know where your husband is in Europe to get in touch with him."

"Oh yes," I said. "I have the address somewhere but I can't remember. I think he and David Niven are in France."

Eventually papers were served on Richard in Europe and he sent word through his lawyer that he would not contest the divorce.

I was hardly aware of the property settlement until I saw a cartoon in the paper which showed a husband telling his wife, "I don't know why they're worrying about the national debt. Dick Powell just settled four million dollars on his wife, June Allyson."

That was a slight exaggeration.

By transatlantic phone and in cables, Giesler and Richard had worked out the agreement and Richard signed it somewhere in Europe. I would get two and a half million dollars. The children would, of course, stay with me. But he could see them as often as he wanted.

And suddenly he was flying back from his sojourn. I took the children and went to the airport to greet him. A good actor can avoid showing surprise. Richard was a good actor. I kissed him as if nothing had happened and if anything, I loved him and wanted him a little more than ever. The children clung to his hands. He smiled benignly.

I took him home with me and we locked the bedroom door

and made love half the night. "That's what you'll be missing, little one," he said. The next morning he started packing and throwing things into his car, which he had parked in front of the house in full view of reporters who were stationed outside watching.

"Richard, what are you doing?" I croaked, fighting an urge to run out and carry his things back from the car.

"Can't you see, I'm moving," he said calmly.

"But, Richard, you can't go now!"

"Oh, can't I? This is what you told Jerry Giesler you wanted."

Now I knew. His pride was at stake. He wanted me to back down and plead with him to stay. I would have if he'd made the slightest concession, but he wasn't saying anything would be different in our battered relationship. I clamped my teeth and waited for a signal from him. None came. I went into another room. I rushed back to him. "But, Richard—where will you go?"

"I'm going to Newport Beach. I need a rest." I heard his car drive away and I couldn't believe what I had thrown away. Well, I thought, grabbing at sanity, I'll sure have to keep busy now. I'll go on a self-improvement kick. I'll have my throat operation—get rid of those polyps on my vocal cords. He'll have to come visit me at the hospital.

Jerry Giesler, suffering from a heart condition at Mt. Sinai Hospital, arranged for my divorce trial to be heard January 31, 1961. I was not a good actress in my big courtroom scene. I wanted to help the judge but obviously he was not pleased with me. He kept shaking his head sadly. "Why are you getting this divorce?" he kept asking me. "Did Mr. Powell ever strike you?"

"Oh no, Richard would never do anything like that."

"It doesn't sound to me like you want this divorce. Maybe you'd better think about it." But the die was cast—I said I wanted the divorce because Richard criticized and laughed at me sometimes and because he never came home for dinner, but just stayed endlessly at the office. The newspapers were amused at these quibbles and headlined a story—THE MAN WHO DID NOT COME TO DINNER. Somehow the divorce was granted and I stumbled out of court and tried to drive home, feeling heartsick and brushing away tears.

I had expected Richard to be in the courtroom and shout, "Stop this divorce!" I got into the house and there he sat in front of the fireplace having a snack, his usual sandwich and glass of milk. "Did you get what you wanted? Are you satisfied?"

"What are you doing here? We just got a divorce."

"No, you did not. You just got an interlocutory decree. That means—he paused and stood up—"according to the law, you have to wait a year before you remarry. But should you cohabit with your spouse—he paused again and I was beginning to blush—"the divorce is null and void—which I believe is about to happen to yours."

And suddenly life was very sweet again. Or was it? I had hoped he would stay with me after we made love, but he was rising from the bed and getting dressed, ready to leave again.

I said, "Richard, what are you doing? Where are you going?"

"Back to my house," he said. "Trust me. We'd be the laughingstock of Hollywood if we went back together so quickly. When the time is right, we'll call a press conference and announce our big reconciliation."

"Oh my God," I said. "What a crazy idea."

"No crazier than your crazy divorce. But meanwhile"—and he leered at me—"we can have this liaison and you can play the role of my fallen woman."

And that's the way it was. He spent as much time as he wanted at the house. After all, a man must see his children.

We did not tell the press immediately that we were back

together. There would be time enough during the course of a year's interlocutory decree. And just maybe he wanted to draw out the lesson to me a little bit longer. But finally he called a press conference in his suite of offices at Republic Studios. Richard had switched there after Howard Hughes had sold RKO to General Tire, and RKO was now known as RKO General.

We sat facing the reporters, holding hands and acting like newlyweds. I was sporting a new diamond ring and new diamond pendant, both of which, Richard volunteered, added up to about four carats.

"But what brought you together again?" the reporters demanded.

"Well, it was a divorce that never should have happened," I said, and Richard nodded.

"But what made you see the light?"

"The children," I said. "They kept telling us we were both idiots." And again Richard nodded his agreement.

"But what finally did it?"

"Look," said Richard. "I'll tell you the real truth. You might say it was June's stew that had something to do with it. She's a lousy cook otherwise, but she does know how to cook a great stew."

It was altogether a most satisfactory press conference.

And then there was the second honeymoon—with the family.

I am so happy that Richard got to go on the trip he had dreamed of—on his own boat, surrounded by those he loved, visiting all the primitive little villages along the Mexican coast. And unaware of approaching tragedy. Had we waited to go on this trip, it would have been too late.

13

RICHARD WAS BASICALLY healthy—very healthy—but when he got sick, it was like a giant redwood falling. Once he had penicillin poisoning and almost died of it.

He was on his way to Cuba, where he was shooting a movie, and had stopped overnight in New York to take care of studio business and catch a new play. He had a bad cold, so before going to the Broadway show, he stopped at a doctor's office and was given an inhalation of penicillin.

As Richard described it to me later, his lower lip felt strange during the course of the play and he looked down. To his horror, he could see the lip had ballooned up. Then his whole face felt a little strange.

It had started to swell, too. Eventually his whole body ballooned.

He was at the hospital in Cuba and then in L.A. for weeks before they got the poisoning under control. He had been brought back on a stretcher. I would sit with him every day, making small talk and funny comments to show I wasn't worried. Later the doctors said it was the worst case of penicillin poisoning they had ever seen. They warned me never, never to let him eat blue cheese or anything with mold.

Richard and I were in New York, where he was doing a show, and suddenly his face started swelling. We thought it was penicillin poisoning and rushed back to his California doctors. But it wasn't a reaction to mold this time. It was cancer of the lymph glands in the neck.

I had to get him bigger and bigger shirt neck sizes as he fought what he nicknamed "the Golden C," the C standing for cancer. Others had licked the Golden C.

He thought he would lick it. He never let on that he thought it was terminal. He may not have known. Around my birthday in early October 1962, the doctors told me there was no hope because the cancer was spreading to too many places.

I told the doctors not to tell Richard but just to let me make life as normal as possible. Unfortunately the cancer had been discovered by the doctors just as Richard was finally going to sell the Alpine house and build our ultimate retirement home. We were to live in our vacation house at Newport Beach while Richard supervised the construction. He had house plans scattered around everywhere.

Morgan Maree came to me and said, "June, Dick is selling the house. Don't you think, in view of the fact he's been diagnosed to have cancer, we ought to stop him?"

"Oh no!" I said. "If we stop him, he'll think it's serious. Anything he wants to do. If he wants to go on a trip to the moon, we have to let him. We can't act worried."

He had already signed the papers to sell when doctors came to see me and said, "June, you can't move him."

I said, "Yes, I can." I told them Richard had already signed the papers and the house was sold.

"Where are you going to move him?"

"I don't know. He's planning on moving to our house at Newport Beach. It's on Lido Isle, across a bridge from the mainland."

"It's too far from his doctors and medical facilities. He can't go." They convinced me it would be better for me to tell Richard I didn't want to move until he was completely cured and then to go see the lady who had bought the house and let her in on the truth.

I told the doctors I would see her but that I wouldn't let Richard know, and maybe she could say she wanted to wait for some reason or other before moving in. Then he wouldn't think it had anything to do with *his* health. She refused, even when I offered to lease her another house or pay for her hotel bill indefinitely.

Now I really had to find a place to move to and quickly. I asked a few friends to help me hunt. Eva Gabor, bless her, overwhelmed me totally when she said she wanted to move out of her house so we could move in.

Tempting as it was, I couldn't let her do it. Anyway, Richard would have been suspicious of such an extreme act of kindness. He'd have seen right through it.

As it was, he was busy and cheerful, even in bed, looking forward to the move that would bring him closer to his retirement house. He even remembered to have me drive him to his dentist to keep an appointment to have his teeth cleaned.

Someone finally found a place for us—in the Marie Antoinette apartments in Beverly Hills between Brentwood and Wilshire. When Richard moved there, it was by ambulance—without siren. Now the news of his illness could no longer be suppressed and the apartment was full of friends, many of whom stopped in almost every day—the Bergens, the Firestones, the Justin Darts. Republican buddies were there—Richard Nixon and Ronnie Reagan. Ronnie told Richard he'd at last become a *conservative* Republican and Richard still threw a few barbs at his old friend, saying, "I'm still not sure about you."

Jimmy Cagney dropped in, and Jack Benny and Richard's good buddy George Burns, still with a cigar. Richard looked at the cigar and said, "What's the matter? You're not puffing very fast—you have to buy your own lately?" George Murphy came, and Eva and Zsa Zsa Gabor. Joan Blondell brought food to tempt Richard and I was just sorry this was something no chicken soup on earth could help. Joan was a standout in the crowd of people who kept Richard company during the long days and nights. Once she stood talking to Norman, her son, whom Richard loved so deeply. Joan sobbed and said, "I should never have divorced Dick." The words cut like a knife.

In the last days, Richard and I grew very close. For hours I sat beside his bed talking and laughing and keeping him company—and afterward I realized every word had been spoken except one—death. We went over our lives together and I confessed that it had hurt all these years to be considered the heavy in his breakup with Joan Blondell. "Even though I had a crush on you, I didn't think I was taking you away from anybody."

"You weren't," he said. "I was a chump. Joan came home with a fur coat and she said Mike Todd gave it to her because he couldn't afford to pay her a salary. Eventually I realized what was going on and she admitted she was living with Mike."

"Thanks for telling me, darling," I said. "I wouldn't trade a hundred fur coats for you."

Richard grinned, "Well, at least one woman traded me for one."

His nightmarish involvement with The Caine Mutiny was on his mind to the end. He no longer cared that he hadn't received credit—he was content to have directed a Broadway smash. He found Henry Fonda the strangest man he'd ever worked with. Richard said, "Hank's a moody guy—the kind you could live with in a house for six months without speaking." But when Hank Fonda did speak he was certainly forceful. He once threatened to quit the play and go back to New York if Richard did not go along with his decision on how he wanted two minor characters to handle their dialogue with him. Richard saw the humor of the minor characters' scenes and Fonda didn't. Richard gave in because Fonda was the top star. But even on his deathbed, Richard was chuckling because he had been proven right and the laughs had come just where he had predicted, in spite of Henry Fonda getting his own way.

We reminisced about Marilyn Monroe and how we'd been floored, both of us, the day that Marilyn, then a young starlet, an unknown, had arrived, wiggling, on the *Right Cross* set, and how neither of us had predicted she'd be a star. We recalled Uncle Ike, Dwight D. Eisenhower, and the fun we'd had with him at Palm Springs, and how we'd stay at Firecliff, which the Firestones owned, not too far from Uncle Ike's house. How cheerful the Eisenhower house always looked with Mamie's chintzes. Later, Mamie would worry about me because I had lost weight, and once she insisted I go along with her to Maine Chance, where she was going to shape up and reduce a little. All the heavy ladies had kidded me for going there to fatten up when they had to diet. They'd watch me and drool as I ate as much as I could of my special diet of fattening foods while they ate carrot sticks—it was the joke of the spa.

Richard told me with pride that Franklin D. Roosevelt had once called him to the White House and they had had a meeting in the famous Oval Office. Dick didn't go along with his politics, but he fell in love with FDR as a man. FDR seemed to know every picture Richard had been in and must have read files on Richard because he knew every detail of his life.

Pammy and her daddy also shared happy memories. They talked of the motor trip they had taken all by themselves through Germany in 1957 while I worked on *Interlude* with Rossano Brazzi.

"Kiddo, Junie face, this time you're going to have the best dressing room yet," Richard said, thinking of the retirement house. "And of course, that sunken tub you talked about. What style are you going to decorate it in?"

"You know. I told you a thousand times. Strictly New England. And I want all my braided rugs back."

"Yes, pet." I could see him start to grimace with pain and I quickly went for the nurse to give him a shot. Once, Richard and I and the nurse were getting ready to go to the boat at Newport Beach when Joan Blondell drove up and parked across the street. She had brought many containers of food she had cooked.

It was a thoughtful thing to do but I couldn't appreciate it. Richard was already in the station wagon and Joan started putting the stuff in the back, calling cheerfully, "Dick, wait till you taste this! Remember when I made it for you—how much you loved it?" And then she went to the side of the car and they started to talk. It was one of Richard's more lucid days. I couldn't stand it. I suddenly turned and walked to the corner. I resented what was happening and thought of how I didn't want to give up one minute of precious time with my husband. I marched back and when Joan saw the look on my face, she headed for her car without speaking again.

Slowly, Richard became less mobile. Morphine was needed now or the pain would be constant. Finally, he was receiving morphine every two hours. I couldn't eat, though people tried to force me to, and once I stepped on the scales and saw that I had dropped below ninety pounds. It didn't matter. Nothing mattered now except taking good care of Richard.

Richard still loved his boat and still had to see her. We used the station wagon so he could lie down in back. A nurse was with us and sometimes we had to pull over to the side of the highway so she could give him a shot for pain.

At the dock, he would pull himself up and go aboard and just sit looking at the water. Once he casually said to his nurse, but so I would hear, "When I'm dead someday, I'm going to have my ashes scattered in that water and be a part of the sea."

He didn't look at me and I didn't look at him and I just kept smiling. "Yeah, a hundred years from now," I said.

Richard still looked at Howard Hughes as his benefactor right to his very death. Once on board the *Sapphire Sea*, he reminisced about Hughes and how his strange hobby was playing God. Hughes, he said, got his kicks by being the invisible force who can make miraculous things happen. Richard told me something that he had learned from Hughes' doctor, who had saved Richard's life when he had appendicitis. Hughes had read about a little girl hovering near death from a terrible accident, and he had anonymously gotten her the best medical care and paid for everything.

"Didn't he want to meet the little girl when she got well—did she get well?"

"Yeah, she got well. He didn't bother to see her—does God summon people for a visit after *He's* made them well?"

In my heart, I prayed that the real God would make Richard well and not call him in for a visit. He looked so weak as he sat on a deck chair, absorbing the sun.

One day he was in a big hurry to get to the boat and said, "Can't you drive a little faster?" He was afraid he would miss seeing the opening of the Dodgers game on shipboard television, and I thought, That's a good sign—he's still interested.

But then he started to fade away before my eyes and he would have lucid moments interspersed with confused states and periods of coma. He would hallucinate. Once he said, "June, how many times have I told you to get Bette Davis' clothes off the foot of the bed." I went through the motions of taking clothes off the bed and he was satisfied.

One morning Ricky came in to tell his father good morning.

Richard said with annoyance, "Son, how many times have I told you when you go out to play tennis, take just one racket and one can of balls."

Ricky said, "I'm sorry, Dad, I'll take them back," and left the room. He was not carrying any rackets or tennis balls.

I comforted Ricky, who was just turning twelve, on Christmas Eve, and explained about the effects of morphine. And that his father wasn't really angry.

Cancer was not a gradual thing with Richard. It was a plummeting that spanned only a matter of months. He dropped halfway, seemed to stabilize—and then he plummeted the rest of the way. His last Christmas showed his true nobility. He insisted that we have a perfectly normal holiday. He was so weak but so game. I wrapped presents and made the children deliver them and on Christmas we opened presents for Richard, knowing he would never use them. But he sounded like he thought he would—and had a lifetime ahead in that house he was going to build just as soon as he licked the Big C.

He was pleased that I had found some gifts he could use and not my usual wild ties. I had found gadgets to make it easier for him to read, by holding books and papers for him. And things to make his sickroom more cheerful.

Curt Jurgens sent an appropriate gift. An exquisite pillbox with a card telling Richard he was sorry to hear he was ill.

Once, during the holidays, Joan Blondell came in all dressed to the teeth on her way to a party and only stayed long enough to say hello to Richard and hover over him for a minute.

Richard held out and saw us into the New Year.

And then the last day, January 2, 1963, the doctor said to me, "It's about over," and I didn't believe him. Richard had been in a coma but seemed to be coming out of it. I had on a sweater and I was sitting on the bed, cradling his head against my shoulder and he was hanging on to my sweater.

I was suddenly angry because I wasn't alone with Richard. I was aware of a roomful of people. And I looked at the foot of the bed and there were a lot of people standing all around there, too—I didn't even know who. And someone's hands were holding on to the foot of the bed.

I followed the hands up and it was Ellen. She was standing there not making a sound, and her face was wet with tears. I looked up at her and it was like my heart just shattered for the three of us. It was as if we three were alone—Ellen, Richard and I, bound together by her silent tears.

Richard opened his eyes, the most beautiful eyes I had ever seen, and I moved him a little so I could look down into those eyes. He took a deep breath and said, "I'm sorry. Oh, I'm so sorry." And he took another deep breath and was gone. I didn't believe it.

I was desperate to have everyone leave us alone. Why couldn't we be alone? Why were all those people there?

I looked at the foot of the bed again and Ellen was still standing there and not making a sound and silent tears were streaming down her face and I melted for her. But why was she crying? I realized that Arthur, my medical brother, kept pulling the sheet over Richard's face and I was pulling it back down.

I kept saying, "Don't do that. He can't breathe with that over his face."

Then I realized I was standing up and hugging Richard's bedroom slippers and people were talking to me but I wasn't registering. A little later, Pammy was tugging at me and moving me this way and that and saying, "Mother, come with me, you simply have to eat something. Mother, look at me. When did you eat last?"

Something out of the corner of my eye caught my attention and I turned from Pammy's grasp just enough to realize white-clad attendants were carrying Richard's body away. Suddenly I was rising above my own pain and seeing it from Pammy's standpoint. She was just fourteen and she was trying to shield me.

I hugged her but I still did not cry. And then I realized everyone was gathered around the dining room table and there seemed to be some sort of conference going on.

I stood behind them as they started to talk about the funeral arrangements—this must be done and that must be done. Suddenly they were involving me and were asking me what hymns I'd like played and everyone was talking at once, making suggestions.

Hymns?

What was I doing? Suddenly I heard myself shout, "Wait a minute. Hold it. *Everybody shut up.*" And they were so shocked, they did. I said, "Nobody in this room knows Richard the way I knew him. He hated hymns. Yes, he did. He sang them to earn money and then he never sang them again."

I realized everyone was shocked but I charged on. "Do you know what I want? This is for Richard and nobody else and I want them to play every song that Richard sang in his career—the songs he loved—and I don't want any eulogies, any fancy words said about Richard. He would have hated that."

I looked around and realized my audience was in a state of shock. But I still had one little thing to say and I said it. "Richard tried and he lived the best way he could with the Lord's Prayer and the Ten Commandments and that was all he lived by and that was his religion. And that's all I want."

I shut up then. Some of them looked at me sheepishly and tried to explain that it couldn't be done that way and it would be sacrilegious to play popular music in church. It wouldn't be allowed.

By now I was exhausted, and it was Andy Maree, the son of Morgan, Richard's friend and financial manager, who jumped up and put his arm around me and said, "This is what she wants and this is what she's getting and I'll see about the special permission from the church."

Funeral day found me dry-eyed and frozen-faced as I was led gently but firmly from place to place only half comprehending, half responding. The sunlight was blinding. It seemed that half of Hollywood was converging on the chapel of the All Saints Episcopal Church in Beverly Hills. Did I want to duck in a side door and avoid the crowd, I was asked. "No," I said. "I just want to be like anyone else."

I was surrounded by those who had loved my husband and some who wanted me just to know they were there if I needed them—Jimmy Stewart, Jack Benny, George Murphy, George Burns, Danny Thomas, Buddy Rogers—and Edgar Bergen, who sobbed so loudly behind me that his wife had to comfort him. Ronnie Reagan was there—he had taken over Richard's TV chores, introducing *The Dick Powell Show* "until you get well," as he would tell Richard. Jane Wyman, with her soft sympathetic eyes, was there. Jimmy Cagney tried to give me a "hang in there, kid" signal. Richard Nixon was there as an honorary pallbearer and with him was Pat, whose eyes expressed sadness and concern. Joan Blondell arrived alone, her eyes red from crying. Now neither of us had him. He belonged to God.

One friend of Richard's who could not be there was Jack Carson, who lived down the hill from us at Mandeville Canyon. Terminally ill, he had died within five minutes of Richard.

Now I was hanging on to the hands of my children, one on each side, dimly conscious of family and friends and the hundreds who stood outside listening to the service on the loudspeaker. Richard's brothers were there—Luther, who had come from Rio de Janeiro, where he represented the International Harvester Company—and Howard from Chicago, where he was vice president of the Illinois Central Railroad. We hugged and comforted each other, but during the ceremony, I hardly looked to the right or left but held tight to Pam and Ricky and kept my eyes glued to the cross. Pammy whispered softly, "Maybe God needed him for a special job." It should have been a comforting thought but I hated God for taking Richard before he had seen his children grow up.

All through the service, they played Richard's songs—"I Only Have Eyes for You," "42nd Street," and "Hollywood Hotel," ending with "Don't Give Up the Ship."

When the organ started playing "Don't Give Up the Ship," I heard a man's racking sobs and it was Johnny Green. He had fallen apart like a little boy, and Bonnie was trying to console him. I couldn't talk as they led me away and took me to the Bergens' house. There I sat dry-eyed on the floor in front of the fire listening to the sounds of voices.

Before Edgar Bergen was to die, he would specify in his will that he wanted his service to be "like my buddy's, Dick Powell's," and Frances would tell me she had tried to have everything like Richard's service.

Jane Dart came up to me where I was sitting and staring into the fireplace, and the next thing I knew, Jane had me on my feet and I was being bundled into the Darts' private airplane with Pammy, Rick, Jane, and Justin and heading for Palm Springs.

And still I did not cry. And right from the beginning, Jane and Justin got me out on the golf course and made me keep going. I was standing around in a daze on the greens and Roz Russell came over and put her arms around me and said, "June, dear, you are a wonderful, brave woman."

And then she was gone. I said to Jane, "Isn't that like Roz, trying to make me better than I am. I'm not brave. I have no choice. I don't even know what I'm doing or why I exist anymore."

I thought of the telegram I had gotten from Lauren Bacall and of all the condolence cards and messages I had received, that telegram said it best. I had it in my purse and carried it for a long time. It was only three words long:

TERRIBLE, TERRIBLE, TERRIBLE.

IV

THE TUNNEL

14

Andy Maree called me and he said, "Are you ready?"

He didn't have to tell me for what—I knew. It was pouring rain, and buckets of tears were coming from heaven. We got into a big limousine with Richard's urn. The place for Richard's ashes to be placed was so high, it took a ladder to reach. But it was comforting to know that Richard's niche at Forest Lawn was in the special area reserved for those who had contributed most to the film industry.

I insisted on being the one to climb the ladder and put the urn with its precious contents in place. "You know, Richard isn't going to like this," I said. "He wanted to be scattered over the ocean where he was the happiest, but they say it's against the law. Isn't that silly? Maybe I should have done it anyway."

"I'm sure he understands you're doing what you think is best."

"I know, but if it had been me instead of him, he wouldn't have listened to anybody. He was such a fighter."

"You're a pretty good fighter, too."

"Oh, Richard, this is so terrible. I miss you." I was placing the urn in the niche and then I ran my fingers in farewell over

the words I had had inscribed under his name below the niche—
GOD IS LOVE. So many images were flashing through my mind. I
remembered how Richard and I had laughed when Gloria
DeHaven had told us what she wanted on her tombstone: HERE
LIES GLORIA DEHAVEN—BUT NOTHING'S DEFINITE.

Morgan Maree, the tough guy in business dealings, had simply fallen apart. His son had taken over with some of the same
strength and tenderness. I leaned on him all through those
unbearable days.

I hadn't cried when Richard died. I hadn't cried at his funeral. Then I cried for eight years. Ricky would find me crying
and say, "Mom, he doesn't hurt anymore." He tried to comfort
me. At twelve, he was the man of the house and he tried to come
up with the right words. I found a letter Ricky had written to his
father, after Richard had been dead only a few weeks.

. . . and once I said come back to me Dad and I'll do
everything you mentioned.

And when you were sick I prayed for you every second
of the day. I loved everything you gave me for my birthday
and Christmas. I've got your swivel chair now that you had
in your office at the studio. And most of all I love you Dad,
and you know that blackboard that you had in your room? I
have that too Dad. Dad I still love you. You were suffering
a lot and I think you're better off in a way because you
don't hurt any more. You're better off but it's our sor-
row.

Everybody misses you very much. Even Bumply does,
you know. It is vacant in the house because instead of setting 4 places for dinner we set 3 places. It is so lonely without Dad. And it just is. I don't know why but it is. Dad
knows how we feel about him going away. We can't touch
him or do anything else that we have done in the past 58
years but we have appreciated everything he's done

. . . but when I go into his room to kiss Dad he isn't there any more to kiss or to hold his hand and to hear him sing the wonderful tunes.

Ah, the word "appreciate." How Richard would have liked seeing that. I cried buckets. One "tune" Ricky was referring to was a little song Richard had written for Pammy just the year before and had recorded—"The Wonderful Teens"—after she turned thirteen. It had become a family favorite. I cried when I found a little box Richard had kept through the years. It was filled with collars and cuffs that had been cut off shirts. He had obviously been saving them to put on other shirts if his fortunes changed—downward.

The world was ugly without Richard. I didn't know how ugly it would get. I had been a princess and didn't know it. I had been championed by a prince and didn't know it. It had been a storybook and the book was closed. Betty Bacall was right. I saw her after Bogie died and she said, "I'm learning a lot and I guess the main thing I've learned is, when your husband dies, you go too."

Richard had drawn up his last will and testament on October 9, 1959. I winced as I realized that while I had been complaining and bitching about Richard's lack of attention and threatening divorce, he had been calmly arranging for my future. I felt sick. If only I could bring him back for just five minutes to say I was sorry and that I understood.

I would never be hungry, that was sure.

A. Morgan Maree, Jr., was named executor and trustee. The will gave me all personal effects outright plus my share of the community property. Also half of all other property and directed that a trust fund be set up for my benefit.

There was also a trust fund for Pamela and Richard and a codicil had been added giving Norman and Ellen, the children born to Joan Blondell, each a sizable number of shares of stock in the Four Star Television Corporation.

Richard had thought of everything, even that if Pammy and Rick ever needed a guardian other than me, they would be put in the custody of Edgar and Frances Bergen. But there were two names he did not even mention in the will—it was as if they had never been—Joan Blondell and Mildred Maund.

Now, for the first time, I saw how busy Richard had been building an empire and providing for the future of his family. There were oil wells and blocks of business property and plain undeveloped land, and cattle and stocks and bonds, and Four Star and other production companies. And now, for the first time, I saw what I had earned from my movies and what he had done to make the money grow.

There was a lesson for Pam and Rick in the will. Richard did not want them to grow up as spoiled rich kids with a big allowance to live on. He wanted them to earn their own way until they finally inherited their money. I could almost hear him telling me again, "Give a man charity and he comes back for more. Give a man a shovel and he earns his own living."

When the will was made public, Hedda Hopper took Richard to task, even in death, for not leaving money to motion picture charities. Something snapped. How dare she tell him what to do with his money after he had provided thousands of jobs and given to charities and helped countless numbers of people while he was alive.

I picked up the phone and got her on the line. She did not get a chance to say a word. It just poured out of me as I told her what I thought of her.

Finally, I stopped for breath and she got a chance to break in. She said just three words: "You're a bitch."

In my sweetest voice, I said, "Yes, I know," and hung up.

In May, when I was still raw with pain, there were the

Emmy Awards and I was told that it was important for me to be there because Dick Powell was to receive a posthumous award for his contribution to the art of television filming—"In grateful remembrance . . ." I was asked to be ready to rise and accept the Emmy.

The Four Star partners had a meeting and decided it would be bad for me to give the acceptance speech. I would sit at the table and they would do it. A photo was taken of the moment when the Emmy was brought to the table and handed to me. I was so emotional that I was not aware of what was happening until I saw the photograph on the front page of the newspaper the next day. I was leaning my forehead against the statuette and large teardrops were rolling down my cheeks.

My escort that evening was a medical man who was divorced from a well-known movie star. Someone had thought it would be nice to get us together. He was very nice indeed and it was comforting to be with him that evening. Another evening, he took me to a restaurant and suddenly his ex-wife entered and walked by angrily, with head held high and without even a hello.

I thought, So this is what it's like in the single world, and I didn't like it.

Four Star was trying to fill the void left by Richard's death and was holding business meetings, which I attended. I insisted that Aaron Spelling be given the reins of Four Star after Richard died—not just because he was a friend but because he was so talented. I felt the current management would let the studio run downhill but that Aaron, with his fresh ideas, could save it and keep it growing. I was voted down and what I predicted happened. I saw disaster ahead and sold my stock.

Now that I was a young widow I concentrated on my children. I was never going to do another movie, I told myself. I was just going to be a good mother—the kind Richard would have been proud of.

Richard. His shadow was everywhere, and to get away from

the apartment with its sad memories and hospital bed, we rented Betty Hutton's former home. How happy I had been to follow in her footsteps onstage in New York, and how sad I was to be following her now. I felt that I was also following her into obscurity. Betty had left Paramount in 1952 after her greatest triumph, The Greatest Show on Earth—and a tremendous screen career was virtually at an end.

I was not happy in Betty Hutton's house. Her bad luck seemed to be rubbing off on me. She had appeared in only one minor movie and gone into an eclipse. She filed for bankruptcy and, all alone, divorced and penniless, tried to fight her drinking problem.

I was seeking solace now and then in a few glasses of wine myself. John Wayne tried to look after me a bit. He invited me to go along on cruises on his yacht, The Blue Goose. I did go once but it was too soon after Richard and I was not a good guest. I did love John, however, for his big heart.

Ricky was fond of John Wayne, too, and one Christmas Rick and a friend decorated The Blue Goose for the annual Christmas Parade of Boats in the harbor at Newport Beach. They did it all in blue lights and it was beautiful.

Judy Garland tried to take me under her wing, phoning me and trying to keep me from brooding. "I know how you feel but you must get out of the house," she kept telling me.

"Where should I go? What should I do?"

"Go anywhere. Do anything. Just get out. Come over here."

"I have to take care of the children."

"Be on my TV program. Come be my guest."

"Don't hurry me. I'll think about it."

"I'm penciling you in," Judy said. "You'll live. Just hang in there, Junie. I love you."

"I love you, too, Judy, even if you don't like the way I sing."

"I like the way you sing. I like it so much I'm going to let you sing on my program. In front of the grown-ups and everybody."

"Shwell, Judy," I said in my best Humphrey Bogart imitation. "Just shwell."

And soon it was a party Judy was insisting I come to. She phoned to say the invitation would be in the mail, but she was not giving me a chance to pretend I hadn't received it.

"I can't go to parties," I said. "It's too soon. Richard's only been gone a little while."

"Five months," Judy said, "and it's my birthday. You have to come. I need you. And Richard wouldn't want you to just quit living. Would he?"

"I don't know. I don't even know who to ask."

"Silly girl, what are agents for? Ask your agent."

So I asked Stan Kamen, who had become my agent after Johnny Hyde—Marilyn Monroe's boyfriend—died. But somehow, in my confused state, I had mentioned my dilemma to two other men as well and I ended up with three escorts sitting in the living room glaring at each other. I called Judy and she said, "Bring 'em all. Bring the army, but just get out of the house!"

Everyone made a fuss over me at the party, and if they noticed I had too many escorts in tow, they were nice enough not to comment. It was lovely, from my standpoint, with three men dancing attendance.

I sank back into my tunnel for a few months but surfaced at La Scala, feeling miserable as I tried to eat dinner. Judy Garland spotted me and came over. After a big greeting she said, "Why don't you do my show like I asked you to? What's your latest excuse?"

I couldn't come come up with one instantly so she started scribbling down the address and time for me to meet her the next day. "We'll have a staff meeting and figure out what songs to sing. Be there," she said, stuffing the note in my purse.

I watched her walk away, thinking how surprised she would be if she knew how wretched I felt. But I did show up and it was a lovely respite from my personal grief.

October 27, 1963—I was on the set with Judy and Steve Lawrence and Jerry Van Dyke, her other guests of the night, hamming it up and having a wonderful time. Mel Torme, who was on her staff, also joined in.

We did medleys and duets that included all our old triumphs and favorites like "Cleopatterrer," "Till the Clouds Roll By," "Thou Swell," and "Look for the Silver Lining."

Mel Torme was her musical director and Judy and I had a secret. We giggled like the MGM brats we used to be so long ago. Judy had found out it was Mel's birthday and so had a huge birthday cake prepared. After the show, Judy and I both came out carrying the cake. The audience was still there. Mel Torme was amazed and showing his delighted surprise when we lifted the cake and pushed it right into his face, laughing hysterically.

Mel did not think it was funny. Years later in his book about Judy, he said we had both been drunk. Wrong!

How I wish I could bring back that night—Judy and I laughing all the way as we skipped along her Yellow Brick Road. CBS had really done it. They had put down a Yellow Brick Road between the stage and Judy's dressing room. And not just a straight line.

We did drink some that night but it was after the show. I don't drink before I work, and I didn't see Judy drink anything until after the show, either. Judy and I drank wine. She had some Blue Nun Liebfraumilch in her dressing room and said this was her favorite. Judy Garland was not much of a drinker, in fact, and neither was I. It didn't take much to get either of us high—Judy was already on pills and I'm allergic to liquor.

In her dressing room she told me that she was separating from Sid Luft. "I'm happy again, Junie—I'm dating my dream man, Glenn Ford. I've had a crush on him ever since he man-handled Rita in *Gilda*. I was so thrilled when Glenn finally noticed me."

"Remember Ty Power," I said. "He was your first Holly-wood crush."

"Yeah," she said. "The nerve. Mayer as usual ruined it. He called me in and told me I had to stop seeing Ty because he was dating all the big, sophisticated glamour girls around Hollywood and he called Tyrone in and told him he had to stop dating me because I was jail bait. Who knows how wonderful life would have been if I had married him? Anyway, I was seventeen, for goodness sakes." She laughed, then paused in reverie. Then she laughed again and said, "Oh God, I can't believe it all happened. And now there's Glenn Ford. He's so concerned and so nice. It's like a second chance."

By the time Judy's divorce from Sid Luft went to trial, Glenn Ford was out of the picture and she was dating Mark Herron, who had acted in a Fellini film. Luft brought the names of both Glenn Ford and Mark Herron into the divorce proceeding. Judy Garland's life and my life were going downhill fast at the same time.

I, too, had jumped into a bad marriage. Unable to cope with loneliness, I had married before 1963 was over.

I managed to get through the New Year and pass January 2, 1964, the first anniversary of Richard's death. Before the month was over came news of Alan Ladd's death. It was somehow my last tie with the good life. When I cried now, I cried alone.

Alan had been alone, too. He went to his hideaway in Palm Springs, January 28, 1964. Only his butler was there. Alan felt so depressed that he sent for a doctor, who gave him a vitamin shot. The next morning his butler served him breakfast in bed and Alan said he was going to take a nap and did not want to be disturbed, no matter what happened. About 3 or 4 P.M., when

Alan still hadn't emerged from the bedroom, the butler went in and found him dead. He was still in bed, wearing his pajamas and a robe.

The year before, when Alan had gotten the news of Richard's death, he'd refused to eat for days. He wrote me a note and proceeded to drink himself into temporary oblivion, despite Sue's efforts to keep him sober. What did he die of? *The Biographical Dictionary of Film* states, "As he grew older, his face puffed up . . . and he developed an alcohol problem. In 1962, he tried to kill himself and after a last memorable performance—as the cowboy movie star in *The Carpetbaggers*—he died as a result of alcohol and sedative poisoning."

I did not go to Alan's funeral. I was torn apart with my private grief but I did not feel it would be right to go. Why stir up the Ladd family and the gossip columnists? I cried as I read that a letter young David Ladd had written to his father had been placed in Alan's casket. I got out the letter Ricky had written to his father after Richard had died and read it again.

It was now all long ago and far away and at least we had not disrupted our families. Both sets of children had had more or less serene and secure family lives until the passing of their fathers, just one year apart.

Now my own life fell apart. I drank, and that, along with a string of nervous breakdowns and my bad rebound marriage, almost finished me off. My husband and I fought constantly and I wanted to die but I was too much of a coward to commit suicide. I waited for the wine to do it for me. If you drink and you don't eat, you will die, doctors kept telling me. It was good news.

It is painful to talk about that marriage even now, almost twenty years later. My life during this period seemed to be written in headlines: JUNE ALLYSON'S BRIEF MARRIAGE AT AN END. That was the first headline after only ten months of marriage. Then came many more including JUNE ALLYSON DELAYS DIVORCE and DISTURBING PEACE CASE DISMISSED and ALLYSON AND EX-MATE MARRY AGAIN.

I am looking at a thick stack of legal papers and I can hardly believe it happened. Things became so hectic between the first marriage and the last divorce action, I still cannot believe it was me. I left him. I took him back. I started divorce proceedings. I dropped the proceedings. I did it again. I got the divorce. I remarried him. I left him. I was so confused, so unhappy, so fearful of being alone. I went back. And more and more, I sought relief in wine.

My brother, Arthur, was concerned for me and invited me to go to Sun Valley with his friends. There were sixty couples from Ventura, where Arthur practiced surgery, and we all boarded a train called the *Snowball Special*.

I was standing outside the train, trying to hide my unhappiness. Suddenly, at my side, there was my brother and with him an attractive tall man with kindly eyes—I could stand and look at them all day and drink up all the understanding they offered. I felt as if we were alone and I was clinging to him. I heard Arthur saying, "And this is my best friend who's always asking about you, June. You've heard me talk about him, Dr. David Ashrow. Dave, this is my sister."

He was holding my hand and for a precious moment it was as if I were gaining strength from him. Then we started talking a mile a minute. He specialized in children's surgical dental problems. "Oh, that's why you look so kind," I said.

"Well, I don't scare kids, if that's what you mean," he replied, laughing, and suddenly Dr. Ashrow's wife was pulling him away on one side and Carol and Arthur were pulling me away on the other. What a pity he was married—he looked like someone who could save me from myself. That was all there was to it. A kidney infection cut my ski trip short and I ended up at a hospital instead of the ski slope.

I was avoiding friends—not returning calls, refusing invitations to dinner. Why would someone want anyone as depressing as me around? I asked myself, certain that they were just trying to be kind. I crawled further down the tunnel, dragging my bottle with me like a security blanket.

Thank God the children were older now—Pam was already thinking about college. She graduated from high school in June 1966 and went on to Marquette to study journalism.

My career had gone downhill and I figured no one remembered me anyway, so no big loss. Then David Merrick wanted me for *40 Carats* to replace Julie Harris on Broadway for six months. Live theater has always frightened me but I thought, Why not a Broadway debut? If I fail, my self-destruction will be complete.

So off to Broadway I went with my dark and destructive thoughts. But my professionalism took over and I never drank before a show. The show seemed to please the audience and only when I was laid low by flu did I miss a few performances during the run of my contract. As in the old days, I was still terrified of the stage. I would throw up before each performance—and sometimes afterward, as well. It was torture, but the sound of the applause was sweet. And I loved seeing that I could make people laugh.

Then it was back to L.A. and more drinking. But because my Broadway run had been such a success, I was asked to star in the first national tour of *No No Nanette*. Again I accepted, hoping I'd fail. And again my professionalism got the better of me and I toured for a year—still feeling deep inside that life was not worth living.

Looking back at that period of my life, it still amazes me that I didn't drink while I was working. Considering my emotional condition, I'm quite proud that I performed as well as I did. When I was deeply depressed, I still sought comfort in wine. But because of my allergy to alcohol it didn't take much wine to have a strong effect on me. If I had two glasses during that period, I would be as drunk as someone who drank two bottles. So although I was drunk, I didn't have to drink a great deal to get that way and stay that way.

And the bottom line was that I detested the taste of wine or any alcoholic drink. Drinking was only a way to self-destruct. Thank God I failed either to self-destruct or to learn to like the stuff.

When it was over, I returned to my home and my solitude. Most of the time I sat reading and drinking in my apartment or outside at the pool, gazing at the foliage.

Once I went to visit Pammy at Marquette and all her classmates made a fuss over me, saying they had seen *Little Women* and asking for career advice. Pam would later leave Marquette and go to work as a reporter on the Orange County *Daily Pilot* and then in public relations for the prestigious firm of Rogers and Cowan.

For a time it looked like Ricky was launched on his own acting career—he was given the role of Dick Powell as a young man in the movie *The Day of the Locust*. After a couple of co-starring film roles, he went on the dinner theater circuit starring, in a series of well-known plays. Later he found his niche in the movie industry as a location manager; ultimately Rick wants to produce or direct.

Peggy Straus and her husband, Jack, chairman of the board of Macy's, were steadfast friends at a time when I needed someone most. She and Jack spent many long hours with me, cheering me up and trying to help me make some sense of my life. When they saw me drunk and full of bruises one time they took me to a hospital. I leaned very strongly on the few friends—like Carolyn Jones—who did not give up on me. I didn't respect myself, yet dear Sissy had faith in me, told me I would find my way back, and offered an arm to lean on. Sissy had gotten an Oscar nomination for *The Bachelor Party* and was in my opinion the best actress of her day. But Sissy was much more interested in writing her novel, which was later published. She came to national attention again as Morticia in *The Addams Family*.

Judy Garland called me from London and told me that she had married Mickey Deans, a former manager of the Arthur discotheque. They had rented a town house and Judy said, "Now I can try my hand at playing housewife and taking care of my little nest and a man. I'm even cooking!" She and Mickey, who was a pianist, were planning another comeback, another concert tour.

Judy was sympathetic about my drinking—she was struggling with uppers and downers herself. Her last batch of pills, I would later hear, had cost $100. Prophetically, Judy said to me, "If I ever die, Junie, make sure they put me in a white casket—and that everybody wears white and yellow."

I said, "That's dumb talk for a bride. You wear the white and yellow and be happy with your new husband."

In June of 1969 I heard of Judy's death. She had been at her home in London with Mickey. They had gone to sleep and he had awakened in the morning to find the bathroom door locked. He pounded. He looked over the transom. She was dead—pills had done Judy Garland in.

My sympathy with Judy was total. If I hadn't committed suicide already it was strictly owing to lack of will, not desire—and it might only be a matter of time, I thought. "What's become of us MGM princesses?" I said out loud, though I was by myself. Through my tears I kept seeing Judy and me skipping down her private CBS Yellow Brick Road and drinking Blue Nun in her dressing room.

Liza was there when her mother's casket was brought down the ramp at Kennedy Airport. "I don't think it was suicide or anything like that," Liza said. "I think she was just tired like a flower that blooms and gives joy to the world and then wilts away."

Judy had put in her will that she wanted the same makeup man who had made her up during her TV series to perform this final service for her in death. Liza tried to get him, but he was now employed with another series in Hollywood, and the show's executives explained it would cost $30,000 for him to drop everything and fly to New York. Someone else helped Judy look her best as 20,000 tearful fans filed past her glass-covered casket in New York.

I was not there. I never went anywhere—I was a hermit now and my companions were a book and a bottle of wine.

And now someone was doing for me what I had once done for Judy Garland. I had never dreamed when I had sat with her in the lonely terror of her nights that I would someday need the same kind of baby-sitter.

I wouldn't go out and yet I couldn't bear to be alone. My dear Pammy found a warm, motherly black woman—Robbie—to come every day and see me through the night. But one person was not enough. I would panic when Robbie was gone and so Pammy found a second woman so that I would not be alone at all. I leaned most on Robbie. It helped to have her there when I fell asleep and to know someone would be there when I woke up. If I cried, she would comfort me and say words I could hang on to—"I know you're suffering, child, but just remember, God never gives you more than you can handle." So why, I wondered, is Judy Garland, who gave me rides in limos, dead in her forties?

I would hear after the funeral that Judy had gotten her wish—her casket was white. That was Liza's triumph, too. There had been no white coffins, but Liza Minnelli and her staunch friend Kay Thompson stood their ground and a brown casket was spray-painted white. And everything at the funeral was a cheerful yellow and white. Liza sent word to all the friends invited to the private service not to wear black.

I found myself dwelling on those early days at MGM, when Judy and I had first become friends and were having our confessional of who we really were and how we had been rechristened. Judy had said, "You know, Junie, I'm a Hoagy Carmichael song combined with a perfect stranger. What are you?"

I said, "I'm a stranger's favorite month combined with an old family name." Judy had laughed as she told how, when she was just a little kid, her mother had maneuvered and finally managed to get "Baby Frances," as she was then called, and her two older sisters booked into the Oriental Theater in Chicago, where George Jessel was the headline performer. But to her mother's disgust, the children's act appeared on the marquee as "The Glum Sisters."

George Jessel had told mother Ethel that the name of Gumm was hopeless and that it rhymed with all the wrong words. He said they'd never get anywhere with it. A newspaper man named Garland happened to be interviewing Jessel at the time, and Jessel said, "Hey, why don't you call them the Garland Sisters?"

Ethel, surprisingly, liked it. But since Baby Frances was the star of the trio, Jessel asked her if she still wanted to be Frances.

"No!" she said.

"What's your favorite name, dear?" he coaxed.

Peggy was the name Judy really liked and the name she gave her doll, but she had fallen in love with a song called "Judy."

"Judy," she said on impulse. That night was the first time the magic name would be spoken. George Jessel said, "And now, ladies and gentlemen, the Garland Sisters, featuring Little Miss Judy Garland with the BIG voice!" Judy would never cease to be grateful to Georgie Jessel.

As I sat alone and pondered my friend's death I could almost see and hear her as she looked that night at Mandeville when she launched into a Hebrew chant with a tremolo and pathos that could tear your heart out.

And Richard nodding his head at Judy and saying, "I've had it all, Judy, had it all—Catholicism, Judaism, Protestantism—and what I've come away with is that all groups are equally noble, equally good. God loves everybody."

Then he had raised his hands over her as if in benediction and said, "God is Love."

Now it was over for both of them—they were the lucky ones.

At night I could not stop crying. Pam worried about me and so did Carol Peters, my sister-in-law.

My weight was down to under eighty pounds and sometimes, when I cried and cried, Robbie would hold me on her ample lap, like a child, and rock me back and forth and say, "Hush now, hush now, child," until I quieted down. Sometimes Robbie would call Carol and say, "She's crying again," if she was unable to get me to stop. There was never a time Carol did not come when Robbie said, "She needs you." She was afraid I was suicidal and I may have been.

I didn't want to live. Life was grim, scary, lonely. I *did* want to die, but I couldn't commit suicide—what would it do to my mother? To my brother? To my children? So drinking myself to death became the solution—slow suicide. The only problem was how to keep the liquor down. I would have to sit very quietly until my stomach settled. Otherwise I would throw up and have to drink more wine.

When I ventured out, I didn't want to be recognized or have to speak to anyone. I took to wearing wigs and ended up with quite a collection. I would wear one when I went to visit a few days with my brother and Carol. I stayed in my room if they had company.

Of course people knew I was there because my nephews would slip and mention it and then someone would say, "Oh, can I meet June Allyson?" Arthur or Carol would have to say, "Let's make it another time, because she isn't feeling well." I knew I was embarrassing them but I was too deep in my tunnel to really care.

After Richard died, both Susan Hayward and eventually John Wayne also developed cancer and died.

Was there a connection? Some thought there was, and the connection that spelled death was the sand that had looked so much like the Gobi Desert. It contained radioactivity from atomic tests that had taken place within fallout range.

Why hadn't the government warned them?

I remember Richard did have some concern and talked about checking the area with Geiger counters, and I seem to recall there was a newspaper clipping about the location scouts and Richard doing just that—using Geiger counters. But the government assured them there was no problem, the radiation level was very safe.

The Utah location chosen was less than 150 miles from Yucca Flat, Nevada, where atomic testing had been going on the year before at something like one blast a month. Not just *one* but *two* atomic bomb tests had spread long-lasting radiation over the surrounding territory in a greater degree than the Hiroshima bomb which had leveled the Japanese city with its 13 kilotons.

In April 1953, Yucca Flat had been the site of a 50-kiloton blast, later nicknamed "Dirty Simon," and the following month, a 32-kiloton blast nicknamed "Dirty Harry," and there we were just one year later being bombarded with sand that blew almost constantly in the wind.

Shocking to think of now, loads of the contaminated soil were even trucked back to the studio for retakes and close-ups. A shuttle truck service began, and before it was over, 120 tons of the red sand and rock were deposited at RKO to make a miniature tent site.

Richard would eventually die of lymph gland and lung cancer early in 1963. And later the same year the government outlawed above-ground testing. Another important member of The Conqueror group was also battling cancer at the same time as my husband—Pedro Armendariz, who played an important Mongol soldier and spent quite a bit of time falling from horses and rolling on the earth.

Pedro had first developed kidney cancer, four or five years after the movie, and doctors thought the cancer had been arrested. But then, at the same time as Richard's battle, Pedro learned he had cancer of the lymph glands and had only months so live. He did not fight his fate as Richard did. Sometime after Richard died, Pedro put a gun to his heart and pulled the trigger, after tricking his wife into going to get him a sandwich.

My dear friend Agnes Moorehead, who had a supporting role in The Conqueror, may have been the first to make the connection between the movie and the cancers which various members of the cast and crew were developing. One character actress had skin cancer, and Agnes herself developed uterine cancer. In fact, in 1974, on her deathbed, Agnes Moorehead told our mutual friend Debbie Reynolds how she regretted having acted in The Conqueror because of all the people connected with it "who have died."

Susan Hayward was also fighting a losing battle, having been struck by cancer in many places—skin, uterus and brain. In the last stages, she returned to the fetal position and that was how she died, in 1975.

John Wayne hung on the longest, finally succumbing in 1979 to a combination of throat, lung and stomach cancers.

In all, over ninety of the 220 actors and crew who made The Conqueror have developed or died of cancer—and they were not alone. Studies have shown that an abnormally large number of the local populace also developed cancer that could be connected with nuclear testing fallout. Even some of the children of the stars who spent full time at the site developed tumors, but so far the Powell children and I have been lucky.

I don't think we've heard the end of the story.

Occasionally I hear that the children of *The Conqueror* cancer victims are considering a class-action suit against the government for not having warned the studio about the known dangers of atomic fallout. How naïve I was at first about the whole matter of possible radioactive contamination. Jim Bacon was interviewing me when he asked about my visit to Richard on the location site of *The Conqueror*. Had I ever heard of Dirty Harry? Jim wanted to know. At first I thought he was talking about Clint Eastwood's movie *Dirty Harry*. My understanding is that the money the relatives may receive from any suit would be used for cancer research. I am certainly all for that.

15

THE FIRST MAN to lure me out of my tunnel was Jon Peterson, a dealer in antiques and an artist. He specialized in making very fine artificial floral arrangements, especially for movies. Talented and handsome, Jon had also designed for several Presidents, and some of his floral arrangements were on coffee tables at President Nixon's western White House—San Clemente.

For the first time in years, I found myself laughing merrily as Jon described his set-designing adventures. He had made snapdragons for Liz Taylor to throw at Richard Burton in *Who's Afraid of Virginia Woolf?* Liz had hit Richard so hard with them, while the couple was feuding, that she broke the flowers four times and they had to be redone. His flowers had helped set the mood of movies as diverse as *Hello, Dolly!* and *Bell, Book and Candle.*

With Jon, I felt safe enough to go to Tana's, his favorite restaurant, which soon became mine too. I was still in my wig, of course, and as an added security blanket, at first Ricky would somehow appear at the restaurant and check up on me.

As Ricky learned to trust Jon, he no longer acted like a duenna. Somehow Jon and I found ourselves talking marriage, but it seemed far in the future. Jon understood my drinking problem,

238

how I still drank to feel safe from the night. I felt he alone understood me and loved me anyway. And I thanked the dear Lord for him. But Jon could not sit around holding my hand all the time and I still needed Robbie to stay with me and watch over me through the night.

Once, I even felt good enough to ask Jon to escort me to my brother's surprise birthday party. We arrived and had just entered the door when again, after years, I was looking into the kindest eyes I had ever seen.

"Dr. David," I said, gazing up at him and clinging to the hand he had given me.

"Junie!" he said, excitedly, "June—you remembered my name."

"Why wouldn't I? You remembered mine."

"That's different. Your brother talks about you all the time."

"Lies. All lies," I said, letting go of his hand and laughing.

He was laughing too. What power he had to make me laugh over nothing. I realized we were standing there while others were waiting, but I couldn't help myself and we went on reminiscing about that ski trip long ago and how I had disappeared into the hospital and he had wanted to come see me.

I wanted to keep the laughter going and I made funny remarks about anything he mentioned. My Kidney? No, I didn't have the operation. They couldn't find my kidney.

Where was it? Beats me, it must have stepped out for a drink.

We stood smiling at each other and then realized we'd better pay attention to our dates. Jon was hurt. And even as Jon and I were making our way to our table, I heard David being told, "You're making a perfect fool of yourself again." They left the party soon after. All I knew was that I could feel something light up inside of me and nobody could take that away.

But soon I sank back to my old routine, only leaving my

tunnel to go to dinner with Jon or to visit a while at my brother's home in Ventura. On one such visit, my brother said, "June, dear, we're having a very dear friend come to dinner tomorrow night. The reason I'm telling you now is to give you plenty of time to adjust to the idea so you'll join us and not disappoint us. He's a very nice person and he's looking forward to this."

I said, "Arthur, how can you do this to me? Invite all the friends you like but just let me stay in my room. You know I don't go on blind dates."

"It's not a date. It's just a man who's going through a divorce and he needs some companionship, too."

"Yes," said Carol. "A divorced man."

"That's the worst kind," I said, cutting her off. "Okay, okay, I'll join you—but I only promise to be polite."

I approached the next evening with dread. I had a new book. I had a new bottle of wine. I could have my party and they could have theirs. But Arthur and Carol were so good to me, if they insisted I meet one of their friends, I could make an exception.

The guest was arriving, I could hear. I made my appearance fifteen minutes late, out of sheer nastiness.

His back was to me. Carol said, "Hi, June," and he turned around. My mouth flew open. It was David. *He* was getting a divorce and they hadn't even told me?

I put my hand out. "Oh, David—it's so nice to see you." Now *he* was holding on to my hand and there was no one to tell him it was stupid. My brother and Carol later said that they could have packed and gone to Europe and we wouldn't have noticed they were gone.

We sat smiling at each other and talking, getting acquainted really, though the words had little to do with our emotions.

HE: Do you like the mountains?

ME: Oh, I *love* the mountains.

240

HE: Do you like to backpack?

ME: Oh, like Boy Scouts. Oh, I love it! Where do you backpack?

HE: Where *don't* you? It's the only way to escape from the world. Deep in the mountains. If you don't mind a few snakes I'll take you.

ME: Snakes? Not at all. That would be great.

HE: I even know where we can catch some fish that are unpolluted. Can you fry a fish?

ME: Well, I'm not sure, but if you can catch a cow, I can milk it for you.

David was drafted to handle the steaks on the outdoor grill, and we all went outside. To demonstrate his expertise, he flipped the steak into the air like a pancake and it landed smack on the concrete deck. He picked it up, blew on it, and said, "Not to worry. We will now sterilize it with heat." He served me a piece and I started sawing away at it without much success.

"How is it?" he called. "Is it tender?"

I still hadn't managed to cut a bite. "Oh, fine, fine," I said. "It's very tender."

At that point, Arthur took my hand and turned my knife over for me. "It cuts better that way," he said. "With the sharp side."

I gave David my unlisted number at the Wilshire Comstock and he called the next morning, inviting me to dinner. I got the shakes—I wasn't ready to see anyone but Jon, who understood me and made no demands. "No," I said, "I can't go to a restaurant, but I have tickets for a children's charity dinner. Want to be my escort?" I should have been taking Jon, but it popped out. "Black tie. All right?"

"Great," he said. "I'll dust off the dinner jacket. This is just where we left off—remember that party for Arthur?"

"Yes," I said, "and this time you can even sit down and eat."

But by the time David arrived, I had drunk too much out of fear and I sat huddled in my bed. Robbie was hovering over me, trying to get me to drink coffee. The truth was that already I felt that I was beginning to care too much about David. I didn't want to hurt him, or me, or anyone else.

"No, no," I said. "I can't go. Just tell Dr. Ashrow I'm sick."

"I just want you to fix yourself up a little."

"No. It's too late. Just don't let him in the door."

He somehow persuaded Robbie to let him see me. We sat up all night talking. And when I cried, he let me cry and held me tenderly. I didn't reform overnight, but with David I eventually started to realize I had been living with a strange sense of guilt—a feeling that I should not love anyone but Richard.

This was never so evident as the night David escorted me to the Thalian ball. The Thalians are a charity to help children, and I was a vice president. Bing Crosby got up to sing, and the first words out of his mouth were "Bésame Mucho," the very song that Richard used to sing to me over the phone to show that he loved me.

I simply fell apart and had to leave the table for a little while, after just sitting there crying and listening. When I got to the rest room, hardly able to see, someone asked for my autograph and I just shook my head no. A few days later a gossip columnist wrote that "June Allyson was too tipsy to even sign an autograph book." Wrong! But David knew the truth and that was all that mattered.

It was strange—mother, son and daughter were all dating at the same time. Even in romance, Ricky and Pam were very unlike. In contrast to Pam, who looked so like me, and dated one person at a time, Ricky fell in and out of love every thirty minutes. His ex-girlfriends somehow remained friends and even would come by his bachelor quarters to check out his new girlfriend. One night he called me to see how I was and I could hear laughter in the background. I asked what was going on. He said he was entertaining and mentioned several girls' names, all of them ex-flames. I said, "Together? You don't have them all there together?"

"Of course," he said. "We're all good friends and we're having a ball."

"Are there any other fellows there?" I hadn't heard any masculine voices. "Nope," he said, "just me and the girls." I hung up and looked at Pam, who was visiting me, and shook my head. "You don't understand Rick's reasoning," she said. "If he likes them, wouldn't the girls automatically like each other?"

"Well, it just confuses me," I said. "His breaking up never seems to make a girl feel rejected."

Pammy finally was ready to study acting and she went to New York. She worked as a model and in TV soap operas—and she was in love. He was such a nice young man that I began calling him Mr. Stability. Then she fell in love with a glamorous young man of royal blood—no less—and gave up Mr. Stability. When Pammy broke up with her titled lover, I was really confused. Then she was back with Mr. Stability. And I was pleased. And then she fell in love with politics and Mr. Stability was confused. She was named national chairman of Young Voters for the President, and spent so much time crisscrossing the country to help re-elect President Nixon that she was given an ultimatum by her boyfriend. She would have to choose between politics or Mr. Stability.

She chose politics.

After the election she went to work at the White House in youth affairs. I was sorry she couldn't have it all—marriage and career. Now she had her own office at the White House, and when Richard Nixon stepped down and Gerald Ford became President, Pam stayed on.

In both Nixon's and Ford's administrations I was a guest at a state dinner, and by strange design, both times I was paired with Secretary of State Henry Kissinger. I was told he was always teamed with Hollywood stars when one was available.

I remember that Kissinger turned on his charm and said, "Why does a little girl like you smoke such long cigarettes?" He was leaning close to me at the table and beaming at me.

With my inevitable great wit, I explained to Dr. Kissinger that I only smoked these extra-long cigarettes when I came to the White House. "You see," I said, waving my cigarette, they have these extremely lovely silver candelabra with the long tapering candles and they are so far away, I have to reach like this and I can only reach them if I smoke these long cigarettes."

And I was waiting for a laugh. But Henry said, "Oh really," and his expression said, "How gauche." He quickly turned to his other dinner partner and started talking to her.

Now and then he would turn and seem to be including me as he talked of world affairs and I would quickly say, "Oh yes," or "Yes, indeed." Finally he turned to me and said, "You must have read it in my book, of course."

I looked at him and said after a painful pause, "No, sir."

Even the Secretary of State didn't know where to go from there. And that made two of us. I turned to my other partner, some great Russian dignitary, only to find he didn't speak English.

Safe at last.

To my delight, Dr. Kissinger signed his place card and gave it to me. It said, "To my favorite actress, June, from her most ardent admirer."

When Pat Nixon had her stroke, I went to visit her at San Clemente. And I remember before San Clemente was sold, I was invited to the party ex-President Nixon gave for the astronauts. David had walked me to the edge of the Nixon property and pointed to a place in the ocean where he used to surf. At that time, David recalled, the Nixon property had been a horse ranch and surfers had walked freely through the property, carrying their surfboards.

David asked how well I had known Pat Nixon. I told him well enough to have luncheon with her in Los Angeles now and then in the old days but not well enough to call her at the White House when I was in Washington and say, "Hi, Pat, I'm here."

I added that my Richard and I had been with the Nixons on the emotional night Nixon had lost his bid for the governorship in California in 1962. I heard Richard Nixon say, "Now I'm going to go out and tell those damn reporters what I really think of them." My Richard threw his hands up and said, "Oh, that did it! Now he did it," meaning Dick Nixon had ruined his chances for the future.

After a couple of dates with David, it was apparent we were in love. But we had our differences—some seemingly unimportant to most people but very important to people contemplating marriage. I smoked and he didn't. I was a fussbudget ashtray emptier and David, bless him, was a bit untidy. And when the subject of marriage came up, I confessed I still harbored guilt feelings about loving someone other than Richard—the feeling of disloyalty was one more reason for my self-destructive attitude. I was coming up with so many reasons why I wouldn't be a good wife for David that I honestly believe I had him convinced.

I was scheduled to go on a celebrity cruise—a luxury cruise during which the movies of the guests are featured—and I invited David to go with me—separate staterooms, of course. We decided we'd postpone any further discussion of marriage until after the cruise.

I learned that Rita Hayworth was going to be on the same cruise. Rita looked so alone and vulnerable that David and I took her under our wing and looked after her. Rita was genuinely afraid of crowds. She appeared haughty because she refused to put on her glasses and was thus unable to recognize people.

One night David, feeling romantic, ordered a table placed on deck for just the two of us. Rita saw us and asked if we'd mind if she joined us. She felt lonely and a little sad.

How could we say no to that? Rita became nostalgic and talked about her daughters—Rebecca and Yasmin—and how proud she was of them. One of them, she said, had a great voice and was training for the opera. "I have produced a singer"—she smiled—"I who can't sing. They always dubbed me."

Rita and I felt very close that night. She had experienced physical violence in a marriage and I sympathized. She had told in court, during her divorce from the famous singer, that Dick Haymes had hit her. "I could hardly believe I could be a princess one minute and be treated like that the next," she said. "If you liked being treated like a princess," I said, "why didn't you stay with Ali Khan?"

"Because he was a playboy and in spite of all that had been written about me, I was not a playgirl. I couldn't stand his playboy habits. I'll say this for Orson. He was the *real* prince. Maybe I tried hardest to be a good wife in my second marriage. I really wanted to be everything Orson wanted of me."

I told Rita that the year I came to Hollywood, 1943, the big news had been her marriage to Orson Welles. Rita nodded her head, remembering sadly and on the verge of tears. David saved the day by quipping, "I don't believe it—I thought the headline news was JUNE ALLYSON ARRIVES IN HOLLYWOOD."

"Dancing has given me everything," Rita said. "It's just natural. You know, everyone credits my father's dancing, but nobody ever gives enough credit to my mother. She'd been a

Ziegfeld beauty." She looked at me sadly and said, "I sometimes wish I could just have had a normal childhood like everyone else." David remembered that Rita's picture had been pasted on the plane that carried the atomic bomb in World War II and Rita laughed and said, "Yes, that's something I'm proud of."

We talked about movies we were most known for, and Rita was amused that with all the movies she'd been in and all the dancing she'd done, the one thing she would be remembered for was the sexy way she had peeled off her long black evening gloves in *Gilda*.

"Don't worry," I said, "you're going to be remembered for your dancing. How I envied you, dancing with Fred Astaire, my idol."

She said he had been her idol, too, and the single thing she was proudest of was that in his memoir, Fred Astaire had said she was his favorite dancing partner.

At first I tried to hide from my adult children the fact that I was "living in sin" with a man—not at the apartment I'd moved to on Wilshire Boulevard but at his house in Ventura. Only Carol and Arthur knew. Only they knew that a man—David— was finally teaching me the basics of housekeeping, including basic cooking. Actually, I had to learn. As David put it, straightforwardly, the inside of the house was my responsibility and the outside was his.

But I was sure that David would help me with at least one tough inside job—the cleaning of the oven. I was mistaken. "That's an *inside* job," he told me as he left for the office that morning.

All day I worked with screwdriver and hammer, and when he returned, what met him outside was the whole oven—still encrusted with burnt grease and dough. Before he had a chance to say a word I said, "Now it's an outside job."

Every day made David more dear to me.

Eventually the subject of marriage arose again, but I felt we couldn't make a success of it. I fell apart completely. A dear friend, Gloria Luckenbill, knew how much I loved David and was so concerned over my depression that she literally dragged me to a private hospital in a distant city, where I hoped I would be cured of my self-destructiveness. It was to be seventeen days of the worst hell I've ever been through.

Gloria stayed with me several days for emotional support until David suddenly arrived on the scene. He told Gloria, "If June is that sincere and cares that much about our future, I can do no less. I want to help as much as I can." He remained nearby for two weeks.

On the day of my release, I walked out of my room and there stood David. The love and trust in his eyes did his proposing for him.

David never actually proposed. He just asked me where I'd like to live. Things took a slightly comical turn soon after when David asked Ricky for my hand in marriage. He already had my brother Arthur's blessing, of course—after all, Arthur was his best friend. Ricky was a lot tougher. He said if David ever hurt me, he'd have to answer to him. David did not like that at all and he replied, "Son, I've lived more than fifty-five years and I don't have to answer to anyone—but I assure you, I will not hurt your mother." Eventually Ricky started calling David "Dad."

And so we married. In fact, the morning of the wedding, October 30, 1976, I woke up with David in bed beside me. And I was not ashamed and I knew it was right and we belonged together.

Though I loved living with David—my gentle David—I couldn't stand the house. It was not a smiling house and it was dressed and painted up in harsh green. I certainly did not want to live in that house after we were married. Besides, David had lived there with his second wife. We went looking for another— I told the real estate dealer I wanted a house with a feeling of charm. "Anything but Spanish," I specified.

Though there was nothing available in the Ojai area, we liked it there and would bring a picnic lunch and sit on the grass looking off in the distance. One day we saw a house up on a mountain and went exploring. We went up a private road and there it was, at the end of its lane—its own little lane—and it smiled at me. I said, "This is the house."

David said, "It's probably not for sale. Anyway, it's Spanish style." I said, "Quick, let's call the real estate woman." She was slightly dazed. She said, "The architect who built it lives in it and it's his own retirement house. He might be willing to sell, but he built it for himself."

"Can I go in?" I asked.

She called him on her other phone.

"Yes," she said. "He said it would be all right to look."

I walked in and it was the same inside. I said, "This house is happy. And it's my house. I want to talk to the architect right away because I want him to break through the ceiling over there and put in a bedroom up there—" I realized I sounded exactly like Richard, and at last I could savor the enjoyment he felt in redecorating and making decisions. David was saying, "It's great just like this, Junie, and the bedroom downstairs is just fine."

"Well, it's fine, but just wait till you see it as part of the living room."

Eventually the house was ready and we named our retreat Shangri-La. And into paradise came Tootie. Her official title was housekeeper but her major role seemed to be to keep us from taking ourselves too seriously. "They're only putting this on for you," she tells guests when David and I smooch a little in front of company.

"I don't have to put up with this," became her favorite line when asked to do something "unreasonable" like change the linen. "I'm leaving."

Tootie has truly caught the spirit of Christmas giving. One year she got tired of David griping that her car was leaking oil on his nice white driveway. "You'll just have to get your car fixed," he told her again and again. Instead, Tootie got him a huge drip pan and propped it up in the living room where it towered over the Christmas tree.

Of course one of the first things we did after we were married was go backpacking. I was ready—I had the cutest camping clothes ever, including nice little gloves. But nobody told me it's 20 or 30 degrees colder way up high in a mountain. And at night, forget it—you're frosted in.

Well, we went, and David was ready for anything, even rain—cold, soaking rain—and that's what we got. So instead of roasted hot dogs and marshmallows over a campfire—I'd packed the marshmallows in myself, to be sure—we had dehydrated mountaineer food. David said it was beef stroganoff that he prepared by adding water to the pot boiling on his little portable mountaineer stove.

But at last, after the rain, after the so-called dinner, came the time for blessed sleep. David got out two sleeping bags. One was a pretty blue that looked very clean and cozy. The other was an old army surplus bag patched together with black tape.

Guess who got the army surplus one?

I was determined to be a good soldier. But I was relieved to see that David had brought along some warm booties to sleep in. "I'm so glad to see those," I said. "My feet are so cold." He was busy putting on the booties, which matched his sleeping bag in heavenly blue.

"Oh, that's no problem," he said. "I brought along an extra pair of woolen socks." He tossed them to me.

I was still a good soldier. I did not chicken out till I realized I had to make one small trip to the bathroom before I could sleep. I nudged him and told him. I felt something cold.

"Here's the flashlight," he said. "You remember where the little privy is."

"Oh, I can't go alone. It's too far. I'm scared."

"Okay. You don't have to go. Just take the shovel that's right outside the door and go about ten feet away."

"Shovel? What do I do with that?"

"Guess," he said, turning over.

It was my first and last backpacking trip.

David thoroughly enjoyed meeting movie stars he had only seen on screen. I introduced him to Cary Grant one night at a party and after a moment's conversation, turned to walk away. I looked back, thinking David was right behind me, but he was leaning over Cary and saying, "You know, you really *do* look like Cary Grant."

I burst out laughing. Life was suddenly so relaxed.

And soon after that, David and I were at another Hollywood party at which I was about to introduce him to Ted Knight. David said, "No, no, don't tell me. You're Lou Grant."

Ted Knight looked at him with that sardonic look and growled, "Ted Knight. But who gives a damn," and walked on by, still grimacing.

David had heard so much about my friend Van Johnson that he was delighted the first time we ran into him on the theater circuit and Van made a big point of inviting us to dinner. It was in New York and I held my breath when the check came, wondering what devilment Van would be up to.

He did not disappoint. He looked at the check and said, dramatically, "Oh God, I wish we were back at Horn and Hardart."

I was not going to let him get away with that. I said, equally dramatically, "A gentleman never shows the lady a check."

Van said, "I am not a gentleman."

David looked at both of us and just shook his head.

I had been asked to do a play, and as David helped me rehearse I realized he had acting talent. My producer agreed. It was a happy discovery because David had retired from dentistry after open-heart surgery. He couldn't backpack *all* the time.

David hasn't turned into another Dick Powell, but he has become a competent actor—appearing as co-star on stage with me on several engagements and doing quite well. Sometimes, in fact, striving a little too hard.

My Daughter, Your Son was David's first play. Perfectionist that he is, he was determined to improve his appearance as well as know every line perfectly. He was busy, busy, all on his own, and suddenly I became aware that his wonderful gray temples were gone and his hair had turned a horrible jet black.

"Oh, David, what did you do?" I wailed.

"I may have made a bit of a mistake," he said, "but the label said dark brown. And I didn't realize it was permanent dye."

"Oh my."

"Not to worry. I think I can fix it."

The next time I saw him, it was even worse. His hair had turned a ghastly red.

"David, David, what happened?"

"Oh, Junie, I tried counteracting it but I got the wrong chemical reaction." He was looking so dejected I didn't have the heart to laugh.

"You know, June, I don't know if I want to be an actor after all. Is this what they have to go through?"

"No, David, I don't know any other actor who dyes his own hair. Have you ever heard of a men's hair stylist?"

He grinned weakly. "Yeah, I guess next time I'll consult an expert."

Visiting Washington, D.C., David and I ran into George Murphy at the Jefferson Hotel. George invited us for cocktails. It was just like the days with Richard, when I sat listening to the men talk politics, world conditions, and finance. George Murphy told me he was almost eighty. He looked like an energetic fifty. "Think old and you'll be old," he said, adding, "I can walk into a room and pick out immediately the people who have retired and let their minds stop."

George Murphy did admit, however, that one leg was a little sore and we had to laugh as he told how it had happened. He had gone to a party where Morton Downey, the famed tenor of years past, had gotten up and sung even more beautifully than in his radio days. And after Downey had sung for a half hour he had said, "All right, I've done the singing. Now, George, you do the dancing."

So George got up after sufficient coaxing and said, "Everybody talks about that old soft-shoe, Ray Bolger. But let me tell you something. I'm the old soft-shoe. Bolger does the tricky stuff. I do the real thing." So then, as George put it, "I danced for half an hour and I was marvelous. I sat down while I still could and I had the most terrible charley horse —and I haven't been the same since." He was going to go to the White House to have a little visit with our old friend Ronnie Reagan, which brought back memories.

I looked at George and said, "You know, George, it's a red letter day when you can run into two happy endings in one day—Ronnie has his happy ending and I have mine."

And I thought, Richard must be somewhere smiling to see his prophecy about old Dutch come true.

I was still uptight about Richard—I wouldn't have any picture that included him out where it could be seen. Back home, David made me get some pictures of Richard with the children and place them about. "They are entitled to see that you are proud of their father. He was an important part of Hollywood and your lives."

Oh, I loved David so for his understanding and for his sensitivity.

And when friends from the past came to visit, he would be aware when they carefully avoided the subject of Richard and he himself would say, "June dear, why don't you tell about the time Dick Powell did such and such." At last Richard was no longer a taboo subject and I could talk freely again.

One day David said, "Is that a wig you are wearing?"

"Yes," I said. "It's easier than taking care of my own hair."

"Do you need a wig?"

"Of course not," I said, "but it gives me confidence."

"I'd like to see the real you."

That night David and Rick built a bonfire outside and a great ceremony took place. One by one they threw the wigs on the fire, after a few words, of course, and a lot of laughter in which I joined in. Voilà! No more wigs.

I did not have to throw a wine bottle on the fire—I was long since emancipated from that dependency. I no longer needed a drink.

Today I am a woman. I'm not the scared little girl anymore. And I guess the truth is that I am who I am today because of David. Most women never find that kind of happiness once. I have found it twice. And this is only the beginning—God willing. I look out the window at David returning with his backpack from a solitary hike and I smile.

Peace.

Glittering lives of famous people!
Bestsellers from Berkley

* *

From the stage, screen and TV—Celebrities you want to read about!

✱ ✱